P-SCREAMERS

THE HISTORY OF THE SURVIVING LOCKHEED P-38 LIGHTNINGS

P-SCREAMERS

THE HISTORY OF THE SURVIVING LOCKHEED P-38 LIGHTNINGS

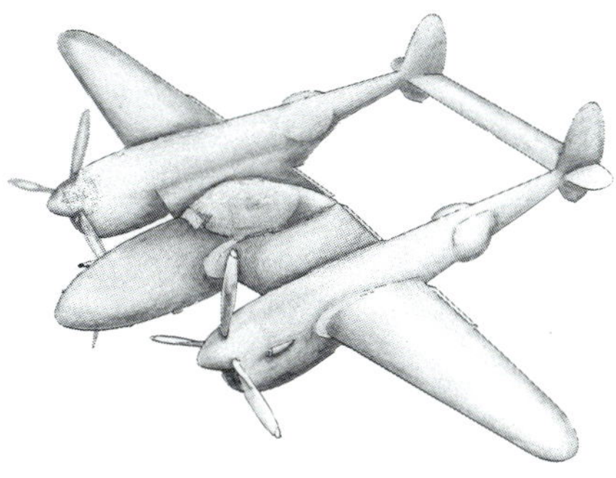

PICTORIAL HISTORIES PUBLISHING COMPANY, INC.
Missoula, Montana

LIBRARY OF CONGRESS
CATALOG CARD NUMBER 94-68089

ISBN 0-929521-90-0

First Printing: July 1994

Typography & Design: Arrow Graphics
Cover Design: Mike Egeler

ABOUT THE COVER PAINTING:

Aviation artist Michael Short has captured the beauty of Lefty Gardner's "White Lightnin" being trailed by a P-51 piloted by Gardner's good friend, the late Bob Love. Michael Short studied at the Surrey College of Art and Design in Farnham, England, before moving to the United States in 1985. Autographed prints of his painting "White Lightnin" can be purchased through AIRRACERS, P.O. Box 42, Lincoln City, OR 97367.

PICTORIAL HISTORIES PUBLISHING COMPANY, INC.
713 South Third West
Missoula, Montana 59801

Contents

Foreword

THE RUGGED AND powerful P-38 was the most outstanding fighter plane of its day in the U.S. arsenal.

In the late 1930s Kelly Johnson and the Lockheed "Skunk Works," working hard to build a fighter that could handle the German ME-109, were revolutionary in their inception, design and development of the P-38.

In the flight test stage, Milo Burcham, Tony LeVier, and others were elated when they discovered that it was 100 mph faster than any other U.S. fighter.

Its unique twin engine, twin boom, and single seat fighter concept enabled many, many pilots to fly long over water flights back to base on one engine . . . and live to fight another day.

The performance of the P-38 compared to other first line fighters of World War II was better in most categories. However, this is still a highly debatable topic in pilot circles depending upon which fighter the pilot was flying when he came under the guns of the Hun or Nip.

Its lack of torque and other design features made it the most stable gun platform of any of the fighters. The four .50 caliber machine guns and a 20mm cannon mounted in the nose, with no convergence angle, made it one of the most deadly accurate of all fighters to find on your tail.

Its top speed is only a few miles slower than the P-51 in military configuration. It will out climb and out cruise a P-51 Mustang at the same power. The L Model with dive and maneuvering flaps is equal to or exceeds most fighters with the exception of the Japanese Zero.

The Southwest Pacific Commander General George Kenny, said the P-38 was his best tool against the Japanese and it shortened the war by at least a year. In the hands of pilots like Dick Bong, the top American Ace with 40 Japanese to his credit, Tommy McGuire with 38 Japanese to his credit, and Rex Barber—who shot down Admiral Yamamoto, the mastermind of the Japanese attack on Pearl Harbor, the Japanese Zero was just no match for this fast and powerful fighting machine.

Personally, after some 30 years and 4,000 hours of flying the P-38 as well as other World War II fighters in airshows and racing, I am convinced it was the best all around fighter of the era. It is the most delightful of all World War II fighters to fly. The comfortable cockpit, a wheel instead of a stick, and two Allison engines make it very smooth and quiet. Control pressures are soft yet responsive with no torque making it docile enough for any Sunday pilot . . . as long as both Allisons are behaving properly, since each is critical.

LEFTY GARDNER COLLECTION

The cost of maintenance and operation of the "Lightning" compared to other single-engine World War II fighters has kept it from being popular with sport aviators. There are only five or six airworthy P-38s flying today.

This chronicle is the most in-depth and interesting research I have ever read concerning the post war history of the remaining few Lockheed Lightnings. It's a story never told before.

You'll only see one P-38 at the Reno race track. The "White Lightnin" with an empty weight of over 12,200 lbs. doesn't do as well around the pylons as the chopped up P-51s, but then who would want to chop up a magnificent aircraft like a P-38 just to win a race, and . . .

After the airshows are over,
and there are no more races to run,
I trust that the good Lord above me,
Will look favorably on all that I've done.

You know it's been like heaven on earth
to fly this magnificent plane,
To pierce the sky and dodge the clouds,
and soar above the rain.

They say you can't take it with you,
when you pass through the pearly gates,
But I hope and pray that the angels above
want a ride in my P-38.

LEFTY GARDNER
August 1992, Austin, Texas

This book is dedicated to the memory of:

Oliver Aldrich

Bob Boughton

Jim Butler

Jim Cook

Roy Degan

Malcolm Gougon

Royal Frey

Paul Fournet

Earl Reinert

Bill Ross

Acknowledgements

The success of any project is seldom due to one person's effort. I was very fortunate to have the assistance of a great number of fine individuals and organizations who share my interest and devotion to preserving aviation history.

My sincere appreciation and affection goes to my lovely wife, Jackie, and to my children, Jennifer, Jill, and Troy. This book would not have been possible without their love and understanding.

I would like to express my greatest appreciation to Oliver Aldrich, Warren Bodie, Bob Boughton, John Brooks, Carroll Haugh, Rolan Clark, Clark Dugan, Paul Fournet, Ervan Hare, Norman Malayney, Dick Phillips, Reagan Register, Earl Reinert, Nick Veronico, and Tim Weinschenker for their trust, guidance, and unselfish support of this project.

My genuine gratitude to the individuals and organizations who allowed me to illustrate the history of the surviving P-38 Lightnings with their superior photographs: Jo Antonson—Alaska's Office of History & Archaeology, Allison Gas Turbine, Walter Bassano, Roger Besecker, Bob Bolivar, Elinor Burchinal, Donna Bushman—Experimental Aircraft Association, Jim Butler, John & Donna Campbell, Marge Carter, Gil Cefaratt, Marcia Clemmens—Collins Commercial Avionics, Colin Crawford, Edward Davies, John Davis—Kansas Aviation Museum, Wally Dietrich, Bude Donato, John Dunbar, Don Downie, Jeff Ethell, Pat Funston—Markhurd Corp., Paddy Gardiner, John Garric, Alan Gruening, John Harjo, Charlie Hyer, Jim Jarboe, Trygve Johansen, Melissa Keiser—National Air & Space Museum, Burton Kemp, Aaron King, Walter Lamb, Ken Lensley, Jack McNulty, Bill Meixner, Ken Molson, Jeff Nichols, Neal Nurmi, Michael Obert—Kelly AFB history office, David Ostrowski, Milo Peltzer, Bob Rocker, Bill Rogers, Robert Rossi—New Line Cinema, Bob Shane, Brian Silcox, The Greenland Expedition Society, Scott Thompson, K.E. Thro, Ralph Willett, Lindsey Youngblood and a special thank you to Warren M. Bodie for giving me unlimited access to his outstanding photographic collection.

Many thanks to the following people who took the time to help me develop the manuscript by offering their recollections and P-38 information: Robert Baker, Sid Baker, Rodney Barnes, Jim Benham, Norman Bergman, Ralph Bills, Joel Bishop, Bob Bolivar, David Boyd, I.N. Burchinal, Doug Champlin, Terry Camp, Leo Childs, Jim Cook, Bob Diemert, Guy Dority, Pat Epps, Joyce Bong—Erickson, Walter Erickson, Jeff Ethell, Jim Farmer, Steve Fletcher, Bruce Fraites, Royal Frey, Bob Gonzales, John Grey, Stephen Grey, Malcolm Gougon, Russ Hall, Dan Hagedorn—National Air & Space Museum, Herb Hansford Jr., James Harp, Robert Hathaway, Ivis Hill, Steve Hinton, Thurston "Jaybo" Hinube, Bruce Hoy, Harvey Hughes, Dr. Frank Ingles, Leslie Knapp, Daryl Lens, William T. Larkins, Gary Levitz, Kent McMakin, Edward Maloney, Wilmont Marlatt, Dick Martin, Birch Matthews, Julian Myers, Frank Onynyk, Bruce Pruett, Bob Rocker, William Ross, Wayne Rothgeb, John Thompson, John Silberman, Revis Sirmon, Richard Smith, Alex Spencer—National Air & Space Museum, Ted Spencer, Richard Taylor, Vernon Thorpe, Charlie Walling, Jack Ward, Larry Wilson—National Air & Space Museum, Mike Wright, Coby Ufferhiede, Carl Vincent—National Archives of Canada, Mike VadeBonCoeur, and to Nick Veronico for his expert assistance in editing the first draft.

A special thank you is due to aviation artist Michael Short and publisher Tom Winter for allowing me to use the painting "White Lightnin" as a cover for this book.

Last but not least, I would like to especially thank Lefty Gardner and his charming wife, Sharon, for their wonderful "Foreword."

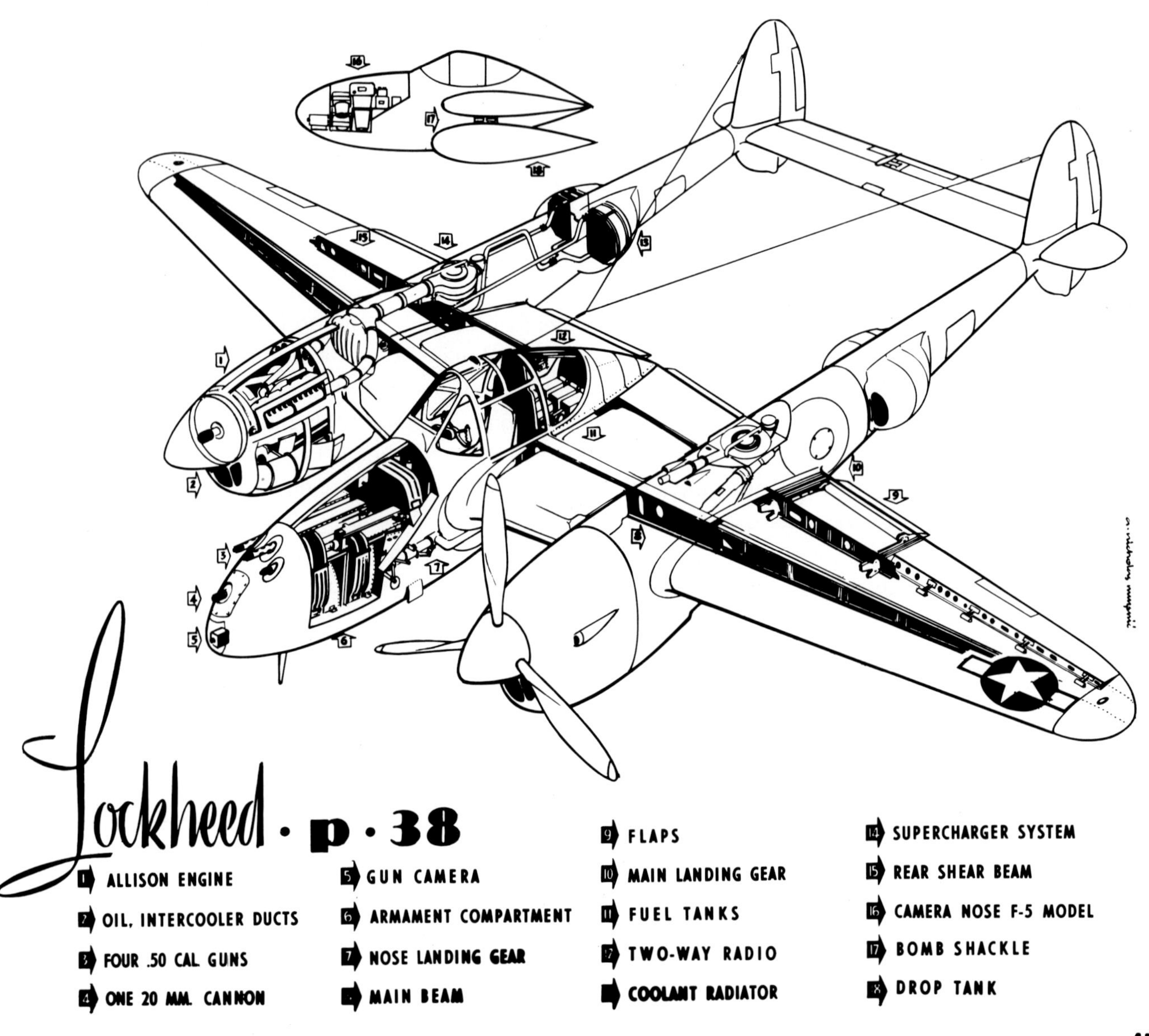

413093

ALLISON ENGINE CORPORATION

Introduction

Volumes have been written about the great fighter aircraft of the Second World War, and the Lightning is certainly no exception. The general military history of Lockheed's famed, but sometimes controversial, fighter has been well documented. However, little has been written about the use of the P-38 during the post-war years, or for that matter, about the individual aircraft that survive today. Therefore, *P-Screamers* is intended to serve as a historical reference that illustrates the history of each of the remaining Lockheed P-38 Lightnings.

Although small in number, the planes that are covered within represent almost every aspect of the P-38's operational history. Included are battle scarred wrecks, post-war racers, civilian survey ships, and impeccably restored museum pieces. The criterion used to categorize these aircraft as survivors is simple. Obviously, airworthy examples and P-38s that are displayed in museums automatically qualified, but some of the aircraft that are included in this volume are not publicly accessible. In these cases additional qualifiers were applied. In order to be considered a survivor, the aircraft in question had to either be historically significant or being currently appraised for restoration.

The geneses of this project really began as a joke. In September 1986 I attended my second warbird airshow as member of the Valiant Air Command. The most prominent feature on the poster advertising the event was a Lockheed P-38. Being somewhat of a novice at airshow work I was assigned the job of dealing with the public as a, so called, "crowd control specialist." Occasionally I was approached, during the static part of the show, and asked when the P-38 was going to arrive. Again, having little knowledge of the availability of a P-38, all I could do was defer their questions to my fellow members. It must have been obvious to some of my newly found friends that they really had a pigeon on their hands, and I suppose it was difficult for them not to take advantage of the situation. As time progressed I found myself being increasingly harassed by spectators who wanted to see a P-38. It was almost analogous to being beaten over the head with an old lady's umbrella. But fortunately, I was able to find sanctuary when the flightline was closed for the active part of the airshow. That evening I had the good pleasure of eating dinner with Roy Deagan who had recently returned from his search for the six P-38s that were lost in Greenland during the Second World War. Over dinner I recounted the ordeal I experienced with the crowd and suddenly a blast of laughter erupted around the table. It then became obvious to me that I had been subject of a practical joke. I learned, in fact, that some of my fellow members were actually responsible for sending the people over to me to complain about the absence of a Lightning. After several rounds of kidding, Roy Deagan entertained our table with recollections of his Greenland adventure. Before we departed for our respective rooms, he mentioned to me, with all kidding aside, that someone should really find out just how many P-38s there are still in existence.

The story of surviving Lockheed P-38 Lightnings can now be told. A story that took me down many a path and rewarded me with friendships and experiences that I will always treasure.

A. Kevin Grantham, *February 1994*

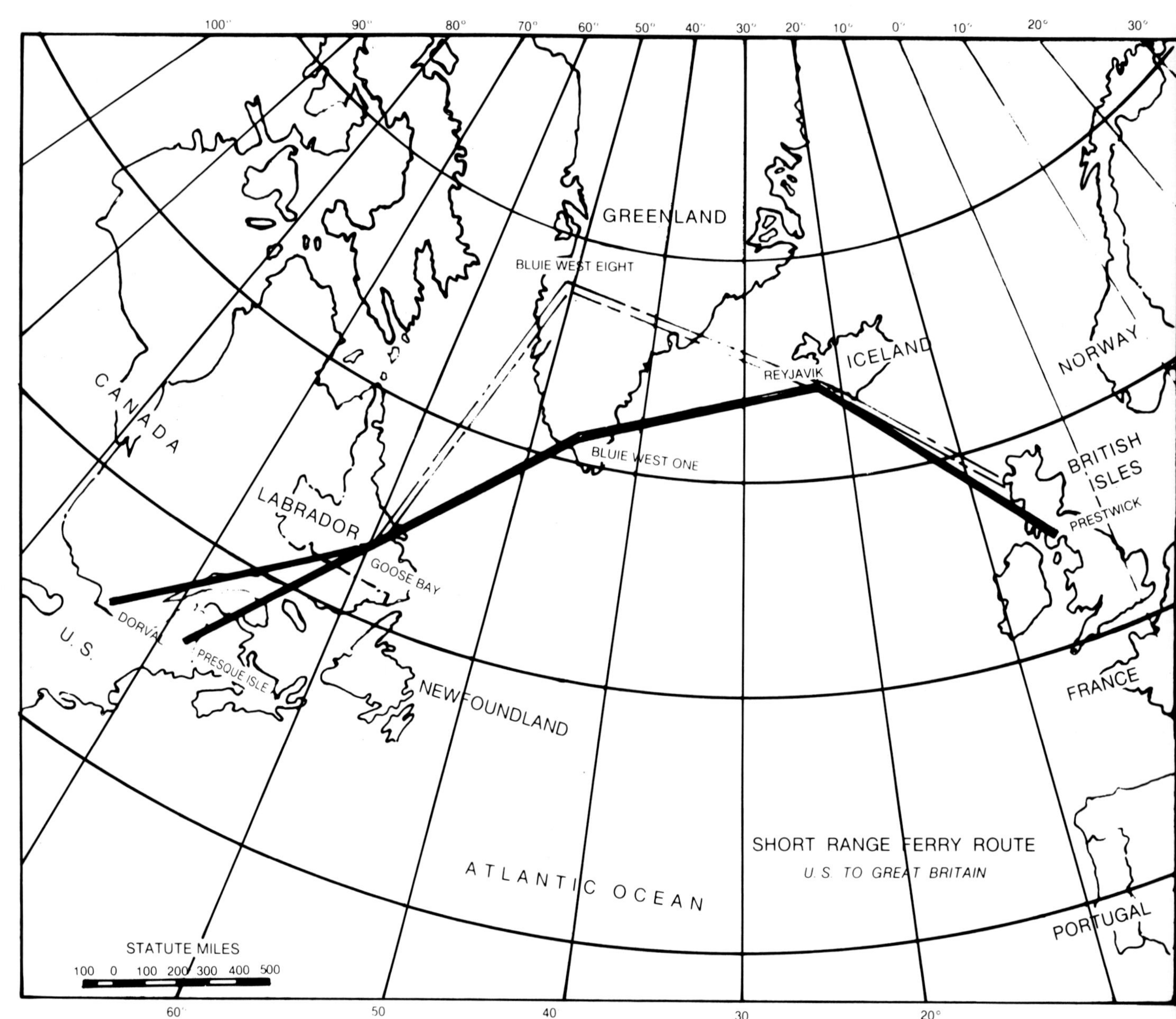

Bolero Ferry Route. USAF

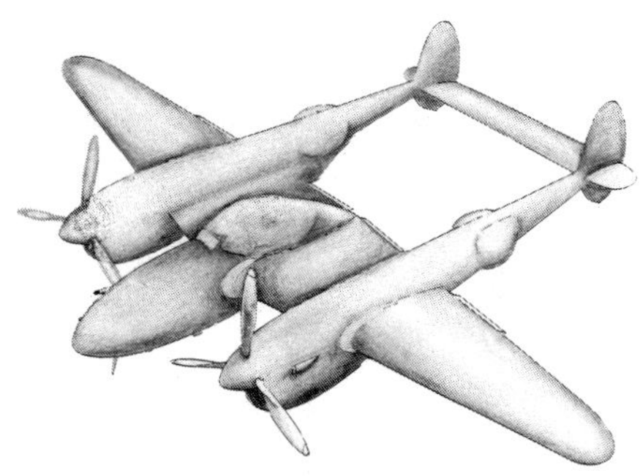

Report to Bolero

America's policy makers began their lengthy involvement in the Second World War by deciding that Germany, with their supposed Atomic bomb program, proposed a far greater threat to the world than Japan. With that in mind, military strategists were asked to devise a plan to rapidly deploy an American expeditionary force to Europe under the code name "Bolero." The Army Air Force's role in this plan called for them to stage a massive build-up of airpower that could aid the Royal Air Force in an offensive action against the enemy held continent. The policy makers in Washington were eager to show both the Germans and the Allies that America was ready to fight. So, the idea was born to ferry the needed aircraft across the Atlantic in stages with stopping points in Canada, Greenland, and Iceland.

The trip was not an easy one for the aircrews of the 97th Bombardment and 1st Fighter Groups that were ordered to "Report To Bolero." Most of these airmen were fresh out of training and had little experience in navigating over the variety of terrains along the ferry route. Weather reports were also frequently in error primarily due to the unpredictability of the weather in the region and because of the primitive forecasting technology of that time. Pilots and navigators often found the approach to Greenland's Bluie West One (BW-1,) and Bluie West Eight (BW-8) obscured by unexpected low-level fog and clouds. To make matters worse, the facilities in Greenland were far below any standards to which these crews had previously been accustomed. The food was bad, air-to-ground communications were bottle-necked, and transient living accommodations were limited. Despite the many aforementioned inconveniences and shortcomings, the "Bolero" mission of June-July 1942 was successful. All in all, 386 aircraft completed the mission with the loss of only 29 planes: eight of which (two B-17Es S/Ns 41-9101, 41-9105 and six P-38Fs S/Ns 417560, 41-7583, 41-7616, 41-7623, 41-7626, 41-7630) were lost at one time.

In recent years the eight airplanes of "Tomcat Yellow" and "Tomcat Green" flights have attracted much media attention. These planes, two B-17Es and six P-38Fs, were lost on July 15, 1942, after departing BW-8 for Iceland. Along the way "Tomcat Flight" encountered heavy weather, which forced them to return to Greenland. On the return trip the flight experienced exceptionally heavy head winds and low visibility. The lead B-17 also received what are believed to have been false weather reports from a German submarine on the conditions in Greenland. By that time the flight had been in the air for more than eight hours and most of the Lightnings were critically low on fuel. Believing they were unable to land at BW-1 or BW-8, the alternative

Bolero Lightnings over the rugged Greenland terrain. RAJANI COLLECTION VIA WARREN BODIE

Lt. Bradley MacManus (left) **was the first to attempt a landing on the ice, but the snow was too soft to support a wheels-down landing. Fortunately, MacManus was not hurt as he is shown in front of his P-38 with Lt. Carl Rudder.** RAJANI COLLECTION VIA WARREN BODIE

was for the planes to make an emergency landing together on the ice. Lt. Bradley McManus, who was flying P-38F, Army Air Forces serial number 41-7560, attempted a wheels-down landing, but the snow in the Ikersuak Fjord district was too soft. The plane's nose gear dug in shortly after touch down and the plane flipped over. Fortunately, McManus was not seriously injured. The rest of the flight soon followed by making wheels-up landings that resulted in only minor damage to the remaining aircraft. A few days later the missing crews were located and supplies were dropped to them from a C-47. Later a Navy PBY was used to guide a rescue team led by Lt. Fred Crockett to the crash site. Eventually, all the men of "Tomcat Flight" made their way through seventeen miles of ice and snow to the Greenland coast where the United States Coast Guard Cutter, USCGC *Northland*, was waiting to take the frozen men to more hospitable surroundings. Back

Aerial view looking west of two B-17s and four of the P-38s that landed approximately 17 miles from the eastern coast of Greenland. The P-38 in the lower right corner is the Lightning that was recovered by the Greenland Expedition Society in July 1992. RAJANI COLLECTION VIA WARREN BODIE

home the news of the ordeal made the pages of the "Colliers" magazine, but soon the memories of what happened to "Tomcat Yellow" and "Tomcat Green" were overshadowed by the more pressing issues of the time.

Renewed interest in the event was generated during the 1970s when *Wings* and *AIRPOWER* magazines published Warren Bodie's lengthy series on the P-38. In this series, Bodie revisited the fate of the eight planes that landed on the ice during the summer of 1942. Russell Rajani, an airline pilot based in Atlanta, Georgia, was one of many that was intrigued by the story. At approximately the same time, his friend Roy Degan, who was also an Atlanta-based airline pilot, by chance met Col. Carl Rudder. Rudder told Degan about his experience as one of "Tomcat Flight's" six P-38 pilots. Soon Degan and Rajani joined forces, and in 1981 negotiated a deal with the Danish Government which gave them exclusive salvage rights to the aircraft. Later that summer they contracted with Pat Epps and Richard Taylor (who formed the Greenland Expedition Society), and the four men then traveled to Greenland equipped with satellite pictures of the region to search for the long forgotten Lightnings. Not really knowing what to expect, the party envisioned the aircraft sticking out of the ice. Much to their surprise, however, they discovered that the planes were buried somewhere under the ice and snow. In 1982 the recovery team, minus Epps and Taylor reappeared in Greenland with additional equipment to aid them in locating the aircraft. But the weather was bad and the results of the search was even worse. In 1983 a break finally came when Rajani convinced a Navy P-3 Orion Crew to help them locate the planes. The P-3 crew flew over the supposed crash location and detected four strong magnetic reflections with their sensitive submarine detection equipment. The search was also aided when Professor Helgi Bjornsson arrived with a radar system he designed to map terrain under glaciers. Bjornsson's "icescope," as it is called, was then used to map the locations of all eight missing aircraft.

Additional trips were made in 1984 and 1985 but the results were much the same as in the previous trips. Mathematical analysis of the radar data indicated that the planes were buried under more than 60 feet of ice. In the interim, some of the original search team members dropped out of the organization, and in 1987 Roy Degan was tragically killed in a flying accident. In spite of these set backs and disappointments, Pat Epps and Richard Taylor were convinced that they would one day succeed in recovering the rare aircraft. The Greenland Expedition Society in 1986 secured the salvage rights to the planes and set out to find an efficient way to recover the aircraft from their icy tomb. They again traveled to the ice-cap but failed to find the aircraft.

A number of proposals for how to extract the planes from under the ice were offered. In 1986 Hamilton Engineering of Seattle, Washington, was brought on board as a consultant to the project. There was some question of what condition the planes would be in after being under the ice for almost fifty years. The opinions concerning the condition of the aircraft seemed to range from finding crushed pieces of junk to discovering fairly well preserved, flyable aircraft.

When the Greenland Expedition Society team returned to Greenland in 1988 their goal was to find the aircraft and determine the depth of their quest. Heli Bjornsson's low frequency radar unit was again used to locate the aircraft. Then a hotwater probe, developed by team member Austin Kovacs, was used to melt the ice. At approximately 250 feet the probe came to an abrupt stop. Again in 1989 the probe was used to reach one of the B-17s, but this time a coring device was also used to bring to the surface a piece of aluminum aircraft skin. Immediately thereafter a new device called a thermal meltdown generator was employed for the attempt to reach the B-17 known as "Big Stoop." This device was developed by team member Don Brooks in collaboration with Richard Taylor and Bobbie Bailey. The idea was to use this huge ice-cream-cone-shaped device to melt a four-foot shaft through the hardened ice by circulating warm fluid through the tubing coils that covered its conical tip. Initially the concept worked fairly well, but at approximately 60 feet the meltdown generator developed guidance problems and turned horizontal instead of vertical. From that time forward the device was referred to as the "Gopher." The "Gopher's" guidance problems forced Epps and Taylor to abandon their attempt to reach the bomber that year. In 1990, a large expedition was launched with Angelo and Remo Pizzagalli of Burlington, Vermont. Their goal was to extract three or more P-38s and view the B-17. The Pizzagalli brothers' extraordinary efforts to cut a 16-foot diameter shaft over one of the P-38s was thwarted by mechanical problems and water. However, a redesigned "Super Gopher" was used by the Greenland Expedition Society and on June 6th it reached "Big Stoop." Unfortunately, the fears that the planes might be crushed from the weight and movement of the ice pack became a realization when the party members finally descended to the depths of the bomber's icy grave. Apparently, the weight of the shifting ice pack had flattened the mighty Boeing bomber. Although the B-17 was not recoverable, all was not lost. The "Super Gopher" concept was a success and many artifacts from the site were brought to the surface. One of these was a piece of fuselage that contained the name of the pilot's wife. Later, on national television, Pat Epps and Richard Taylor donated this artifact to Phyllis Hanna who in turn gave them the keys to the ill-fated bomber.

The condition of the bomber was a disappoint-

It looks as though this Lightning's propellers departed the aircraft about 100 feet before it came to a complete stop. RAJANI COLLECTION VIA WARREN BODIE

The aftermath of Lt. "Spider" Webb's crash landing. RAJANI COLLECTION VIA WARREN BODIE

One of the downed airmen lounging on a P-38 shortly after the landing. RAJANI COLLECTION VIA WARREN BODIE

The USCGC *Northland* patrolled the icy waters in the Greenland area and was responsible for saving the lives of the Tomcat flight's stranded airmen. During the course of the war the *Northland* was called on repeatedly to provide rescue support for both allied and enemy personnel. RAJANI COLLECTION VIA WARREN BODIE

The icy tomb that once enclosed Lt. Smith's P-38 (41-7630). Surprisingly, the aircraft was well preserved. Inset: **The cockpit of Lt. Smith's Lightning complete with the helmet he placed on the seat just before he departed the plane.** LOUIS SAPIENZA/ GREENLAND EXPEDITION SOCIETY

ment, but plans to return to Greenland went forward anyway. By the spring of 1992 the quest was on again. This time they reached P-38F, serial number 41-7630, that had been piloted fifty years earlier by Lt. H.L. Smith. Well-known pilot and aircraft recovery expert Gary Larkins was brought on board to help the team dismantle the plane. Larkins recalled:

> I had offered my services to the Greenland Expedition Society about the time they first started their plans to recover the planes. When I got the call, I really didn't know what to expect. The first time you look down that 264-foot shaft it's a little scary. All you can see is a string of small lights that seem to fade into the darkness. It took about twenty minutes to descend to the bottom. Along the way you quickly lose sight of the surface and beneath you all you can see is a string of lights. Once you reach the bottom you are committed to being down there for several hours. The inside of the frozen cavern was extremely wet which made dismantling the airplane difficult. It was also common to slip off the plane into the icy pool of water which surrounded it. Occasionally, the generators above the ice that were supplying power would kick a circuit breaker and all would go black. I can't say that I ever got used to being totally wet for long hours in a 32-degree environment but the Societies' crew was exceptional and we managed to accomplish the job despite the many difficulties.

On July 15, 1992, fifty years to the day when Tomcat Flight crash-landed on the ice, Bradley McManus and O. Earl Toole, a member of the original rescue team, were on hand to help celebrate the recovery of the P-38 by firing the plane's 20mm cannon. The final piece of the P-38F emerged from the bowels of the glacier on August 1, 1992, through the great efforts of the small final crew which was led by Bob Cardin and Roy Shoffner. The aircraft paint seemed to suffer little after being frozen under tons of ice and snow for 50 years—the tail number 17630 was clearly visible. Some of these parts were brought to the Experimental Aircraft Association's convention at Oshkosh, Wisconsin, where they were the hit of the event.

By early fall 1992 most of the Lightning's parts had been transported to Epps' FBO at Atlanta's DeKalb-Peachtree Airport. The center section arrived by ship in Savannah, Georgia, in October. Then the unassembled aircraft was moved to Middlesboro, Kentucky, where Roy Shoffner will oversee its restoration.

This is not the end of the story for the Society intends to return to the crash site and recover the remaining five P-38s. It is hard to say how history will rank the Greenland Expedition Society's endeavors after the last plane is extracted from the ice. But certainly the Society's remarkable accomplishments will rank high in the minds of P-38 admirers and will not be soon forgotten.

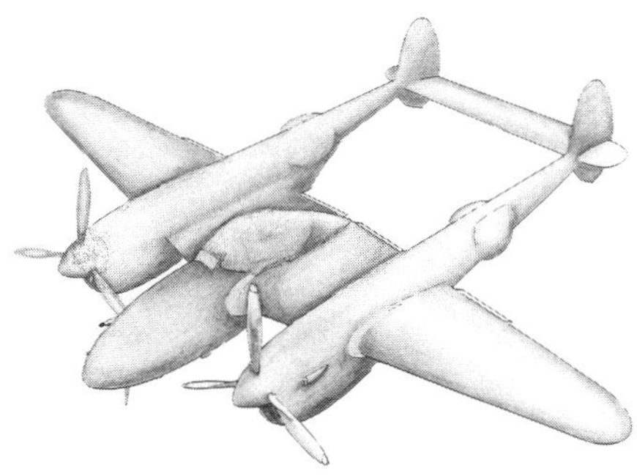

NUMBER 34 OF THE 39TH FIGHTER SQUADRON

THE NATIONAL MUSEUM of Papua New Guinea has two P-38s on display in their outside storage area. The first of these is an unrestorable F-5A-10-LO, Serial Number 42-13084, which the museum plans to use as a source of spare parts for future Lightning restorations. Unfortunately, little is known about this particular aircraft.

On the other hand, their second P-38 is an F-5-LO model Lightning, serial number 42-12647, which is the oldest of its type to be included in any museum today. It is also the only surviving restorable P-38 that has a true combat record, and uniquely most of the pilots who made victory claims while piloting Number 34 are still around to tell their stories.

In September 1942, Number 34 was among the first group of "F" model Lightings to arrive in Australia. These planes were immediately attached to the Fifth Air Force's 39th Fighter Squadron of the 35th Fighter Group, which at that time was returning from its first combat tour in New Guinea. During their first tour the squadron's Bell P-39s were quickly out-maneuvered by their more nimble Japanese fighters. But the P-38 gave the 39th a plane that could out-perform their adversary in many areas. Lt. Ralph Bills was given the assignment of checking out the former P-39 pilots from the group to P-38s as well as checking out the Lightnings that were arriving unassembled by ship. On September 14, the 39th started their move back to Port Moresby, New Guinea, and set up operations near 14-Mile Drome. Ralph Bills piloted his newly assigned Number 34 to Port Moresby on September 21, and flew his first combat mission the following day.

"I went to 33,000 feet, the first to be above 12,000 and use oxygen," recalled Bills. "I didn't see any enemy aircraft but I was COMBAT READY! From September 22 to December 31, 1942 I flew 33 combat missions, the majority of which was in Number 34."

Number 34's first recorded victory was on December 31, when pilot Ralph Bills dispatched a Zero in the vicinity of Lae New Guinea. It was his second victory. On January 8, 1943, Number 34 was again in combat, but this time the pilot was Lt. Hoyt Eason who on the last day of 1942 became the first P-38 ace in the Southwest Pacific Theater of Operation. Eason's combat mission was on the third day of an air-sea battle over Lae Harbor in which the 39th destroyed a total of fifteen (10 Oscars, 5 Zeros) aircraft in the largest aerial victory the 39th ever had in one engagement. Eason was credited with downing one Oscar, given probable credit for another, and damaging yet another Oscar.

In early March 1943, Number 34 was piloted by 1st Lt. Wilmot R. Marlatt. The following is Marlatt's description of what transpired that day as well as his recollections of the Battle of The Bismarck Sea.

Lt. Ralph Bills in front of his P-38. Inset: **Ralph Bills.** JOHN DUNBAR COLLECTION. INSET: NATIONAL AIR & SPACE MUSEUM (NASM).

On March 2, 1943 I was in one of eight P-38's on a mission escorting our bombers which were to attack an enemy convoy. The weather was cloudy, and as we approached the New Britain coast near Arawe, three enemy planes popped out of the clouds directly below us. As we were flying in two flights of four (two elements each), the lower flight hit the three Zero's first, downing one of them. Then our flight took over as the other two Zero's tried to maneuver. Being in the first element of our flight, flying the wing of Capt. Curran L. Jones, we attacked the two Zero's remaining. Jones took a burst at one which dashed back into the clouds. As I was inside Jones, I locked onto the second Zero by several maneuvers and spiraled into position to destroy him, firing from 100 yards and sending him down in smoke and flames.

One of the results of this mission was that our bombers did not find the Jap convoy, except for one B-17 that had engine trouble and turned away from the bomber flight and by luck sighted the Jap convoy. The convoy consisted of approximately 20 transports plus cruisers and destroyers headed out of Rabaul, New Britain, for Lae, New Guinea. This convoy being reported led to the Battle of the Bismarck Sea on March 3, 1943. The Bismarck Sea Battle saw sixteen P-38s in action and also every plane (American and Aussie) that could fly out of Port Moresby, New Guinea. At this time there was no Navy, except for a few PT boats. In this action the Air Force destroyed many Zeros and convoy ships. About ten to fifteen Japs were lost.

As for the P-38, it had excellent fire power, four 50-cal. machine guns and a twenty millimeter cannon, free firing in the nose of the plane, right in front of the pilot. The plane had a top altitude of 37,000 ft. which was 7,000 ft. above the Japs. The P-38 could also attain dive speeds between 450 and 500 mph. The P-40s and P-39s I flew during 1942 had an altitude of 24,000 ft. fully loaded and at that time the Japs could go to 30,000 ft. The P-38 had good maneuverability. One of the favorite maneuvers in combat with Zeros was hit and run. In action, after firing, I would go into a steep climb to almost stalling speed and cut one motor, turn, and put full power on the other motor and be back in action in no time at all. There was no way to go into circle combat with a Zero. They could out-maneuver you in close combat.

1st Lt. Wilmont R. Marlatt (in flight suit) with fellow members of his squadron. MARLATT COLLECTION

The Japanese lost their entire fleet of reinforcements in the Bismarck Sea Battle. The 39th accounted for 16 confirmed victories, but the squadron was not without its losses. On the first day of the conflict three P-38s, piloted by Bob Faurot, Hoyt Eason and Fred Schifflet, came to the aid of a lone B-17 that was being attacked by a swarm of enemy fighters. Sadly, the B-17 crew and all three of the P-38 pilots were lost.

The last victory to be credit to Number 34 was recorded at 10:15 a.m. on April 12, 1943, when Lt. Richard "Snuffy" Smith shot down a Betty bomber about 20 miles north of Kokoda. Smith kept a diary of his exploits during the war and what follows are his entries for that day.

> Went out to the flight line to gather up a few things and to put new earphones in my helmet. I wasn't on alert—dayoff. Sully (Charles O'Sullivan) gave me an airplane to fly and said they were expecting a raid. We took off a few minutes later (just six of us) and headed North. At about 20,000 feet we saw the "Silver Fleet" straight ahead; about 7,000 feet above us. Dick Suehr was leading. We climbed up and to the side then came back behind them. At 33,000 feet we stopped climbing. We were told not to attack the Bettys yet because of the ack ack ground fire. So we waited until they had dropped their bombs and then we attacked. There were about 45 Bettys and about 30 or more fighters. Sully and I attacked a formation of nine Bettys. We damaged three and Sully and I both shot one down. The Betty's right engine started burning, and I also hit him in the cabin and side of the fuselage: my third Victory.

Number 34 made its next recorded flight on May 14, 1943. Lt. Wayne P. Rothgeb, who was a new arrival, was at the controls and got his first taste of combat that May morning. Rothgeb also kept a diary of his wartime experiences, and has subsequently written a book titled *NEW GUINEA SKIES*. Here is his account of his first combat encounter.

> May 14, 1943. Today I had my first taste of a real scramble. It was my first day on alert. At about 9:30 a.m. it was reported that Japanese bombers were headed for Lea. I had a little trouble starting my left engine. I think that it was buck fever. When I got it started almost everyone was in the air. All were in trail and headed hell bent for altitude, straight up at about 30 degrees. I tacked on to a fellow's wing. Suddenly there was an explosion and it took my right engine out.

Number 34 preparing to take off. ROTHGEB COLLECTION

Lt. Wayne Rothgeb. ROTHGEB COLLECTION

With pieces of metal penetrating the cockpit, Rothgeb first thought he had been jumped by an enemy aircraft and instinctively headed down to evade his attacker. When he pulled out of his frantic dive he began to feel the drag of the windmilling prop and realized that Number 34's right supercharger had exploded and pelted his aircraft with projectiles of hot metal. Rothgeb knew that the prop would have to be feathered, but his experience with the P-38 was limited. Before his ill-fated flight he had been given a quick course on the Lightning but prop feathering was one topic that was absent from the curriculum. He quickly remembered reading about the magic feathering switch and was very careful not to feather the working engine. Once he got the plane under control he attempted to get his bearings. Again remembering a lesson from his training days, Rothgeb picked a compass heading and started looking for landmarks. Before long the shore line of New Guinea presented itself, and he figured that by flying south he would be heading away from enemy-held territory. After several minutes of worrying about fuel consumption and whether he was heading in the right direction Rothgeb spotted a sod field near Port Moresby. He then executed a very frightening, but nonetheless perfect, one-engine landing (his first) on a mudcovered strip. When the plane finally came to a stop, Rothgeb took the time to thank his maker for allowing him to survive the events of the day.

Rothgeb, in a way, expected a hero's welcome when he later returned to his outfit. After all, he had experienced in one engagement just about everything that could go wrong with a P-38 and still managed to return with the badly needed airplane. However, it didn't exactly turn out that way. Wayne Rothgeb eloquently described his return in his book *NEW GUINEA SKIES*:

> The conversation din was high pitch and the adrenaline was still flowing as each pilot looped his arms and cocked his hands as he recreated his Japanese connection that day. At dinner's end squadron commander Tommy Lynch asked for pilots who had fired their guns that day to give a report. The reports were toned down. They were modest and brief. Lynch was the leading ace in the Pacific. He knew what had happened in the air that day. No one was going to stretch the truth on him. In closing Lynch said, "Oh, yes Rothgeb came home on a single engine, but he landed at the wrong field." Ralph Bills cut in the conversation. "Yea and he was flying my plane—Number 34." Momentarily, I was hurt; but then I swelled with pride to be a member of this all business, crack 39th Fighter Squadron.

Air Force records indicate that Number 34 was again in combat on July 18, 1943. On this day 42-12647 was one of six P38s that were assigned to cover a flight of transport aircraft that were bound for Marilinan. Piloting Number 34 was Lt. Walter C. Baker. After escorting the C-47s back to their base at Yule Island the flight of P-38s were called back to the Salammaua where they engaged approximately 50 enemy aircraft. Lt. Baker was credited with the probable destruction of a Zero during this combat.

What happened to Number 34 after the Lt. Baker's combat is uncertain. According to Bruce Hoy, former curator of Papua New Guinea's National Museum and Art Gallery, an inspection plate was found on the aircraft's left engine which showed that it had been overhauled in November 1943. The plane was also found on its belly in a swamp about 30 miles from 14 Mile Drome. Therefore, it is likely that the plane was flown several times before it was officially written off the Air Force's books in July 1944.

In November 1978 Number 34 was recovered by the Papua New Guinea's Defense Forces on behalf of the National Museum and Art Gallery. Many of the aircraft's parts, most noticeably its gun filled nose, were

42-12647 at Milne Bay, January 1943. BRUCE HOY VIA JEFF ETHELL

Much the way it looked when it was first discovered by Bruce Hoy in 1967. It is believed that Number 34's original nose was salvaged by David Tallichet and used in the restoration of 44-53015. BRUCE HOY (1967)

missing. However, Papuá New Guinea is littered with numerous P-38 wreck sites. In fact, the nose that is presently attached to Number 34 came from the remains of Lt. John Dunbar's Number 37 (P- 38G-5-LO, Serial Number 42-12847) which also served with the 39th Fighter Squadron.

In the late 1980s the Travis Air Force Base Historical Society began negotiating with the Papua New Guinea Government for salvage rights to a rare B-17E, Serial Number 41-2446, which was nicknamed "Swamp Ghost" during the 1970s. They proposed the idea of bringing this rare battle veteran back to the States and displaying it. In exchange for granting rights to the B-17, Travis' Historical Society offered to also restore Number 34 to static museum standards and return it to Papua New Guinea's National Museum, as well as paint a B-25 Mitchell bomber, which is located at Popondetta, Papua New Guinea, in an authentic paint scheme. Project Coordinator, Kenneth W. Fields and Project Manager, Bob Gonzales realized the fruits of their successful quest in December 1989 when their proposal was given verbal approval by the Papua New Guinea Government. But then came the Copper mine strike in Bougainville. The strike hurt the Papua New Guinea economy, led to civil unrest, and ultimately hampered the Society's recovery efforts. This setback and delay did not dampen the spirit of the dedicated team, for negotiations with governmental authorities continued.

Wayne Rothgeb returned to New Guinea in April 1990 where he was reunited with his beloved Number 34, and he was quoted as saying: "You have not been forgotten. During the past years, every time I heard the beautiful sound of a P-38's twin Allison engines, I looked skyward and remembered you. I've come back after 47 years to New Guinea to say, 'Thank you, loyal and trusted friend—Plane Number 34.'"

In late 1991 the director of the Papua New Guinea National Museum sent the word to the Travis organization that they were no longer interested in having their P-38 restored because of a lack of display space. One hopes a deal can be struck in the near future that will save this truly historic Lightning.

Parties interested in helping the Travis Air Force Base Historical Society with their recovery efforts can contact them at 2700 Waltrip Lane, Concord, CA 94518.

Number 34 lying abandoned in a field about 30 miles from 14 Mile Drome. It was later recovered, at the instigation of Bruce Hoy, by the Papua New Guinea Defense Force on behalf of the Nation Museum. BRUCE HOY (1978)

42-12647 as it awaits restoration at Papua New Guinea's National Museum and Art Gallery. BOB GONZALES (1989)

Richard "Snuffy" Smith (right)**, at the invitation of Bruce Hoy** (left) **then curator of Papua New Guinea's National Museum, was reunited with Number 34 in 1986.** RICHARD SMITH

Wayne Rothgeb again at the controls of his ill-fated P-38 during his 1990 tour of Papua New Guinea. ROTHGEB COLLECTION

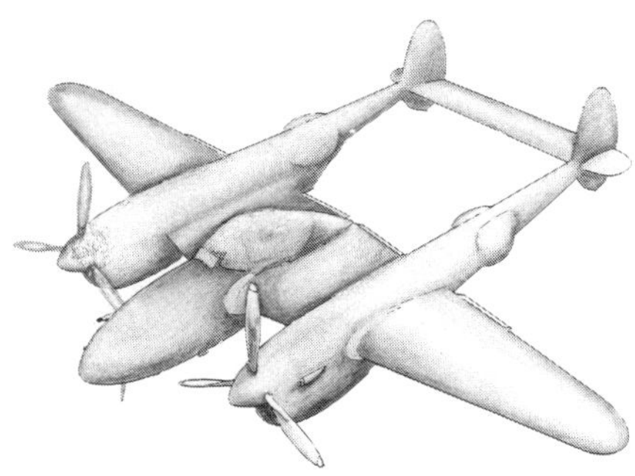

Aleutian Lightning

In the early afternoon of January 1, 1945, a four-element flight of P-38s, code named "Otter Green," departed their home base to patrol the skies above the Aleutian Islands. Missions of this type had been routine in nature and mostly uneventful since the defeat of the Japanese forces on the island of Attu in 1943. However, this particular mission would prove to be more than routine for the young lieutenant who was piloting this flight's number three aircraft.

Shortly after takeoff, "Otter Green" flight headed for the island of Shemya where they frequently flew patrol and practiced formation flying. After about an hour, the flight reversed its course and headed toward the island of Attu for gunnery practice. While flying in an easterly direction, near the mouth of Temnack Bay, the four Lightnings formed up in a 200-yard interval trailing formation. The first two aircraft made an uneventful low-altitude gunnery pass through the surrounding mountains. But 2nd Lt. Robert L. Nesmith's aircraft developed a propeller malfunction as he initiated his run through the pass. Shortly thereafter, his aircraft struck the ground at a shallow angle while he was checking the oscillating propeller and its associated control mechanism. The momentum of the plane's impact propelled it back into the air momentarily before finally coming to rest on the snow-covered terrain. The pilot of the number four aircraft immediately radioed "Mayday," and pulled his Lightning up and circled Lt. Nesmith's ill-fated bird. Fortunately, Nesmith emerged from the wreckage unhurt but was noticeably shaken. "Otter Green's" flight leader, 1st Lt. James E. Danaher, instructed the remaining two aircraft to form up and return to base. He then departed en route to the crash scene. Upon arriving, Lt. Danaher dropped a note, which instructed Nesmith to remove all forms and anything of value from his ship and that a crash boat was on its way to pick him up. The flight leader then left the scene in order to lead the rescue boat to the crash location. A few hours later, Lt. Nesmith was returned safely to his home base.

The P-38G-10-LO, serial number 42-13400, that Lt. Nesmith piloted that day was constructed at Lockheed's Burbank factory in April 1943. The plane was then assigned to the 11th Air Force's 343rd Fighter Group, 54th Fighter Squadron. 42-13400 initially cost the American taxpayer $98,441, but the pressures of war put little value on an aircraft which was severely damaged in a combat zone. So, Lt. Nesmith's Lightning was salvaged for usable parts and forgotten.

In the years following World War II, the monetary and historical value of war-related artifacts increased substantially. Early on, weak attempts were made to control the removal of vintage war material that littered many areas of Alaska. However, in the 1970s steps

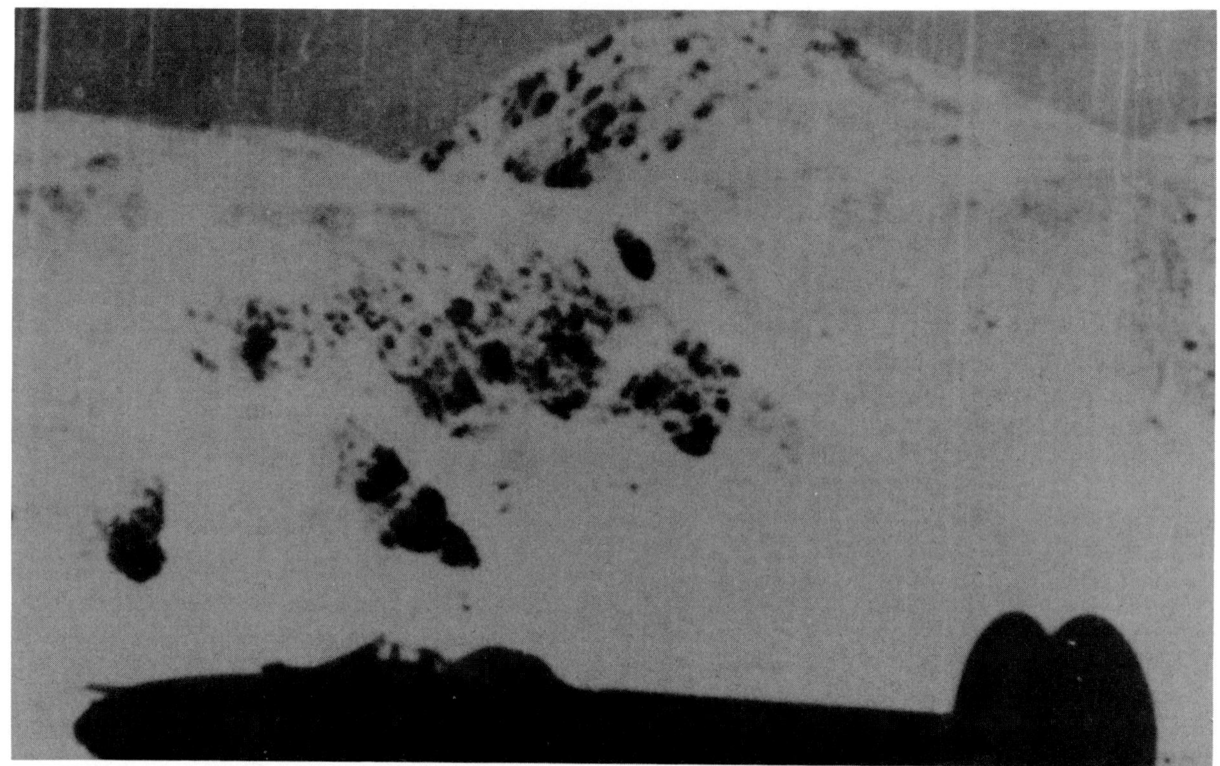

Rare photo of Lt. Nesmith's P-38G, taken after its accident. USAF (1945)

The last known G-model Lightning resting in the tall grass on the island of Attu. Inset: **The degree of vandalism that once plagued this rare aircraft is evident by the way its cockpit has been gutted.** TED SPENCER PHOTO VIA OFFICE OF HISTORY & ARCHAEOLOGY, ALASKA DIVISION OF PARKS

The aircraft's tail number (413400) is still visible despite almost 50 years of exposure to the harsh Aleutian environment. TED SPENCER PHOTO VIA OFFICE OF HISTORY & ARCHAEOLOGY, ALASKA DIVISION OF PARKS

were taken to better control the removal of such items. Lt. Nesmith's once forgotten P-38G was one of the first items to be put under the protection of the Coast Guard and added to the National Register of Historical Places as a historical object. Ted Spencer, president of the Alaska Aviation Heritage Museum, pioneered the efforts to save the remains of Alaska's war relics.

Many Alaskans, including myself, felt that Alaska's historical relics were simply not there for the taking. In fact, there are procedures that govern the removal of such items, but it is difficult to police an area as big as Alaska. So, we started to perform historical surveys of crash sites. The P-38 which is located at Temnac Bay is one of the aircraft that has been successfully documented.

We expect the museum will be given the final approval to recover this rare plane as soon as the United States Fish and Wild Life Service concludes their survey of the crash site. Once the plane is brought to the museum's facility we are hoping we can coordinate our restoration efforts with the Air Force's History Program. The aircraft will then be restored so it can be statically displayed.

Alaska has the distinction of being the first and the last place that P-38s were used in an operational combat capacity. It is, therefore, appropriate that the last known "G" model Lightning be preserved so that future Alaskans can appreciate the role these fighters played on the stage of World War II.

Lt. Smith and the "JAPANESE SANDMAN II" shortly before the 39th Fighter Squadron's transition to the Thunderbolt. RICHARD SMITH COLLECTION

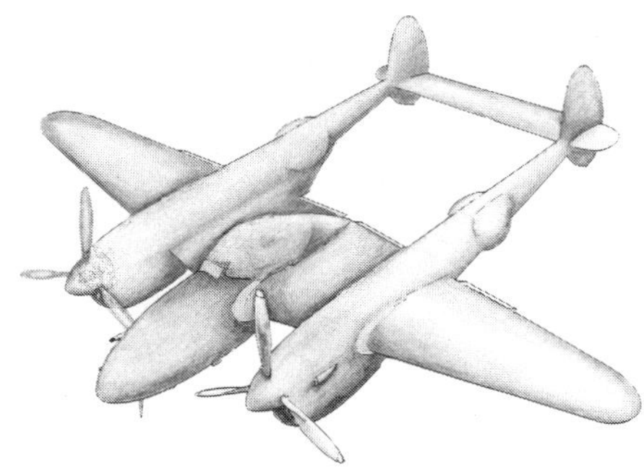

THE JAPANESE SANDMAN II

LT. RICHARD E. SMITH was already an ace by the time the 39th Fighter Squadron began to receive replacement aircraft for their battle weary "F" model Lightnings. On September 22, 1943, Smith scored his seventh victory while flying his newly assigned P-38H-5-LO, Serial Number 42-66905, which he had nicknamed "Japanese Sandman II." Smith, like most of the 39th's pilots had become truly attached to the Lockheed fighter and looked forward to finishing his combat tour in the P-38. However, in November the 39th reluctantly began their transition from P-38s to P-47s. What follows are the entries Lt. Smith made in his diary the day the 39th gave up their trusty Lightnings.

> November 19, 1943. We got rid of our P-38s this morning. Took off at 08:30 and buzzed the camp and strip; then headed for Dobodura. Gave them to the 475th Group. Came home on a transport—got home about noon.

After the war Richard Smith often wondered whatever became of the "Japanese Sandman II," and dreamed about someday returning to the South West Pacific Area (SWPA) to revisit Australia, New Zealand and New Guinea. In 1986 Smith and his wife, Dorothy, decided to fulfill their long-time dream and made arrangements to go to the area. At about the same time, Smith received a letter from Bruce Hoy, who was the curator of Papua New Guinea's National Museum and Art Gallery. Hoy was no stranger to Smith for they had been friends for a number of years, but the contents of Hoy's letter had much more significant meaning than a mere cordial exchange of greetings. To Smith's amazement Hoy informed him that an avid collector of World War II memorabilia had discovered the remains of the "Japanese Sandman II." Needless to say, the normal anticipation and excitement that Smith and his wife already had for the trip was increased beyond description.

Some weeks later, the Smiths arrived in New Guinea and were accompanied to the crash site by David Pennifather who had initially discovered the wreckage. The trek through the jungle wasn't an easy one, but once the Smiths arrived at the site it all seemed worth it. "After all," recalled Smith, "it isn't often a fighter pilot's wife gets to see the aircraft her husband flew in combat. We wanted to shout, cry, and pray at the same time." He learned from Hoy that the plane was lost about two weeks after the 39th had turned over their Lightnings to the 431st Fighter Squadron of the 475th Fighter Group. Lt. Dawson, who was flying Smith's former Lightning on the day of the accident, managed to escape without serious injury.

Although, Smith's "Japanese Sandman II" is far beyond the point of being recovered, it remains a constant reminder, to visitors that make the journey to view this historical treasure, of the bravery and the sacrifice pilots like Richard Smith made in the defense of freedom.

Forty-three years later Richard Smith is reunited with his wartime mount. RICHARD SMITH COLLECTION

Although the olive drab paint has long relinquished its pigment, visitors to the site can still see the aircraft's tail number and other fine decorative details that once adorned Smith's P-38. RICHARD SMITH COLLECTION

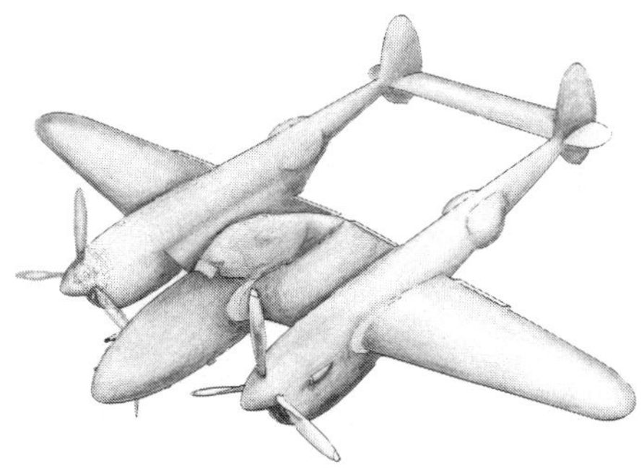

The Last F-5C

The versatility of the Lightning's airframe spawned an entire family of combat aircraft. The most successful of the fighter spinoffs were the airplanes that were modified to fill the reconnaissance role. The early photoreconnaissance (F-4/F-5B) variants of the Lightning were initially produced at Lockheed's Burbank facility. The War Production Board, being very aware that mission requirements for aircraft would be ever-changing during the course of the war, decided that it would be more efficient to set-up a network of modification centers around the country. In theory, these centers would then make the desired changes to combat aircraft and free the main production lines from incorporating design changes in mid-stream. In early 1942 Lockheed was chosen to establish and manage one of these modification centers at Love Field in Dallas, Texas.

A tall, lanky young man name Leo Childs was asked to return to his native Texas to help run Lockheed's modification center. Although Childs, as an engineer, worked on many different airplanes during his Dallas tenure, he is most proud of the contributions he made to the F-5 projects that were completed between 1943 and the end of the war. Childs recalled:

> The Army Air Corps specified the photorecon systems to be installed in the P-38 to satisfy the strategic and tactical intelligence requirements of the Air Force. In this sense, strategic intelligence referred to the enemy's capability to sustain a long duration war; whereas, tactical intelligence referred to more dynamic activities of the day-to-day basis. Photo systems to satisfy strategic requirements usually implies long focal length, large scale, reduced field of view, small area coverage, high-altitude systems. Tactical intelligence implies short focal length, wide area coverage and low altitude systems. In many cases the two systems complement each other and, in some cases, both are required, depending upon the intelligence requirements of the mission. Beginning in 1942, a series of P-38 photo reconnaissance models evolved (as follows) which required the replacement of guns with cameras.

Childs was the project engineer on the F-5C program, and he recalls some of the major differences it had from its predecessors:

> The most obvious difference between the F-5C and the F-5B was the bug-eyed windows on each side of the nose cowlings. These were required to make room for the protruding nose cones of the left and right oblique cameras of the trimetrogon configuration. This change added additional installation space required for larger capacity film magazines and the new K-22-40-inch focal length cameras. Production of these mods was phased out at the Dallas Mod Center in mid-1944. As part of the plan to develop the F-5G, the F-5C program was moved to another mod center in Alabama.

One hundred twenty-three F-5C-1-LOs were produced, but very few of these survived the war. On March 12, 1945, an F-5C (Serial Number 42-67574) had the distinction of being the first surplus Lightning to be sold to a private individual. Arthur D.

J-model P-38s waiting to be converted to F-5s at the Dallas Modification Center. LEO CHILDS COLLECTION

Knapp, president of Mechanical Products, Inc. of Jackson, Michigan, paid $18,000 for his F-5C. Knapp operated his Lightning for only a short time before selling it James De Santo who raced the plane in the 1946 Sohio Trophy Race. The aircraft was later sold to John Saum who also raced the it in the Cleveland National Air Races before finally dealing the plane to a Baltimore, Maryland, based salvage company in 1950.

The only other F-5C to survive both the war and the ravages of the post-war salvage companies is currently operated by the world famous Fighter Collection, at Duxford, England, founded by Stephen Grey. The actual model number and serial number of Grey's Lightning was unknown at the time of purchase from Lefty Gardner in 1988. Apparently, weather and vandalism devoided this mystery ship of any apparent means of identification during the years that it sat abandoned near the Ragsdale Flying Service at Robert Muhler Field in Austin, Texas. Fortunately, however, the aircraft had been photographed several times over the years, and from these photos a partial tail number was discovered. Then in 1988 the author, while visiting Lefty Gardner's hanger, noticed a very interesting wing panel that supplied the missing digits that were needed to identify this Lightning as 42-67543. This serial number was further confirmed by similar identification numbers that were found on the aircraft's center section.

P-38J-10-LO, Serial Number 42-67543 was produced in October 1943 and later sent to Dallas to be configured as an F-5C-1-LO. It was then assigned to Will Rogers Field in Oklahoma where it served in the training role. In July 1944 it was transferred to the 37th Photographic Reconnaissance Squadron (PRS) at Okmulgee Field, Oklahoma. The following month, 42-67543 was attached to the 36th PRS at Muskogee Field, Oklahoma, before being transferred to the 379th Base Unit at Coffeyville Army Air Field, Kansas. In February 1945 the plane was ferry-delivered to an as-yet-unknown surplus depot (it is likely it was transferred to Bush Field, Georgia) and was dropped from the Army Air Force's inventory.

Who purchased 42-67543 from the War Assets Administration remains a mystery. Registration records from the Federal Aviation Administration indicate that no F-5C/P-38 with the serial number 42-67543 was ever issued a license. Unlicensed surplus military aircraft were common place during the surplus sales boom of 1945–46. The surplus depot manager had the auth-

The last F-5C being prepared to make its journey from Lefty Gardner's hangar in Mercedes, Texas, to Chino, California. JOHN GARRIC (1988)

ority to give the purchaser a one-time ferry permit without having to officially register the plane with the Civil Aeronautics Administration. It is, therefore, possible that 42-67543 was ferried to Austin and never flown again.

The Fighter Collection's Lightning was sent to Steve Hinton's Fighter Rebuilders, Chino, California, for restoration shortly after Grey purchased it from Lefty Gardner. When it arrived, Hinton's experienced crew of warbird rebuilders were already in the process of restoring The Air Museum's Lightning. The Fighter Collection's P-38 differed a bit from their ongoing P-38 restoration for it was lacking a number of components, and P-38 parts are not stock items these days. Therefore, the workers at Fighter Rebuilders had to resort, in some cases, to surveying P-38 crash sites for minor usable parts such as the canopy locking mechanisms. One such location that was surveyed is an area near Los Olivos, California, where N504MH—formerly Tony LeVier's N21764, had crashed in August 1965.

On January 11, 1992, the payoff for the 15,000 man hours of restoration work to original specifications came when the newly registered NX3145X flew once again. The brief test flight produced no problems for pilot Steve Hinton. Shortly after "The Last F5C" completed its airworthiness shakedown it was shipped to England in time to celebrate the 50th anniversary of the first American P-38s to arrive in Great Britain during the Second World War.

The outer wing panel that provided the clue to this plane's true military serial number, 42-67543. AUTHOR'S COLLECTION (1988)

Steve Hinton (center) **and the rest of the Fighter Rebuilders' gang pose for the camera after one of the more remarkable restorations of all time.** JOHN HARJO

On January 11, 1992, 42-67543 once again took to the sky. JOHN HARJO

42-67543 was decorated in the colors of 8th Air Force fighter ace Jack Ilfrey's P38 "HAPPY JACK'S GO BUGGY" after it arrived in England during the summer of 1992. PETER HADINGUE VIA HARJO

"HAPPY JACK'S GO BUGGY" being trailed over the cliffs of Dover by a Spanish built 109. PATRICK BUNCE VIA THE FIGHTER COLLECTION

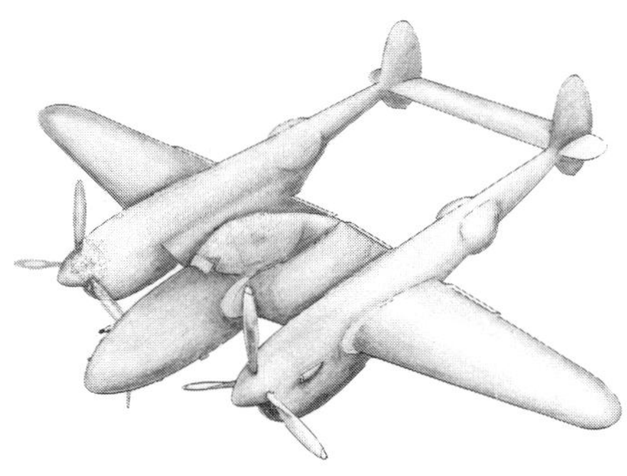

Lightning in the National Air and Space Museum

The National Air and Space Museum, located in Washington, D.C., is one of the most popular museums in the world. Each year more than nine million visitors come and view the relics and historical treasures that trace the evolution of aviation technology. Displayed inside the massive museum building are impeccably restored aircraft and rocket-powered space vehicles, ranging from the original 1903 Wright Flyer to contemporary spacecraft. A lesser known, but nonetheless important, part of the museum is located in Suitland, Maryland.

This suburban facility is named after the late Paul E. Garber, who, for more than sixty years, had been instrumental in acquiring a large number of the museum's most significant aircraft. The Garber Facility functions as a separate storage and restoration annex, which houses more than one hundred eighty aircraft. Amongst the vast array of aircraft stored at this facility is an early "J" model P-38.

The museum's Lightning, number 42-67762, is a typical J-10 model P-38. This aircraft was accepted by the Army Air Force on November 10, 1943, and was first assigned to Wright Field near Dayton, Ohio. On October 9, 1945, the plane was transferred to the Army Air Force Museum's collection at Freeman Field, Seymour, Indiana. The following year 42-67762 was added to the Army Air Force Museum's storage facility at Park Ridge, Illinois.

During the war the United States Government constructed a large aircraft assembly plant at Orchard Place Airport (which is now known as Chicago O'Hare International Airport) at Park Ridge, Illinois. This massive large wooden structure was given to the Douglas Aircraft Company who used the facility to build C-54 Skymaster transport aircraft. After the war, the building was utilized as a storage facility for many of the aircraft that had been collected for the futuristic National Air Museum.

The Air Force decided they needed the Park Ridge complex not long after hostilities commenced in Korea. Their idea was to turn the building back into an aircraft factory that could produce Fairchild C-119 aircraft for the war effort. Therefore, the custodians of the National Air Museum's collection were ordered to either evacuate the premises or the Air Force would destroy the stored aircraft on sight. Paul Garber, sensing the gravity of the situation, hurriedly organized a rescue mission, which successfully transported many of the endangered aircraft to the Smithsonian's new storage facility in Suitland, Maryland. Fortunately, 42-67762 was one of the planes that was saved.

P-38J, serial number 42-67762, in flight over the Ohio countryside. DUSTIN CARTER COLLECTION

Little is known about 42-67762's operational history other than it had only 174.25 hours of flying time logged before being acquired by the Smithsonian.

The museum plans to restore this rare bird in the colors of Fifth Air Force's 432nd Fighter Squadron of the 475th Fighter Group. But presently, this plane can be viewed in Building 20 of the Garber Facility, much as it appeared forty years ago: making it one of the most original military configured Lightnings in existence today.

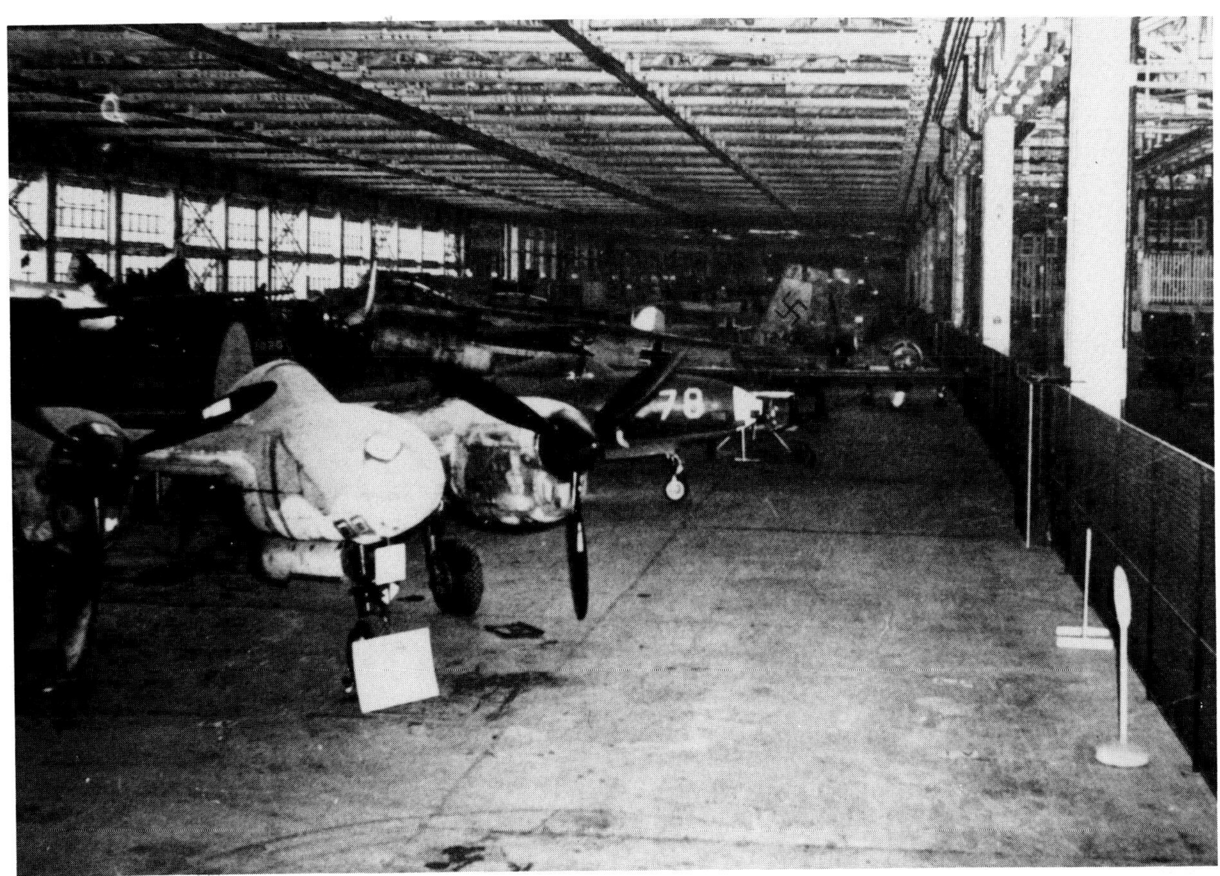

Park Ridge's massive wooden hangar, the largest of its kind ever built, was an ideal temporary storage location for the future National Air Museum's collection of aircraft. NASM

The collection was later moved outside after the Air Force issued an order to evacuate the Park Ridge factory. NASM's future Lightning is depicted amongst many of its World War II contemporaries. NASM

Some of the aircraft in the collection were dismantled and put in shipping containers in preparation for their trip to Silver Hill, Maryland. Others were considered to be of no real historical value and discarded. NASM

The National Air & Space Museum's P-38J-10-LO is scheduled for restoration sometime in the future. Until then, the plane is a truly authentic time capsule of a war era Lightning. NASM

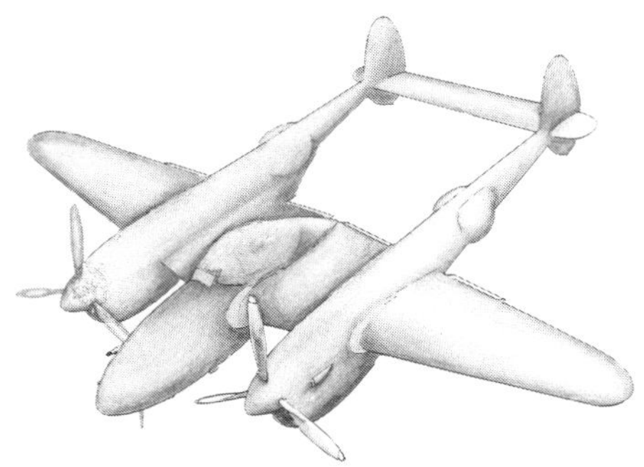

The Scatterbrain Kid

It would be hard to find two individuals who have a more enthusiastic admiration for the P-38 than Paul Fournet and Revis Sirmon. Both of these fine aviators fell in love with this aircraft type while flying the Lightning in combat during the Second World War. In the late 1960s they also realized their dream of actually owning one of Lockheed's wonders which they nicknamed the "Scatterbrain Kid," in honor of Sirmon's wife.

Sirmon flew the fighter version of the Lightning with the 49th Fighter Squadron, 14th Fighter Group, while Paul Fournet was flying F-5s for the Second Photo Recon Group in the Southwest Pacific. After the war, the two Louisiana natives renewed their friendship and went about starting their families and tackling the problems associated with life. Fournet established a thriving FBO at Lafayette Airport. During the same time period his best friend, Revis Sirmon, rose to lead a major petrochemical company. Their business successes offered them the opportunity to purchase a P-38 in the late 1960s, and Paul Fournet still recalls the day their dream came true:

> Revis called, all excited and told me about this red colored P-38 he had seen at the Las Vegas Airport. He gave me the plane's N number and told me to find out who owned the plane and see if it was for sale.

Fournet soon learned that Darryl Greenamyer was the owner of N138X, and, it was for sale. He also learned from the plane's serial number, 43-50281, that it was one of the 113 P-38L-5-VNs produced by Consolidated Vultee at its plant in Nashville, Tennessee, and is believed to have been converted to a "Droop Shoot Bomber." Shortly after the war ended the plane was declared surplus and sent to the Kingman, Arizona, storage depot. In 1946 it was sold to Fairchild Aerial Surveys who registered it with the Civil Aeronautics Administration as N33638. Fairchild operated the plane as a mapping platform for the next 17 years before selling it to Luther Eldridge and Darryl G. Greenamyer in September 1963.

Greenamyer was working for Lockheed as a test pilot at the time he purchased the Vultee Lightning. It was, therefore, natural that he would have it painted red and decorated like Lockheed's 5000th production P-38 "YIPPEE." In 1965 Greenamyer entered N138X in the Lancaster Air Races where he finished in fourth place, but afterwards it was seldom flown before being purchased by Sirmon. Fournet recalled:

> Revis picked up the plane in June 1968 and flew it directly to Louisiana. When he arrived it was obvious that we had a sick bird on our hands. My mechanic Jimmy DeLahoussaye along with some volunteers spent a great many long hours going over the airplane system by system correcting things as they found them. We replaced the photo nose with a gun nose we acquired from a derelict P-38 that Lefty Gardner had acquired from Ragsdale Flying Service in Austin some years earlier. In a short time the plane was really looking great. The only thing left was to decide how we were going to decorate it.

Fournet conferred with Royal Frey, who at that time was a curator with the Air Force Museum, and between them they developed a paint scheme that was similar to the one that adorned the British Lightning I. To highlight this unique paint scheme, Fournet's war time squadron's emblem was painted on the plane's tail. The panels that cover the aircraft's glycol coolers were also given a splash of color with the unofficial emblem of the 49th Fighter Squadron. Finally, the nickname of Sirmon's war time P-38 "Scatterbrain Kid" was painted on both of N38LL's engine nacelles. In 1969 Sirmon and Fournet took their prize to Harlingen, Texas, for the "Gathering of Eagles." It was an instant hit. It was also the first aircraft in the Confederate Air Force to be painted in something other than the standard white with red and blue trim. Col. Jethro E. Culpeper, the mythical leader of the CAF, was so taken with Lafayette's Lightning Brigade that he issued the following citation:

CITATION

For their contribution in the restoration of the P-38 Lightning, the Officers of the Lafayette Lightning Brigade are commended as follows.

PAUL FOURNET, Colonel, CAF, Chief Advisor and Reconteur, is commended for his foresight and dedication in conceiving the P-38 restoration project. Colonel Fournet served as P-38 pilot with the 25th Photo Recon Squadron of the 5th Air Force, 1943-1945, in the Southwest Pacific from New Guinea to Japan. He was noted throughout this combat area for his outstanding Reconnaissance photos of numerous schools of the rare Balanoptera whale, photos of the secret hunting grounds of the Moro tribes of Mindanao—and his extremely accurate mapping of all Geisha establishments from Kyushu to Hokkaido. Colonel Fournet and General Douglas MacArthur were credited, in varying degrees, with the ultimate surrender of the Japanese Empire on September 2, 1945.

REVIS SIRMON, Colonel, CAF, Hero and Pilot, is commended for his superior airmanship and skill in the operation of aeronautical apparatus as demonstrated in the repeated sojourns in the P-38 of the Lafayette Lightning Brigade. Colonel Sirmon served as a P-38 pilot with the 14th Fighter Group of the 15th Air Force, 1943-1945. He served with distinction in the ETO, CBI, and with particular gallantry in the USO. Perhaps indicative of Colonel Sirmon's renown in aerial combat is the fact that it was immediately after his arrival in Italy that Benito Mussolini departed in hast for his conference with Adolf Hitler.

JIM DELAHOUSSAYE, Colonel, CAF, Mechanical Genius of the Lafayette Lightning Brigade is commended for his outstanding ability to restore a tired and neglected aerial warrior to the proud and beau-

N33638 was painted orange with blue trim while serving with Fairchild Aerial Surveys from 1946 to 1963. BUDE DONATO (1960)

Darryl Greenamyer raced his bright red P-38 "YIPPEE" in the 1965 Lancaster Air Races while his Bearcat was being modified. DUSTIN CARTER

tiful eagle of the United States Army Air Force of twenty-five years past. The magnificent contours of the propeller spinners as moulded by his expert hands are said to be envied by possessors of other notable appendages—Sophia Loren, Mae West, Jane Russell and others.

Every part of this P-38 was removed, inspected and returned to new condition under the expert supervision of Colonel DeLahoussaye. Completed in record time, this aircraft is now in new condition and is without question, the most beautiful and mechanically perfect P-38 in the world today. (Due to his outstanding accomplishments in all other phases of this restoration project, the fact that one of the engines runs backwards will be disregarded.)

Colonel DeLahoussaye personally assisted General Curtis LeMay in operation of the Strategic Air Command from 1951 through 1954. He had been one of the greatest proponents of the strategic bombing capabilities of the B-29 since Robert Taylor dropped the atomic bomb on Hiroshima.

Through the efforts of these dedicated CAF Officers in restoring this historic aircraft and flying it with the CAF Ghost Squadron, millions of Americans will

Left to right: **Jimmy DeLahoussaye, Tony LeVier, Paul Fournet and Revis Sirmon at the CAF's "Gathering of Eagles" in 1969. LeVier took this opportunity to demonstrate his Lightning prowess in Sirmon's Vultee P-38.** PAUL FOURNET COLLECTION (1969)

> be reminded that our freedom must always be preserved by superior men and machines—as it was from 1939 to 1945.
>
> Their efforts have materially aided the development of this organization and their dedication to its objectives reflect great credit upon themselves and the Confederate Air Force.

Anyone who visited the Lafayette Airport in the years that followed undoubtedly noticed Sirmon's Lightning parked on the hardstand near Fournet's FBO. Having such an attractive and extremely rare airplane on display courted a certain amount of celebrity status for Sirmon and Fournet. Hardly a week went by that Fournet didn't receive a phone call or a letter of appreciation for the "Kid." One letter that was received from the Associate Director of Louisiana State University deserves particular attention. Paul Fournet tells the story:

> Any one that lives around Louisiana knows how important LSU football is to the people of Louisiana. One day we were sitting around watching LSU get beat when Revis and some of his friends came up with the idea of buzzing the stadium. A few days later the following letter arrived at CAF headquarters from LSU's Associate Director.
>
> "I am a football fan—an LSU Tiger football fan, and when I go to Tiger Stadium I fully expect to receive many football thrills.
>
> "Last Saturday night we received our full quota of football thrills, even though the Tigers lost . . . (no disgrace in being defeated by a superior team!).
>
> "The biggest thrill, however, was not on the field but over the stadium when your P-47, P- 38, and F4U made their several passes. How great it was! It was like suddenly seeing three old and very dear friends after a long, long absence. To say that I was thrilled is inadequate.
>
> "I am grateful that your organization is in existence for the purpose of keeping World War II 'birds' in the sky where they belong. After all, they won the right to be there the hard way, and I am glad that they will not be forgotten."

A sad shadow was cast over Lafayette on October 19, 1974, when pilot George Harper and N38LL were lost in a landing accident. Harper was on a solo training flight from Lafayette to Abbeville, Louisiana. Upon

Lefty Gardner, as a lark, convinced his good friend Revis Sirmon, standing on the wing, to bring his "SCATTERBRAIN KID" to the Reno National Air Races in 1970. There Sirmon put on an aerobatics demonstration and placed 6th in the Harrah's Consolation Race.
MILO PELTZER COLLECTION

his arrival in Abbeville, he mentioned to a co-worker that "he had to keep the left mixture full to keep the engine running right" and that "he had better get back before he lost his nerve." A witness saw the aircraft suddenly veer to the left as it approached the Lafayette Airport. At this point several other witnesses heard popping or surging noises coming from the aircraft's engines. The airplane then suddenly banked to the left to the inverted position, the nose of the aircraft dropped, and it disappeared behind the trees and buildings while continuing the roll before it struck the ground.

A few months later Fournet started the quest for another P-38. He was able to secure a derelict airframe that had been donated to the CAF by Gary Levitz. This particular Lightning was located in Yukon, Oklahoma, and was one of several P-38s that were previously owned by Clarence Page, owner and operator of Page Aircraft Industries.

During the early 1950s Page made a living at supplying aircraft parts for P-38s to various survey companies, that included Spartan Air Services Limited of Canada. The post-war aerial mapping boom was just starting so Page figured he could quickly turn the planes he acquired from Dale Myers around at a profit. But his efforts ran aground when he attempted to register the subject aircraft with the CAA. The CAA informed Page that his request for certification was denied due to incomplete title chain. The letter from the CAA went on to say:

> We contacted the General Services Administration (successor to War Assets Administration) in an endeavor to secure the bills of sale to complete the chain of ownership to Dale Myers, from whom he purchased the aircraft; however, there is no record of Lockheed aircraft, serial number 43-21917. Please advise us as to the numbers appearing on the name plate.

Page pressured Myers for the proper title information while he continued his search elsewhere for documents that would lead him to the plane's true identity. He discovered that it was likely that his P-38 had originally been purchased by Interstate Aircraft Co. prior to selling it to Dale Myers, but he was unable to locate the specific information he needed to register his P-38. In June 1953 Page gave up his search and informed the CAA that the aircraft he attempted to register as N5260N had been salvaged for parts.

Fournet solved the problem of finding a P-38, but now had to devise a way to get it to Louisiana. Fournet picks up the story:

> A P-38, with its outer wing panels removed, is about 28 feet boom to boom. The maximum width that can be towed on the highway is 18 feet so we had ourselves a real problem. While attending an airshow

In the early 1970s the Confederate Air Force found itself with three P-38s. (Revis Sirmon's N38LL, Lefty Gardner's N25Y and Gary Levitz' N345.) Jethro Culpeper, mythical leader of the CAF, understood the significance of this event and issued an order to have photos taken of the three planes on the ground and in the air. CAF VIA PAUL FOURNET

Above: **The "SCATTERBRAIN KID."** Inset: **Sirmon and his prize "SCATTERBRAIN KID."**
SIRMON VIA JOHN CAMPBELL

> in Mississippi we met an Army General that was willing to airlift the airframe for us with one of his helicopters, provided we paid for the fuel. Well, we found the money for the fuel and the plane was picked up at Yukon, Oklahoma and delivered to Sherman, Texas. I might add, that I heard that the Oklahoma authorities were none too happy about our helicopter airlift. We then acquired a variance from both the states of Texas and Louisiana that allowed us to transport the plane to Lafayette.

A deal was made with England Air Force Base to bring the plane to Alexandria, Louisiana, for restoration. The idea was to use off-duty, skilled and unskilled volunteers to do much of the restoration work. The plane arrived at the base in September 1977; however, before the project was finished the base went through a change in command. The new commander, after learning that the project had no liability insurance, ordered the plane off the base. It was then returned to Lafayette and eventually went to Harlingen where fellow CAF member John Stokes took an interest in the project and agreed to underwrite its restoration. In 1981 the aircraft was moved to San Marcos, Texas, where rebuilding the future "Scatterbrain Kid II" got under way once again.

Veteran World War II aviator Virgil "Sandy" Sansing took responsibility for the aircraft's restoration that would take the Central Texas Wing of the CAF more than ten years to complete. In the intervening years, Sansing; mechanics Jim Benham and Ed Carr; and a sea of volunteers found themselves rebuilding most of the plane's deteriorated systems. Finding replacement parts for the ones that had been removed during the years it sat in Oklahoma was a major challenge for the Central Texas Wing members. Locat-

October 19, 1974, pilot George Harper was tragically killed while attempting to land the "SCATTERBRAIN KID" at the Lafayette Airport.
NTSB (1974)

ing a gun nose was high on the list of priorities, but none could be found with a reasonable price tag. Somewhere along the line it was decided to mate a civilian nose, more commonly know as a Spartan Photo Nose, to the plane. A deal was also struck with the Champlin Fighter Museum to trade the "Kid's" existing single canopy setup for the museum's two seat M-model canopy configuration.

Throughout the period of restoration the question of the plane's true identity often surfaced. In the process of stripping the "Kid," Jim Benham discovered three small Lockheed data plates that were attached in different locations on the aircraft's center section. Common to all of these plates was the number 2922-( ). Many of the CAF's membership believe that 2922 are the last four digits of the aircraft's Lockheed Constructors Number and, therefore, can be used to derive N38LL's true military identity.

Lockheed C/N 422-2922 cross references to a P-38J-10-LO serial number 44-104088. The Army Air Force Record Card for 44-104088 shows that it was produced by Lockheed and accepted by the Air Force on January 9, 1944. The plane was subsequently sent to the 8th Air Force in England. The following month, 44-104088, was transferred to the 12th Air Force before being transferred again in April to the 9th Air Force's 370th Fighter Group where it was condemned to salvage in August of the same year.

Ownership of any aircraft that saw combat in World War II carries a considerable amount of historical significance and, therefore, should not be taken lightly. To some, the discovery of the three data plates answered the question of the plane's true identity; however, at the same time, others disagree with the CAF's interpretation of the numbers that appear on these three plates. The author, in an attempt to settle the question once and for all, sent photos of the plates to Lockheed and asked for their help in deciphering the controversial series of numbers. T.L. Crawford, manager of Lockheed's Operations Support, answered with the following:

> In early P-38 production the (Lockheed) serial number of the airplane was stamped on subassembly nameplates. It appears from the photos that the 2922 would be a serial number except for the three digit dash number suffix, which is inconsistent with the Lockheed serialization method at the time in ques-

A derelict airframe that was formerly owned by Page Airmovtive of Yukon, Oklahoma was acquired as a replacement for the "SCATTER-BRAIN KID." EARL REINERT (YUKON, 1964)

> tion. In all probability 2922-( ) is a basic work order and manufacturing designation number to allow traceability back to a particular contract. The second number is the assembly part number corresponding to the engineering blueprint number. The last number listed is the personal impression stamp number issued to the particular inspector who approved the finished subassembly.

To take matters a step further, the author gained permission to examine the National Air & Space Museum's P-38J-10-LO, Army Air Force serial number 42-67762. This seemed to be a reasonable way to see if the numbers contained on these small data plates were in any way related to a P-38's constructors number. NASM's Lightning, although from a different block sequence, is of the same vintage as the plane in question. It is also an excellent test vehicle for examination purposes because it is still in its original war time condition and, therefore, its Lockheed and military identities are not in question. The results of examining NASM's P-38 revealed the numbers 2431-( ) which appear to have no relation to the aircraft's constructors number of 422-2273. This not to say that the CAF's interpretation of their P-38's numbers is wrong. It's perhaps better to say that the identity if the "Scatterbrain Kid II" is unknown; however, there exist the possibility that 44-104088 is the aircraft's Army Air Force serial number.

On February 28, 1992, Col. Sandy Sansing pushed the "Kid's" throttles forward and guided the plane down the runway for its first flight in more than forty years. Later, on the ground, many of the people who had contributed to the success of this first flight were on hand to celebrate with champagne and stories of the long journey to get the "Scatterbrain Kid II" in the air. The ripples of the celebration propagated across the Texas border deep into Louisiana's Cajun land where Paul Fournet finally realized the dream he started some years earlier. Regrettably, Fournet, who referred to the P-38 as "The P-Screamer" and to whom the title of this volume is dedicated, slipped away into a better world the following May. He will be remembered for many of the good things he brought to this world but perhaps most of all, he will be remembered as a true devotee of the P-38 Lightning.

A P-80 nose was mated to the "SCATTERBRAIN KID II" during its restoration tenure at England A.F.B. in 1978. USAF

One of the small data plates that could be a clue to the aircraft's true military serial number. AUTHOR'S COLLECTION (1988)

In 1981 John Stokes took over the restoration of the "KID" and moved the project to San Marcos, Texas. Some of the parts that were used in this lengthy rebuild came from the remains of a RP-38E (AAF S/N 41-2260) that was lost during a training mission near Mt. Hood, Oregon, in March 1943. AUTHOR'S COLLECTION (1988)

On February 28, 1992, the "SCATTERBRAIN KID II" reached for the clouds once again. JIM BENHAM COLLECTION

The "KID's" restoration team.
Left to right: **Jim Benham, Pete Guessner, Mr. and Mrs. Sandy San**

The War Assets Administration donated an outstanding selection of aircraft to Santa Maria's Hancock College of Aeronautics. Hidden in the center of this collection is the future N29Q. WILLIAM T. LARKINS

Painted gloss black with white registration numbers, N29Q spent most of its time between 1954 and 1959 parked along side N79123 at Brackett Field near Lavern, California. DUSTIN CARTER COLLECTION

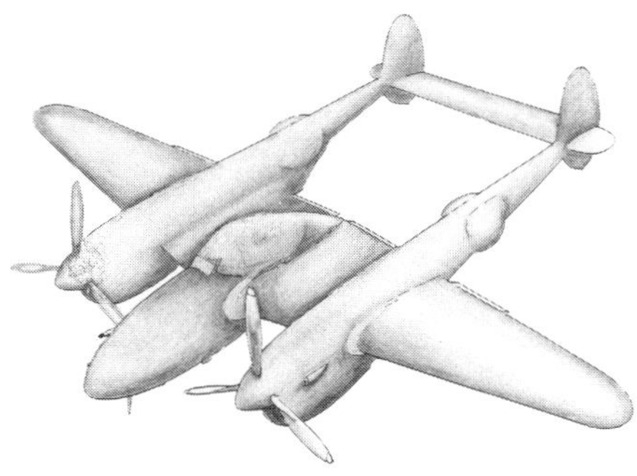

Planes of Fame Lightning

At 8:00 p.m. on July 22, 1988, the Planes of Fame Museum's rare "J" model Lightning, after being statically displayed for more than twenty-five years, reached for the skies once again. This historic event culminated eighteen months and countless man hours of meticulous restoration work by Steve Hinton's Fighter Rebuilders of Chino, California. It was also a continuation of Ed Maloney's philosophy of preserving aviation history by maintaining a flying museum.

Ed Maloney started collecting historical flying machines long before it became fashionable to do so. It was during the 1940s that he realized, unless something was done, future generations would not be offered the opportunity to enjoy the sights and sounds of the planes that once blanketed the war-torn skies of World War II. He, therefore, set out on his personal campaign to save as many of these aircraft from the scrapman's graveyard as he could. In the process, he has collected an unequalled assortment of historic planes, many of which are the only existing airworthy examples of their respective type. The platinum prize among the museum's selection of precious metal is their Mitsubishi A6M5 "Zero" fighter. This aircraft made its way back into the sky in 1978 and is the only surviving airworthy "Zero" that is powered by an original Nakajimia "Sakae" engine. It is only fitting that this great Japanese fighter would someday be complemented by its war-time nemesis—the P-38.

The Air Museum acquired their P-38 from Jack Hardwick of El Monte, California. Hardwick had been a post-war race pilot, and was one of the colorful and unique individuals of that era. He also had a reputation for being quite a "wheeler dealer" in the aircraft parts business and purportedly referred to himself as "The Mad Man Muntz of The Air." Prior to Hardwick's purchase, P-38J-20-LO, serial number 44-23314, was donated to the University of Southern California, which was leasing the Hancock College of Aeronautics of Santa Maria, California, as their aviation campus. The plane was given to the school after being turned over to the Reconstruction Finance Corporation in September 1945. Before that this Lightning spent most of its time serving in a training capacity with the 379th Base Unit at Coffeyville, Kansas, and was, therefore, redesignated as TP-38J-20-LO.

44-23314 is likely the last surplus P-38 to be sold by the United States Government. This possibly came about because the Reconstruction Finance Corporation failed to issue a proper title of ownership at the time the plane was donated. Therefore, Alan Hancock, director of the Hancock College of Aeronautics, had to officially purchase the plane from the Department of Health, Education and Welfare for $799.36 before

N29Q at the Ontario Airport before the Planes of Fame Museum relocated to Cal Aero Field in Chino, California. SCOTT THOMPSON (1975)

By 1986 N29Q's external appearance had waned somewhat. Late in the same year a program was initiated to save this rare bird from further deterioration. AUTHOR'S COLLECTION

it could be re-sold to Hardwick. Apparently, the bureaucratic difficulties that usually accompany such transactions were hurtled and Hardwick took possession of the plane in April 1954. The aircraft was given a limited certification and was entered into the civil aircraft registry as NL29Q. Hardwick kept NL29Q in open air storage at Brackett Field near LaVern, California, until he donated the plane to Maloney's collection in December of 1959.

N29Q has been displayed in several different locations since Maloney first opened his collection to the public. "We flew our P- 38J briefly in the Summer of 1961," recalled Maloney. "We realized that a major overhaul was necessary, but we didn't have the money. [Most P-38s require tons on maintenance, just check with some of the World War II mechanics who work on the Lightnings.] So, we put the aircraft on static display until such time we could afford it."

In 1986 a campaign was initiated to raise funds for this rare bird's restoration. Bob Pond, noted warbird collector, was chiefly responsible for funding the project.

When the plane finally emerged from its protective surrounding it was evident that Steve Hinton's Fighter Rebuilders had outdone themselves. Not only was N29Q aesthetically beautiful, but many technical improvements such as new engines, updated electrical system, stainless-steel control cables, and better corrosion control techniques, were incorporated to make this plane better than when it originally departed the factory.

Over the last ten years the P-38's value has outdistanced most of the other warbirds, and as a result, very few of the existing airworthy Lightnings are actively flown. P-38 admirers are fortunate that there are owners like Ed Maloney and Bob Pond who believe in keeping their Lightning in the air.

N29Q emerged from the Fighter Rebuilder's hangar in better condition than the day it left Lockheed's assembly line. SCOTT THOMPSON (1989)

Twenty-Nine Quebec once again gracing the blue heavens at the 1989 Planes of Fame Airshow. AUTHOR'S COLLECTION

Over the years many of Ed Maloney's aircraft have been used in movies and television programs. The latest of which is "Aces, Iron Eagle III." Here the now registered N38BP is depicted coming in for an emergency landing. MERIE WALLACE VIA NEW LINE CINEMA, 1992

CF-GKE in Spartan colors at Uplands Airport in Ottawa, Ontario. JACK McNULTY (1954)

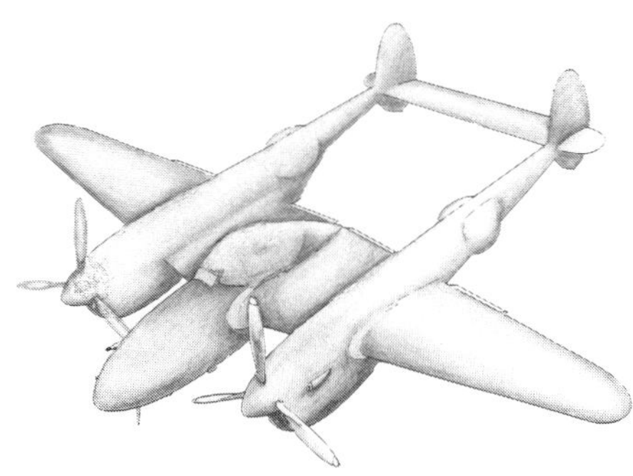

THE WEEKS AIR MUSEUM'S LIGHTNING

In March 1987 Kermit Weeks, world-renowned aerobatic pilot and vintage aircraft collector, officially opened his flying museum at the Tamiami Airport near Miami, Florida. The museum is a non-profit, charitable organization, which is dedicated to the preservation and restoration of vintage flying machines. Most notable of the museum's displayed aircraft includes a rare Douglas B-23 "Dragon," a P-51K that won the Grand Champion Warbird competition at the 1987 EAA convention, and the only airworthy De Havilland Mosquito in the western hemisphere. Also included in the museum's collection is a very interesting P-38 Lightning.

The museum's Lightning began its inauspicious military career after being accepted by the Army Air Force in March 1945. The plane was then sent to Lockheed's Dallas Modification Center where it was converted to a F-5G-6-LO. Subsequent to its photo reconnaissance conversation, it was assigned to the 379th Base Unit at Coffeyville, Kansas. From there the aircraft was stationed with the 5828th Base Unit at Tulsa, Oklahoma, before returning to the 379th in September. The following month 4426761's military career ended when the plane was sent to the Altus, Oklahoma, storage facility for disposal.

Altus Field, like many other Army Air Force Bases during this time period, was utilized as an aircraft storage and disposal center by the War Assets Administration. Most of the nearly 2,500 aircraft that were stored at this complex were stripped of usable parts and melted down into aluminum ingots. However, some of the aircraft that were stored at Altus were sold as surplus property.

In October 1947, Everett L. Moore of Tulsa, Oklahoma, purchased 44-26761 from the WAA for $800. The aircraft was given a limited certification by the Civil Aeronautics Administration, and was registered as NL5054N. Moore removed the camera mounts from the aircraft's nose compartment and replaced them with a Fairchild view finder and a seat from a Cessna T-50. The following February the plane was sold to Clark Smith of Cumberland, Pennsylvania, who, in turn, sold it to Luis Struck of Mexico. In 1951 Kenting Aerial Surveys of Canada purchased 44-26761 from Struck and changed its registration to CF-GKE. Kenting then traded the plane to Spartan Air Services, one of its Canadian competitors, for a De Havilland Hornet in August of the same year.

Spartan Air Service began as a collection of ideas from a number of Royal Canadian Air Force airmen. Many of these men, after returning from their overseas assignments, were recruited to perform aerial photographic mapping services for various Canadian military and governmental agencies.

"These agencies," recalled Russ Hall, co-founder of Spartan Air Services, Ltd., "had been given the task of bringing Canada's map coverage up to date—a big job since there were vast areas of the country which were virtually unmapped." It was while serving with the Number 14 Squadron when Hall realized that aerial photography could be useful in other areas of industry such as forestry, agriculture, and engineering.

After enduring a number of setbacks, Spartan Air Service was officially incorporated in August 1946. "So, we had a company, but no money and no equipment," recalled Hall. "We beat the bushes for investors, but without much encouragement. Finally, we got the break we needed in the form of Barnett MacLaren who owned Laurentian Airways at Uplands. Mr. MacLaren knew the flying business and also, through his involvement with the MacLaren Power Paper Company, knew the value of air photography to the forestry industry. In any case, he invested $10,000, which was enough to get the company underway; and his presence on our board of directors for the first three years probably made bank financing a little easier."

This initial investment provided enough funds for the fledgling aerial photography company to purchase three K17B cameras with 12-inch lenses and a number of surplus Avro Anson aircraft from the Crown Assets Disposal Corporation. By January of the following year, the company was fully operational, and it wasn't long before Spartan began to diversify its flying operations, which included developmental work on the Aerial Profile Recorder and magnetometer work for the Geological Survey Section.

During the early 1950s Spartan began to acquire a fleet of aircraft that could fly at the higher altitudes which were required to produce quality photographs of a scale of ½ mile to an inch. Initially, Spartan tried Lockheed Ventura type aircraft, but eventually ended up using P-38s.

Hall continues:

> As it happened, our timing couldn't have been better, because we had just become operational with a fleet of P-38s when the Korean War developed. Suddenly the RCAF dropped their commitment to provide photography for the government mapping agencies, and it was contracted to commercial firms.
>
> The government also decided to decrease the scale of the photography to one mile per inch which meant running up to 32,000 feet. It was a tremendous break for Spartan since our P-38s were able to cope immediately with the higher altitudes and the vastly increased size of the jobs.

To accommodate the newer cameras, support equipment, and a camera operator in the nose compartment of their newly acquired Lightnings, Spartan decided to expand on the "Droop Snoop Bomber" concept which was briefly used by the United States Army Air Force. Sid Baker, long-time employee with Spartan, recalled the degree to which Spartan's aircraft were modified:

> The major modification carried out by Spartan Air Service was to the nose section. The largest section of the nose was extended about 24 inches and closed by a clear plastic bubble. The nose then accommodated a navigator/camera operator and a Fairchild F24 (9 inch by 9 inch) aerial survey camera. Access to this compartment was through a hatch in the top of this extension.
>
> The oxygen system was modified to low pressure (500 PSI) type using A14 Demand type regulators. This allowed us to refill the system from high pressure cylinders when operating in remote parts of northern Canada.

One of the more interesting events involving this aircraft occurred during the Summer of 1954 when Bob Bolivar (navigator/camera operator) became one of the few to experience a wheels-up landing in a P-38 while occupying its nose compartment. Bolivar recalled:

> During the Summer of 1954, pilot John Tustin and I were assigned several large areas to be photographed in the Yukon territory. Upon returning from one of our photo missions, we were waved off by our aircraft engineer and upon investigation, discovered the nose wheel had not been retracted. As Dawson City (their base of operation) was a rather short grass strip, we decided to proceed to Whitehorse, and attempt a wheels-up landing. We jettisoned our drop tanks into Lake Laberge and successfully landed on a secondary gravel runway. The aircraft sustained minimal damage during the landing; however, it was subsequently dropped during removal from the runway and broke the left wing off. Weldy Phipps, Chief Pilot for Spartan, flew in with his own unmodified P-38, and we exchanged wings—locked the undercarriage down and ferried the aircraft back to Spartan's main base for repairs. Upon completion of repairs, we returned to the Yukon to finish the season.

The Lightning proved to be a very successful aircraft for Spartan; however, at the same time it was also an expensive and difficult plane to maintain. Between the years of 1952 and 1956 Spartan also lost a number of airmen to fatal crashes in the P38. This, coupled

Pilot Jack Tustin (right) **and Navigator Camera Operator Bob Bolivar** (left) **posing in front of CF-GKE.** BOB BOLIVAR

Jack Tustin demonstrated his expert piloting skills by making a near perfect wheels-up landing in CF-GKE at Whitehorse Airport in Canada. The only thing that was really damaged during this landing was the focus of the camera that Bob Bolivar used to take this picture. BOB BOLIVAR

with the company's opportunity to purchase cheap RAF surplus De Havilland Mosquito aircraft from the British War Assetts Commission, marked the end of Spartan's operational use of the Lightning.

In May 1956, CF-GKE was sold to Hycon Aerial Surveys of Pasadena, California. Hycon changed CF-GKE's registration to N6190C, and operated this plane until the late 1950s. Many of Hycon's Lightnings had highly modified nose sections that could carry a wide range of cameras and instrumentation, but this particular aircraft was primarily used for photo-mapping purposes.

Hycon retired its fleet of P-38s in December 1959, and N6190C was included with the aircraft that were placed on consignment with Alamo Airways of Las Vegas, Nevada. In December of the following year, N6190C was purchased by Buce & Gunn, Inc. This Dallas, Texas, based corporation owned the plane for two years before selling it to Kucera & Associates of Cleveland, Ohio, in November 1962.

While under the ownership of Kucera, N6190C was operated as a photo-mapping platform in South America. This plane, along with another P-38 (N1107V), was contracted to do aerial survey work for the Inter-American Geodesic Survey Program. Their primary mission was to map the remote regions of countries such as Bolivia, Colombia, and Paraguay.

In January 1965 both of Kucera's P-38s were operating out of Asuncion, Paraguay. It was at this time when N6190C's hydraulic system was undergoing periodic maintenance. Once the work was completed the pilot started the plane's engines and began to taxi it out to the runway. However, after noticing that the "gear unsafe" light was lit, he immediately turned the plane around and headed back to the maintenance

CF-GKE was one of three Spartan P-38s that were purchased by Hycon Aerial Surveys during the mid 1950s. The newly registered N6190C is shown undergoing check out and modifications at Hycon's facility in 1956. JIM JARBOE

area. (The warning light was lit because a shut-off valve, which isolates the port-side landing gear hydraulics from the main hydraulic system, had inadvertently been left in the closed position.) The pilot successfully maneuvered the plane into its original parking space, but the port-side landing gear collapsed before he shut down the engines. As a result, the plane's left prop, gear faring, boom and stabilizer were extensively damaged. The damage to N6190C was far beyond any repairs that could be done in a reasonable amount of time, so the plane was pushed to one side of the airport and used as a source of spare parts while the other P-38 completed the contracted work.

Kucera planned to retrieve the plane at some point, but ended up selling it in January 1968 to Ronald Bryant of Jacksonville, Florida. Unfortunately, Bryant had no idea of the difficulties he would experience in attempting to recover his stricken bird.

Bryant shipped a number of parts and tools to Paraguay with the intent of flying his newly purchased P-38 out of the country once it was repaired. Upon his arrival at Asuncion, he discovered that his tools and spare parts had been seized by customs. The customs officials informed him that his parts and tools would be released as soon as he paid the import duty assessment on the items he had shipped. The price he was asked to pay amounted to approximately two hundred percent of what the items were worth.

It appeared that Bryant's good intentions of recovering N6190C were caught up in a typical bureaucratic technicality. When Kucera initially sent his two P-38s to Paraguay, each plane was given a temporary sojourner, which excluded the contractor from paying duty. It was also stipulated that these planes would be removed upon completion of the contract. The Paraguayan government considered their original

N6109C sitting at Alamo Airways near Las Vegas, Nevada in 1960. MILO PELTZER COLLECTION

N6109C shortly after its accident in Paraguay. E. BURCHINAL

agreement with Kucera to be void because N6190C had not been removed at the time the contract obligations were fulfilled. Therefore, the plane and any parts related to the damaged bird would be subject to import and export duty assessments.

The American Council attempted to intervene on Bryant's behalf, but was unsuccessful. Bryant then returned to the United States in February 1968 and sold the plane to movie stunt-pilot I.N. "Junior" Burchinal.

Burchinal ran into the same type of problems with import/export duty as Bryant had experienced. The American Council also answered Burchinal's requests for help with three suggestions on how he might try to export the plane.

1. Pay the import/export duty.
2. Have the aircraft dismantled and shipped to the U.S.
3. Obtain a power of attorney from Kucera giving him permission to remove the plane.

Burchinal opted for the second suggestion and attempted to have the plane shipped but the Paraguayan customs officials would not allow the plane to leave the country by way of ship duty-free because the plane had not originally arrived by sea. Burchinal became totally frustrated with the whole ordeal. He then returned to Texas and sold the plane to William C. Padden of Studio City, California.

It wasn't long after he purchased the plane from Burchinal when Padden was contacted by Dr. Rodney Barnes who had noticed the derelict Lightning while on a missionary tour of Paraguay. But Dr. Barnes lost interest in the airplane after he reviewed the cost of restoring a P-38.

The final person to enter N6190C's recovery story, and the person who would ultimately succeed in getting the plane out of Paraguay, was Bob Diemert of Canada. After talking to both Padden and Burchinal, it was apparent to Diemert that the most difficult part of his recovery effort would be in dealing with the local customs officials. The benefit of knowing what to expect when he finally made his recovery attempt had its definite advantages. However, a seemingly unimportant dinner conversation would prove to be the real difference between Diemert's success and his predecessors failures. Diemert recalls:

> My wife and I were in Los Angeles visiting relatives shortly after I purchased the P-38. During dinner one night I mentioned to one of my wife's uncles, who worked for Lockheed, that I had purchased a P-38 that was stranded in Paraguay. He responded by telling me

The way Bob Diemert found the plane in 1974. BOB DIEMERT

Bob Diemert (center) **and his trusty crew of helpers.** BOB DIEMERT (1974)

that one of Lockheed's tech-reps had just returned from Paraguay after instructing the local airline on how to extend the life of their Electra-type transport aircraft, and apparently they liked him so well that the airline tried to hire him away from Lockheed. He went on to say that all I would have to do is mention the tech-rep's name to the people who run Lineas Aereas Paraguayas and they "should treat you like a long-lost brother."

Diemert arrived at Asuncion in 1974 with just a few tools because he knew that he would have to pay two hundred percent import duty on any items he brought into Paraguay. He then went about hiring a few men to help him dismantle the plane, but it wasn't long before he too ran into problems with the customs officials. Diemert continues:

> I got hooked up with a Custom's Broker who was really taking me for a ride. In the mean time, I was taking the airplane apart, and I hadn't taken the time to look-up the airline people that my wife's uncle had suggested. Quite frankly, my Spanish wasn't very good, and I really didn't know how to go about contacting them. But one day I went to the airline's hangar to see if I could borrow a jack, and I ran into the guy (Mr. Guerrero) who was running the airline. We got to talking and I told him I knew all about their dealings with Lockheed's tech-rep and it had been suggested that I look him up and say hello. After Mr. Guerrero learned that I knew about the tech-rep who helped them with their airplanes, he proceeded to help me put my P-38 through customs. (You see, the airline down there is really an arm of the military, and Mr. Guerrero, in addition to running the airline, was also a Major in the Paraguayan Air Force.) He instructed the military customs officer (who by the way was a Lieutenant) to immediately process my P-38. Initially, the customs officer resisted Major Guerrero's order but he quickly changed his mind once he realized that he would be replaced if he didn't clear the plane for export by the following day. Needless to say, my airplane was cleared for export, but if it hadn't been for Major Guerrero's influence with the local officials, my attempt to recover the plane most certainly would have ended in failure.

The obstacle that had thwarted all previous attempts to recover N6190C had finally been hurdled. However, there were other problems that had to be addressed.

"I had a hell of a time dismantling and packaging the plane so it could be transported to the local shipping docks," recalled Diemert. "You don't have the kind of clearances for power lines, trees and things in Paraguay that you do here in North America. Everything down there is smaller, neater and tighter. Therefore, the airplane simply would not make it to the docks without major surgery. So, I pulled the nose off of it, cut the booms off, and packaged all the plane's parts in a box which I thought would clear any obstacles. But I still ended up having to lift power lines when we finally moved the plane to the docks."

A few days later N6190C was finally sent on its way to Norfolk, Virginia. All of Diemert's planning and hard work, not to mention the luck of running into Guerrero, had paid off. In retrospect Diemert never doubted that he would succeed where others had failed, but there was a time when he wasn't sure if he would survive his Paraguayan adventure. Again, Diemert picks up the story:

> The airplane, as I found it, was pushed up against the back of the local Cessna dealer's lot. Bordering this lot was a big slough complete with green algae. Apparently, all the houses around the area ran their

Diemert used a trailer he made from automobile differential units to move his "Do it yourself P-38 kit" from the airport in Asuncion, Paraguay to the shipping docks. He gave great care to support and cover the aircraft components with wood so that it would not be further damaged during its long voyage to Norfolk, Virginia. When his P-38 finally arrived, Diemert he was disgusted to learn that his carefully constructed wooden structure had been dismantled en route and used for deck fires to keep the crew warm.
BOB DIEMERT (1974)

N2897S on display at the Weeks's Air Museum prior to the devastation caused by Hurricane Andrew in 1992.
AUTHOR'S COLLECTION (1992)

sewage into it, and there were a number of drainage ditches (one of which ran underneath the airplane) that drained into this stinking mess of a slough, as well. In any case, it's so hot down there that you have to drink about two and a half gallons of water a day just to keep up with the water your body loses due to the oppressive heat. At that time, I was getting my water out of a cooler which was located inside the Cessna dealer's hangar. One day, I was sitting on top of the P-38 removing the wing bolts when I noticed the hangar rat (the kid who washes the airplanes and runs errands for the Cessna dealer) strike out across the back lot. He walked up to the slough, cupped the slime aside, and scooped up a bucket of water. At first I thought he was going to wash an airplane; however, my second thought was to keep an eye on him. Sure enough, he went into the hangar and dumped the water into the cooler that I had been using. My toes then curled and I damn near died on the spot. After recovering from the shock of it all I immediately switched to "Coca Cola." However, soda water didn't seem to satisfy my thirst, so a few days later I switched back to drinking the water from the cooler. I figured if the water was going to kill me it would have already done so; although, I still can't understand why I didn't get sick.

Unfortunately, Diemert lost interest in the aircraft shortly after it arrived in Norfolk, Virginia, and in February of 1974 sold it to Dick Lambert of Plainefield, Illinois. In 1981 Kermit Weeks purchased the plane from Lambert and changed its registration number to N2897S. The aircraft was then moved to Florida, and in 1987 was put on display in the Weeks Air Museum.

The Weeks Air Museum was completely destroyed by Hurricane Andrew in August 1992. Many of the aircraft housed in the facility were extensively damaged when the museum's roof collapsed. At present the museum has no plans to restore its Lightning to airworthy status.

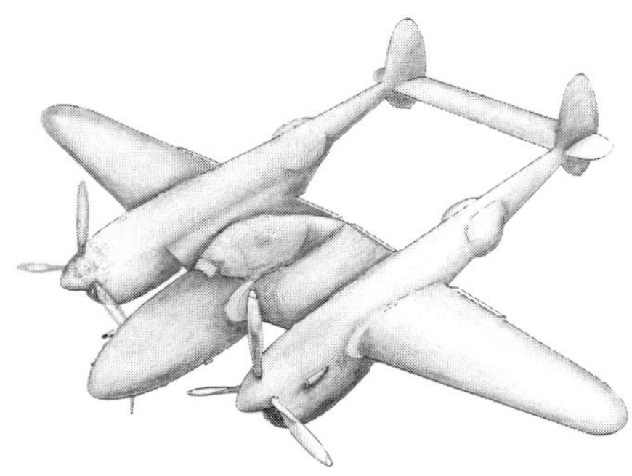

TALE OF TWO LIGHTNINGS

RETIREMENT, TO MOST PEOPLE, conjures up mental images of having the time to finally do things that they have always wanted to do. This couldn't be more true for Bruce Pruett who has chosen to devote his eventual retirement to rebuilding the two P-38s he purchased from the Mark Hurd Corporation in the late 1960s.

Pruett's P-38s were manufactured by Lockheed in the Spring of 1945. The first to be completed was P-38L-5-LO, serial number 44-26969. One hundred and fourteen L-5 models later, serial number 44-27083 also entered active military service. Both of these aircraft were sent to Dallas where they were converted to F-5G-6-LOs before being transferred to Tinker Field, Oklahoma. In January 1946, 44-26969 and 44-27083 were dropped from the Army Air Force's inventory after being delivered to the Kingman storage facility in Arizona. Two months later 44-26969 was sold to Aero Exploration Company of Tulsa, Oklahoma, for $1,250. 44-27083 was also sold for the same amount to Russell C. Reeves of Tulsa, who in turn sold it to Raymond H. Miller for $1,500. 44-26969 and 4427083 were respectively registered with the Civil Aeronautics Administration as N53753 and N75551. Miller later sold N75551 to the Mark Hurd Mapping Company of Minneapolis, Minnesota, shortly after he became a partner in the company. The following year N53753 was reunited with N75551 when it also was sold to Mark Hurd Mapping Company.

The namesake of the Mark Hurd Mapping Company was the fifth person in the United States to be issued a private pilot's license. He also served with the Lafayette Escadrille as a fighter pilot in World War I, and it was during his time in France that he became interested in aerial photography. In the years following the war, he formed the Aerial Photographic Service, Inc., which produced one of the first American made aerial cameras, organized the Aircraft Owners and Operators Association, barnstormed, sold aircraft, and set up flying schools. In 1932 Hurd returned to the aerial photography business by forming a partnership with John Holmberg. The company survived until 1935 when Hurd organized the Mark Hurd Mapping Company. He also established a new manufacturing company that developed the successful Hurd aerial mapping camera. Hurd's manufacturing company continued to be an innovator in the field of aerial photography by producing cameras and aerial photographic equipment that became the heart of most of the photogrammetric systems that were used through the end of World War II.

The conclusion of the Second World War marked an end to the Depression that had plagued the world since the early 1930s. As a result, the world's post-war

Rare photo of what is believed to be Aero Exploration's fleet of F-5Gs. The tail of aircraft in the foreground is the future N502MH. The F-5 in the extreme right background is N53752 now N5596V. The two remaining Lightnings [serial numbers (L to R) 44-27096 & 44-27092] were never given civil registrations. MARKHURD CORPORATION

N75551 in Hurd's early colors of gray with blue trim. WARREN M. BODIE COLLECTION

expansion increased the demand for useable land and natural resources. Aerial mapping was recognized as the most cost effective and efficient methods of exploring previously unmapped regions around the globe. The experience that Hurd's mapping company had obtained over the years put them in a good position to capitalize on the post-war mapping boom. Hurd was also one of the first companies to recognize that the P-38, with its stable, high-altitude performance was an ideal photo mapping platform. Jack Ward, long-time navigator camera-operator, recalls some of his experiences with Hurd's P-38s:

We did flying in Alaska, Ethiopia, Chili, Honduras, Bolivia, The Dominican Republic, and a good portion of the United States. Most of the work overseas was for third world countries and the World Bank. In the United States, we did work for the Forestry Service, Geological Survey, and several other government agencies. We would usually base out of a small town.

Line-up of Mark Hurd's Lightnings outside their Santa Barbara, California, facility. MARKHURD CORPORATION

Close-up of the camera mounting system that was used in many of Mark Hurd's P-38s. MARKHURD CORPORATION

We stayed away from the high-density big cities and it was amazing to find out how many small airport managers would call us and ask us to base out of their airport. They would promise cheap fuel and cars to use while we were based there. One time in Jamestown, South Dakota, the manager of this little airport said we paid off the mortgage on his house just from the gasoline we bought in a season. After all, the airplane used about one hundred gallons an hour and we burned an awful lot of fuel.

In the early days we generally set out to a job with a three-man crew. We had a photographer in the nose, a pilot, and a navigator. The navigator sat piggyback behind the pilot. This arrangement was very uncomfortable for the navigator especially after three hours in the air. After one of our extended hops, we met with Fritz Miller who was a mechanic and also quite a technician with cameras and camera mounts. He figured he could build kind of a cubical for me so I could sit upright instead of leaning over the pilots shoulder. That winter we built a cubical, or bubble, with two windows in the side and it worked real well. The following winter Fritz installed a self-leveling camera mount that he had developed which operated on a pendulum system. He perfected it to the point where we could operate it from my bubble. We used the electrically operated Fairchild camera and tied it with the line to the B-3 bombsight and from there to the cockpit. This arrangement allowed the navigator to operate the camera and thereby eliminating the need for the third man in the nose.

Fritz was always coming up with new ideas and improving on the old ones. I think this is one of the reasons that Mark Hurd was number one in the mapping business.

Our net gain on the flightline was approximately eight linear miles per minute. As I remember, Mark Hurd's average charge was two dollars per square mile. To put it in picture and due to the side lap and end lap, our net gain per picture was about sixteen square miles. That was two hundred twenty dollars a picture and we took a picture every 25 seconds. That's over four hundred dollars a minute!

I always got a bang out of the P-38. Every once in a while we would look out and see an Air Force jet sitting on our wing or trying to sneak up on us. Occasionally, we would play with these boys, who had quite possibly never seen a P-38 in the air before. One

A few of the parts that have been restored by Bruce Pruett. NICK VERONICO (1989)

> time we feathered an engine and this F-89 had to put on the brakes to keep from overshooting us. We then unfeathered our prop and pulled away from the jet. It took a little time for him to catch up with us. It was all in fun.

In 1957, N75551 and N53753 were re-registered with the Federal Aviation Administration as N502MH and N503MH. Ten years later both of these aircraft were retired and subsequently sold to Bruce Pruett of Livermore, California.

Pruett purchased the Hurd Lightnings because he had a sincere admiration for the planes and didn't want to see them broken down for scrap. He was told by many that he would never accomplish the monumental task of dismantling his Lightnings to their component level. He was also harassed by a number of people who thought he was out of his mind for expending so much effort and money on two airplanes which, at that time, were generally regarded as worthless. Despite his critics he successfully dismantled his Lightnings and moved them to a storage location in north central California where they remain today.

Over the past twenty plus years Bruce Pruett has lost little of his enthusiasm for his retirement project. He has started to slowly rebuild one of the airframes, and he is continually on the lookout for parts that might come in handy. Seeing how a P-38, in any condition, is worth a considerable amount of money these days, he also has the satisfaction of having the last laugh at the people who had once poked fun at him.

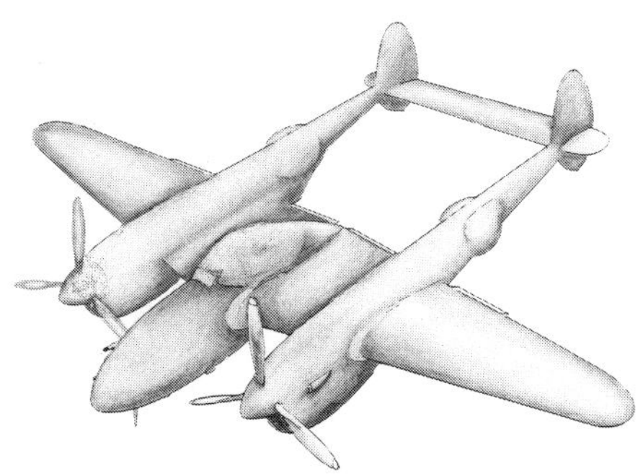

Endangered Species

P-38 RESTORATIONS reached an all-time high during the 1980s. Not since the days of Spartan and Hycon had aviation enthusiasts experienced as many efforts to bring one of America's greatest fighter aircraft back from the point of extinction. One of the more remarkable restorations to make its public debut, during this heightened period of P-38 awareness, was John Silberman's N5596V.

Silberman had financed and managed the rebuilding process of a number of vintage aircraft since purchasing his first warbird in 1967. He was, therefore, no stranger to the aircraft restoration business. But this project was unlike any he had tackled before because this plane was literally a wreck.

During the early 1970s, N5596V belonged to Isaac Newton "Junior" Burchinal, who operated a small museum and flying school in Paris, Texas. His "School For Warbirds" was one of the few flying establishments that offered the average pilot the unique opportunity to fly and be type rated in the likes of the Mustang, Bearcat, and Corsair. In August 1970 he added N5596V to his stable of warbirds and was soon demonstrating the capabilities of the Lockheed fighter at airshows around the area. It was while practicing for one of these airshows in May 1971 that he, and his newly acquired P-38, were involved in a landing accident. Burchinal picks up the story:

> I was practicing for an airshow when a sudden thunderstorm saturated my 3,000-foot grass strip. In an attempt to avoid skidding, I decided to feather the props and just let the plane roll in without using the brakes. (When you feather the props and cut the engines on a P-38 you lose hydraulic power which includes the power needed for braking.) The plane did skid a little when I touched down, but everything was under control until I noticed that a car pulling a trailer had stopped in front of my runway. I knew there wasn't time to pump up the brakes manually, so I pushed the mixture forward and tried to bring the engines back in. I got the right engine turning but the left one wouldn't start. By that time I was a good distance down the runway and it appeared that I was going to crash into the parked car. So, I goosed the right engine, and the plane skidded slightly to the left. That last skid moved the plane enough to miss the car but I ended up crashing into the trailer. Fortunately, no one in the car got hurt.

When Burchinal's P-38 finally came to rest, he found himself in the middle of US Highway 82. A tractor was used to remove the plane from blocking the highway, and, as it turned out, N5596V suffered more damage from the removal process than from its initial impact with the trailer.

For the time being, it appeared that N5596V's career had come to an end: A career which started a quarter of a century earlier when P-38L-5-LO, serial

Aerial view of the War Assets Administration's Depot #41 at Kingman, Arizona. LINDSEY YOUNGBLOOD COLLECTION (1946)

number 44-26996, was officially accepted by the United States Army Air Force in April 1945. Like many of its counterparts, this plane was sent to the Dallas Modification Center where its gun-filled nose was replaced with one that would better accommodate aerial cameras. The aircraft's official designation was then changed to F-5G-6-LO, and after a brief stay at Tinker Field, Oklahoma, it was declared surplus and transferred to the Reconstruction Finance Corporation at Kingman Field, Arizona.

Kingman Field was one of America's busiest airports during the near post-war era. Thousands of the propeller-driven aircraft that helped the Allies defeat the Axis were flown to Kingman to be chopped-up, smelted down, and sold as scrap. Kingman also served as one of the War Assets Administration's surplus sales depots. A number of the aircraft that were stored there were sold outright to individuals under the Surplus Property Act of 1944. In fact, most of the Lightnings that survive today began their civilian careers after being purchased from the Kingman depot.

In March 1946, Aero Exploration Corporation of Tulsa, Oklahoma, purchased 44-26996 and a number of additional P-38s from the War Assets Administration. 44-26996 was registered with the Civil Aeronautics Administration as N53752. Aero operated this plane until December 1951. It was then sold to the Canadian-based Spartan Air Service Limited and re-registered as CF-GCH. During the early 1950s, Spartan was looking to purchase aircraft that could expand their high-altitude capabilities. The P-38 turned out to be the right plane for the job.

CF-GCH's career with Spartan was routine and mostly uneventful with the exception of an engine failure that forced the pilot to make an emergency landing at Duluth's Municipal Airport in May 1953. The pilot executed a perfect single-engine landing, but the plane's port-side gear collapsed shortly after the aircraft started its roll out. The pilot was unhurt and the plane received minimal damage. It wasn't long before CF-GCH was back in the air. In 1956, Spartan was offered the opportunity to purchase cheap surplus military aircraft from the British Government. In doing so, Spartan decided to sell its remaining P-38s to Hycon Aerial Surveys of California.

The formation of Hycon Aerial Surveys, Inc., oc-

CF-CGH at Steenson Field, Winnipeg while being operated by Spartan Air Service Ltd. of Canada. WARREN M. BODIE COLLECTION

curred in November 1954, when its parent company, Hycon Manufacturing, entered into an agreement with Varian Associates of California to form a company that would offer a wide range of services, which included aerial mapping and geophysical surveys. The creation of this new corporation was based upon the needs of both companies. Russell Varian, namesake of Varian Associates, had invented a device, called a magnetometer that was capable of measuring small deviations in the earth's magnetic field. The possibilities offered by this device in the areas of oil and mineral exploration were almost unlimited. However, to deploy such an instrument in a profitable manner required a fleet of aircraft capable of performing tasks similar to aerial survey work. Hycon's Aerial Survey Division was so equipped and was looking for a way to break into the geophysical surveying field; hence, the merger.

Between 1956 and 1959, N5596V was primarily utilized as a high-altitude photo mapping platform. In December 1959, Hycon closed its hangar in Ontario, California. All of Hycon's remaining P-38s were then flown to Las Vegas, Nevada, and put on consignment with Alamo Airways. Over the next 10 years N5596V's title of ownership passed through 10 different owners.

In the years that followed Burchinal's accident in 1971, N5596V was primarily used as a source of spare parts for other P-38s that were flying during that time period. In 1975 David Boyd, who had already purchased one P-38 from Burchinal, took an interest in N5596V and further cannibalized the plane in order to rebuild his other P-38. Four years later N5596V was finally rescued by John Silberman when he purchased what was left of the airframe from Boyd.

Silberman bought the plane as a restorable aircraft, but many of its parts were missing. "You would have had to have been there to believe it," recalls Silberman. "Among some of the parts that were missing were the engines, props, spinners, essentially both firewalls forward, coolers, radiators, gear doors, etc. The aircraft actually had two unserviceable engine mounts and one very rusty engine. It had no accessories, no hydraulic valves, cylinders or actuators. The cockpit had been stripped (no seat or instruments). The wheels were cracked and the landing gear needed a great deal of work. Having the gear pulled out from under it, there were no trunnions. They had to be manufactured and installed. (Lots of sheet metal work.)" Regrettably, P-38 parts were, and still are, scarce; but Silberman and his chief pilot and mechanic, Jan "Jaybo" Hinube, persevered through the six years that was needed to save N5596V from extinction. The reward of their labor was finally realized in March 1986 when the plane made its first public appearance at the Valiant Air Command's annual airshow. Needless to say, Silberman's Lightning was the hit of that year's show.

In 1989 Silberman sold his P-38 to the Santa Monica Museum of Flying in California. At that time

Hycon Aerial Survey's President Aldon E. Acker (right) **and Dr. Russell Varian shown holding a Magnetometer, which is used to measure absolute values of the earth's magnetic field.** HYCON VIA DON DOWNIE (1955).

After Hycon's demise, N5596V spent several years (1960–1962) in Las Vegas, Nevada. N5596V was later bought and subsequently re-sold nine times before ending up in the ownership of I.N. Burchinal in 1970. MILO PELTZER COLLECTION

The aftermath of Burchinal's May 24, 1971, landing accident. N5596V is shown spread across US Highway 82 West near Paris, Texas. WALTER BASSANO

Luck was on Burchinal's side when he narrowly missed the people in car that had stopped to watch his P-38 land. He wasn't as fortunate with the U-HAUL trailer which the car was pulling. WALTER BASSANO (1971)

N5596V minus nose and propellers spent the next nine years on Burchinal's junk pile while it was used as a source of spare parts for other P-38 projects. JOHN SILBERMAN COLLECTION

John Silberman bought what was left of N5596V in 1979. It would take him the better part of six years and a bucket of money to bring this battered bird back to airworthy status. The black cat on the plane's nose is the insignia of the 282nd Helicopter Assault Company. Silberman flew more than 700 combat hours with the 282nd during his tour in Vietnam. Inset: **It has been said that a picture is worth a thousand words. This drawing depicts the condition of N5596V at the time of Silberman's rescue.** JOHN SILBERMAN COLLECTION

Silberman's P-38 made its first post-restoration appearance at the Valiant Air Command's air show in March 1986. The man, sitting in the cockpit waving to the crowd is Thurston Hinube. "Jaybo," as he is called by his friends, soloed at the tender age of twelve and went on to carve out a career in the Air Force as a pilot. He is also a Vietnam Veteran with over 100 night interdiction mission's in the Douglas A-26K to his credit. KEN LENSLEY (1986)

N5596V freshly decorated in the colors of the 435th Fighter Squadron awaits bidders at the Museum of Flying's auction on May 20, 1990. NICK VERONICO

Beautiful aerial view of N5596V caught during Hinton's test flight. COLIN CRAWFORD

N5596V's photo nose was replaced with a fabricated gun nose that was developed by Steve Hinton's Fighter Rebuilders. On May 20, 1990, N5596V was offered up for bid at the Museum of Flying's now-famous warbird auction. William Lyons, former chairman of AirCal, and a telephone bidder were the principal competitors for this P-38. The outcome of the competition acknowledged Lyons as the winner with a record $1,550,000 bid for the rare plane. Lyons was later asked what he was going to do with his prize. He replied, "I'm going to fly it!" Coincidentally, the man who will be keeping the Lyons' P-38 in working order is Vern Hickey, who cared for this plane in the 1950s when he served as Hycon's Chief Mechanic.

In spite of the many P-38 restorations that were completed in the past few years, the Lightning will undoubtedly continue to be an endangered species. However, with price tags in excess of a million dollars, and with the recession of the early 1990s cutting into the military budgets, Lockheed might someday consider putting the plane back into production.

Although N5596V was cosmetically a good looking airplane, it was still in need of some extra work before it was truly ready for flight status. Vern Hickey, who cut his teeth on P38s during his tenure with Hycon Aerial Surveys, was given the responsibility of bringing N5596V up to flight standards. The first test flight was flown in 1992 by renowned test pilot Steve Hinton. COLIN CRAWFORD

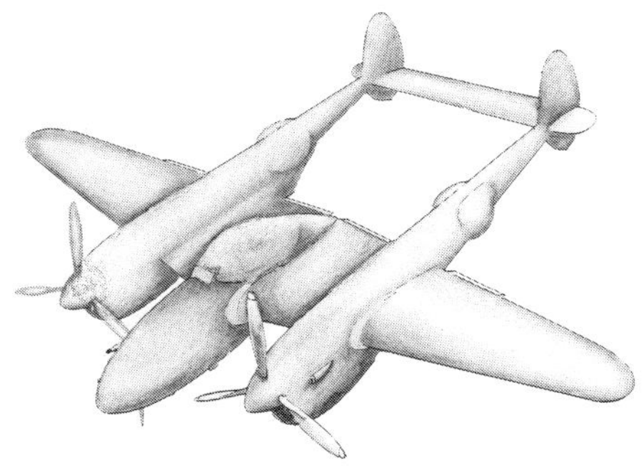

The Weather Hunter

The P-38 was one of the most versatile aircraft to be deployed in World War II. Its unique design offered the Army Air Force great latitude in using the Lightning as a fighter, bomber, or reconnaissance aircraft. The same design features that gave the military such flexibility also made the P-38 successful in the post-war realm. Many of the surviving airframes have performed a wide variety of missions in the course of their respective careers, but few were flown in more hazardous conditions or in as many different configurations as the Lightning that the late Jim Cook used to conduct weather research.

Jim Cook learned to fly in 1935 by trading his skills at guiding the local coyote and wolf exterminator around west Texas in exchange for flight time in a Curtiss Junior. Later Cook went on to contract his flying abilities to the Army Air Corps as a primary flight instructor, and also enlisted in the Royal Air Force with the promise that he would be added to the roster of the Eagle Squadron. However, when the United States entered the war, Cook's RAF enlistment was canceled by the War Department. He then joined Trans World Airlines and flew with both its international and domestic divisions for the duration of the war. But the repetitive nature of airline duty was simply not for Cook. He's the kind of man who gets bored doing the same thing twice.

He once witnessed an aircraft conducting weather experiments and realized the possibility of controlling rainfall. His interest in weather modification soon grew into studying and experimenting with cloud seeding.

"I found out very early that a cloud would dissipate if it was overseeded," recalled Cook. "The cloud dissipation that I observed was caused by the cloud's super cooled water vapor or droplets being attracted to a greater number of sodium iodide crystals. You see, natural rain is caused by water droplets collecting on ice crystals until they are heavy enough to fall. Silver iodide, when released in a cloud, generates a crystal which has about the same geometry as ice crystals. However, if a cloud is overseeded it never builds up enough mass to create artificial rain. Anyway, I got the idea that cloud overseeding might be a way to prevent hail."

Cook purchased a Curtiss P-40 and set out to experiment with his idea of hail prevention in an area of Nebraska which was known for its high incident of hail. His initial results were promising, but the P-40 left much to be desired. Cook continues:

> The engineers that designed the P-40, this is what I think, anyway, figured the guy flying the plane might get his ass shot off because this airplane is too heavy to turn inside of a Zero. But at least it's not going to

Aero Service Corporation used N65485 as a photo mapping platform for several years. Here the aircraft is shown after experiencing a nose gear failure while taxiing. AERO SERVICE CORPORATION

Jim Cook on his P-38. COOK COLLECTION

No, this is not something out of Buck Rogers! This is the business end of Jim Cook's P-38. The hole in the tip of the nose is actually an air intake to an absolute filter that was used to capture particles suspended in the atmosphere. Cook used this device to determine how far the jet stream would carry radiation fallout from atomic bomb tests. The square port above the air intake is a one-way mirror and camera view window. The mirror picked up a reflection from an instrument panel in the nose and projected it in a fashion so the camera could include the instrument readings on the photos that were taken (in time lapse) of weather phenomenon. The two horizontal masts on either side of the nose are electric field strength probes, and the ringed device mounted on the aircraft's left side is a corona ring and detection device that was used to measure the electric charge associated with rain drops. External radar units could also be carried on the strut that is shown connected to the aircraft's right-hand point or pylon. JIM COOK COLLECTION

come apart. I guarantee you that the P-40 is as tough as the back end of a shooting gallery. But it just couldn't get high enough to produce the results I was after.

At about the same time I got a yin to break the record of flying around the world. I tried to purchase Jimmy Stewart's and Joe DeBona's F-6C (recon version of the P-51), but they wouldn't sell it to me because it held several speed records. Finally the Navy broke DeBona's Los Angles-to-New York speed run, and Joe agreed to sell me the plane. I used it successfully for some time, but one day I retracted the gear after take off and only one side came up. I then tried to extend the gear but the side that retracted wouldn't come down. This particular Mustang had a wet wing which at the time of the malfunction was full of fuel. I realized that the wet wing would burst into flames as soon as it touched the ground, so I ended up jumping out of it.

Cook's weather experiments opened many doors for him, and he was soon contracting his services to various governmental agencies that were interested in pursuing severe weather research. He replaced his ill-fated F-6C with a "D" model Mustang and immediately went back to work. In the meantime, he also purchased an F-5G that had been operated as an aerial mapping plane by Aero Service Corporation.

The reconnaissance variant of the P-38 he purchased was built by Lockheed and modified at their Dallas Modification Center in May 1945. Army Air Force 44-27087 was then assigned to Tinker Field, Oklahoma, before being declared excess in January 1946. The following April, 44-27087 was purchased from the Kingman, Arizona, storage depot for $1,250 by Russell C. Reeves of Tulsa, Oklahoma. Reeves registered his new Lightning with the Civil Aeronautics Administration as N65485. The aircraft was bought and sold several times between Reeves' and Aero Service's ownership. When Jim Cook purchased the plane in 1957, he changed its registration to N345. A few months later he experienced an engine failure on takeoff while piloting his second P-51. The ensuing crash-landing damaged the plane beyond economical repair, so Cook removed the instrumentation, which had been installed behind P-51s seat, and put it in the nose of his P-38.

I have never flown an airplane, before or since, that I loved like the 38. I've flown quite a few jets, and none of these so called modern airplanes performed like my P-38. In fact, it was an ideal aircraft for severe weather research, and if I was to build an airplane today to do the kind of work I did, it would look like a Lightning.

Unlike the other airplanes that I have used, the P-38 had ample room in its nose compartment to install equipment. The cockpit had so much room, as compared to the Mustang, that I sometimes felt like a "BB in a bucket." One thing I enjoyed about flying the P-38 was its counter-rotating props, which made the plane very stable and easy to fly. In many cases, I flew temperature lines or humidity lines while breathing pressure oxygen, running a twenty pin recorder, voice recorder, radar set and nose camera, communicating with ATC for clearance, communicating with my base of operations on HF; all while navigating with respect to weather. I can't think of any other airplane, modern or otherwise, that would allow a pilot to do as many things as I did without an autopilot.

One of the things that made the P-38 ideal for weather research was its temperature compensating flight control system. Kelly Johnson's team designed the P-38 to perform equally when subjected to large temperature gradients. This was accomplished by connecting the cockpit control cables to one end of a lever, which pivots in the center. The other end of this lever was connected to the cables which ran to the control surfaces. This design feature enabled the control linkage to expand or contract while not affecting the overall handling performance of the aircraft.

Another advantage the Lightning had over other aircraft that I have flown is its dive flaps, or speed brakes as some people like to call them. If you got into turbulence you could pop those brakes and you would slow up. Plus the airplane did what it was supposed to do. The speed brakes would come out underneath and pitch the plane up. In most modern airplanes the pitch is down or at best neutral. Many times I have been forced into compressibility dives by the strong winds and micro bursts that accompany thunderstorms. This never really concerned me when I was flying my 38 because I knew I had a well built airplane under me, and I had confidence that I could regain control by merely engaging the speed brakes. However, there was one occasion when I found myself in a high-speed dive while being twisted every which way by a violent storm. The plane started to tuck under and, at that point, I

Side view of Cook's P-38 complete with air intake cover. Ten mil wires ran from the mast that is located above the camera window to standoffs on the wing tips. The mast end of these wires were connected to an X-ray power supply that was concealed in the nose compartment. When switched on, this power supply elevated the entire aircraft and its occupant to 30 thousand volts. Cook recalled that while conducting experiments with this device, the hair on his arms would stand up. The first time Cook operated the high-voltage power supply at night he was taken back by the presence of tiny blue-violet lights that seemed to outline the aircraft. These tiny lights were actually the areas of the plane in which the charge of the power supply gathered to form point discharges. It would be interesting to find out how often Cook's P-38 might have been mistaken for a UFO. BURTON KEMP COLLECTION

Another configuration that was used by Cook. The boom sticking out of the nose is a 12-foot-long electric field strength probe connected to the airframe at the base of the plane's nose. Temperature measuring devices, including a vortex thermometer, were incorporated in the tip of this probe. Some of the instrumentation carried in the plane's nose can be seen through the small nose window. MILO PELTZER COLLECTION

figured I'd had enough, so I reached to engage the dive flaps. Then I noticed that the flaps were already extended, and to make matters worse, I looked down at my lap and noticed a rivet. Needless to say, the situation got my attention, but there wasn't much I could do but ride it down. I eventually regained control, and when I got back on the ground I took a closer look at the rivet and discovered that it was one that had its head drilled, and apparently had been floating around in the cockpit for years. I had to put a lot of rivets in the Mustangs I used to conduct weather work, but I never had to replace a rivet in my 38.

Although the P-38 had many advantages over other types of aircraft, it is not without its weaknesses. Cook continues:

The P-38's counter-rotating propellers, when all is working right, kind of spoils the pilot because you don't have to deal with torque. The only time you need to touch the rudder while taking off is to compensate for turbo surging. However, when things go wrong, like an engine failure on takeoff, you really have to know what you are doing or you won't live to fly another day. You see, the torque of the turning engine is in the same direction the plane wants to yaw. Therefore, when an engine fails, you have to give it opposite rudder and hold it until you can throttle back and trim the plane for one engine operation. Well, as I said before, the P-38 spoils you because you don't build up the leg strength that is needed to hold hard opposite rudder for any length of time. One thing you can do to help control the yawing moment is to adjust the trim at the same time you apply opposite rudder. Unfortunately, Lockheed put the rudder trim adjustment on the floor just in front of the pilot's seat. I figured that if I had an engine failure on takeoff, there was no way I could hold hard opposite rudder and keep the plane's nose level while bending over to adjust the trim. So, I built a little box and extended the trim shaft so it could be reached without having to bend over. I experienced several engine failures, and my little trim modification worked very well.

Another weakness the P-38 had was its coolant radiators. In the kind of work I was in, I frequently encountered hail, and I was shot down on two different occasions due to hail clogging the plane's coolant radiators.

The P-38 is often confused with Northrop's P-61 Black Widow. Jim Cook likes to tell a humorous story about his first flight in his Lightning and his chance encounter with a P-61 expert.

I picked up the plane in New Jersey and started home. It had been my experience that when you buy an airplane, the seller generally gives you the sorriest

An example of Cook's working environment. Photo of a tornado taken from N345's camera. Although Cook never flew through a funnel, he often skirted these dangerous clouds in the course of his researching endeavors. JIM COOK COLLECTION

batteries they have on hand. So, when I got around Little Rock, I decided to see if I could land a P-38. I went on into the airport and as I was getting out of the plane this guy dressed in a white tee-shirt and Delta Airlines cap came up to me. He said, "I'll be damned: A P-61. The first one I have seen since I left India." I responded by telling him that I thought it was a P-38. He said, "No, I work for Delta. That's a P-61." Well, I wasn't sure what Delta had to do with it, so I asked him if Delta used P-61s. He said, "No, but that's a P-61." I figured that guy was pulling my chain because those Arkansasers are capable of doing that, but I went on and I told him that I had bought it for a P-38. He said, "You've been took!" I then told him that I was flying it with a P-38 manual. He said, "You're going to get hurt!" At that point it was obvious to me that I wasn't going to convince him that my plane was a P-38, so I went in the terminal and got a bit of lunch. Not long after lunch, I went to start my plane and couldn't get the right engine to turn. The batteries that were given to me were pure junk. I finally found a fellow and I asked him if anyone had a ground power unit I could use. He told me that the Delta people had one. I walked down to the Delta shack and asked the P-61 expert if I could borrow their ground power unit. He said, "You mean for that P-61?" I said: "Yeah on that P-61!"

In the mid-1960s Jim Cook retired; however, it wasn't long before he was again called on to conduct weather research. This time, instead of doing basic research he was asked to produce a training film for the airlines on the use of radar to detect weather conditions. Again the N345 proved to be the right plane for the job. Collins Radio had no trouble with installing its radar packages in the plane's nose compartment. Cook's work over the following two years established him as one of the world authorities on the use of radar. (This led to a contract that brought Cook to Vietnam to help the Army train pilots on the use of radar.) At the conclusion of this project Cook again decided to retire and put N345 up for sale. He wanted to find someone that would take care of his Lightning, and in 1969 he found just such a person in Gary Levitz.

During the fourteen years that followed Levitz successfully raced N345 in several different configurations and paint schemes. In the early years John Brooks, John Rador (whose P-38 experience dates back to the YP-38), Richard Ransophre and Vernon Thorpe provided much of the maintenance that was required to keep Levitz's Lightning in competitive form. John Rador recalled some of the things that were done to make this plane a better racer:

N345 in its final configuration while under the ownership of Jim Cook. Collins Radio installed two radar units in the plane's nose and Cook used this configuration to conduct radar research. Inset: **A view of the radar screen in N345's cockpit. This unit was actually installed behind the pilot's seat.**
COLLINS COMMERCIAL AVIONICS. INSET: JIM COOK COLLECTION

> We installed a fighter nose and removed the turbo superchargers and intercooler ducting and related parts. We also replaced the "L" model cowlings with "H" model versions which were a little more streamlined. The plane's weight was also reduced by removing the wing flaps and all parts including the adel clamps and brackets. Of course, we went through the oil and coolant systems and replaced or overhauled parts as necessary. The wing tips were clipped and about three inches were cut off of each propeller blade. All-in-all, the plane's total weight was reduced by 1,600 pounds.

Some of the parts that were used to rebuild N345 were obtained from a derelict Lightning that Levitz had purchased from Page Airmotive of Yukon, Oklahoma. The remainder of the derelict airframe was donated to the Confederate Air Force, as was N345 in 1972. Although, Levitz donated his P-38 to the CAF he maintained controlling interest by sponsoring the aircraft. In 1981 he traded the CAF two P-63s for total ownership of his P-38.

In 1983 Levitz arrived at the Reno Air Races with his P-38 sporting a gloss black paint scheme. Sadly, an accidental gear retraction in the pit area precluded N345 from competing in the races. Not long after the accident Levitz lost interest in the plane and sold it to Invader Aviation, Inc., of Wilmington, Delaware. The following year, noted aircraft collector John McGuire added N345 to his collection and changed its registration to N577JB. For several years the plane was stored at McGuire's ranch near El Paso, Texas. In 1990 the plane was flown to McGuire's spectacular new museum in Santa Teresa, New Mexico.

MacGuire's War Eagles Air Museum houses a large selection of vintage and rare aircraft and features educational exhibits that explain the significance of each of these airplanes. The museum is staffed by approximately 40 volunteers and is blessed with an outstanding assortment of veteran pilots and mechanics. One of the museum's volunteers is Guy Dority who was a crew member of "Jarrin' Jenny," which was the first Army Air Force B-17 (41-9085) to land in Great Britain the summer of 1942. Although Dority enjoys all the immaculately restored aircraft that are included in the museum's collection, he has a particular fondness for the P-38. No doubt, visitors that tour the museum with Dority benefit from his first-person perspective of what the P-38 meant to the bomber crews during the early days of the European air war.

Gary Levitz brought N345 to the Mojave for the California 1,000-mile race in 1970 and 1971 as shown. Levitz placed 15th in 1970. He and his relief pilot Vernon Thorpe managed to place 22nd in the 1971 event in spite of a having a tire blow on their second pit stop.
WARREN BODIE COLLECTION

Levitz' P-38 appeared at the 1973 Reno Championship Air Races with an attractive overall gray paint scheme highlighted with shark's teeth. Levitz placed 16th with an average speed of 340.541 mph.
DUSTIN CARTER COLLECTION

"Double Trouble" as it appeared in 1975. MILO PELTZER COLLECTION

N577JB in flight over the Texas/New Mexico desert. WAR EAGLES AIR MUSEUM

The majestic lines of race #38 as caught by the lens of Neal Nurmi in 1977.
NEAL NURMI

The racing career of Levitz' beautiful P-38 came to an end with an accidental gear retraction in the pit area during the 1983 National Championship Air Races. BILL ROGERS

N577JB on display in the War Eagles Air Museum, which is located a few miles west of El Paso, in Santa Teresa, New Mexico. Inset: **Interior view of the museum's black P-38.** AUTHOR'S COLLECTION (1990)

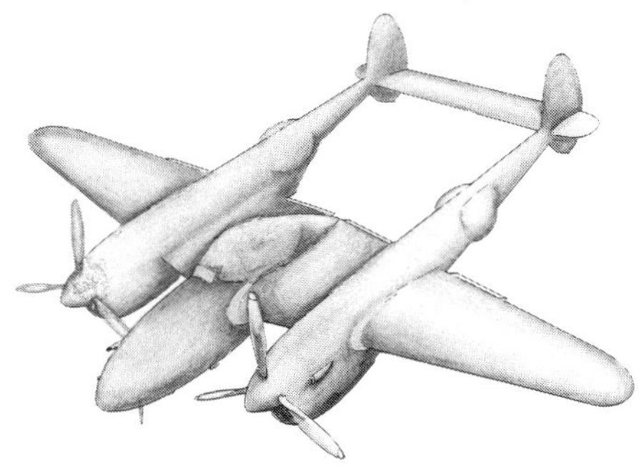

N79123

N79123 WAS ONE of the 2,520 P-38L-5-LOs that were produced at Lockheed Burbank during the last year of the Second World War. After being accepted by the Army Air Force the plane was assigned 44-27231 as its serial number and radio call sign. In the closing months of the war there was an ever-increasing need for photo intelligence, so 44-27231 and many other P-38s were sent to the Dallas Modification Center where they were converted to fill the needs of the war effort. The military designation of these aircraft were changed to F-5G-6-LO.

The photo variants that evolved from the basic Lightning airframe and the pilots who flew the unarmed F-4s and F-5s are, in many ways, the unsung heros of World War II. Equally unsung are the engineers and technical support people who endured the pressures of wartime to upgrade and redesign the F-5 series. Leo Childs, the principal engineer and designer of the F-5G nose configuration, recalls the wartime atmosphere of the Dallas Modification Center:

> The operation took on somewhat of a battle-front atmosphere with planes being flown in directly from the factories or back from the war zones for modification. Individual projects were assigned to project engineers or program managers with full authority to work with military or factory representatives to get the job done in keeping with established schedules. In some cases it was necessary for the Project Engineer to do conceptual design, detail drafting, follow the work through the shops, participate in flight testing, and delivery of the finished product to the Air Corps' Acceptance Officer. Basically, you were given the authority and expected to use it to keep your projects on schedule or . . . get the hell out of the way and let someone else do it.

Childs had previously worked on the project to upgrade the capabilities of the F-5B. This led to the development of the F-5C. This particular variant was designed to carry the Trimetrogon camera configuration, which was ideal for capturing high-quality, low-level tactical intelligence. On the other hand, mission requirements often called for strategic intelligence as well. Missions of this type were generally carried out by two separate aircraft: one equipped with the Trimetrogon configuration and another with cameras that had longer focal lengths. It was obvious to the military planners that mission survivability and efficiency could be increased by incorporating a combination of both camera setups in one plane. Childs remembers the proposal that set in motion the development of what became the F-5G.

> In early 1944 Lockheed submitted a proposal for a new photo recon modification to the P-38 to replace earlier models. The proposal included the following recommendations:

NX79123 was one of ten P-38s/F-5Gs to compete in the 1946 Bendix Trophy Race. Number 95, piloted by James Harp, managed to place fifth in the event with an average speed of 370.447 mph. HUDEK COLLECTION (CLEVELAND 1946)

Removal of the existing gun nose and replacement with a completely new nose assembly from the windshield forward. The nose assembly would be fabricated in kit form, ready for installation at the Mod Center or at the theaters of operation and include all provisions necessary for installation and check-out. This included electrical systems, camera controls, camera bay heaters, intervalometers, and vacuum systems. All provisions were for easy installation of specified cameras. These kits would be prefabricated and ready for swap-out with the gun nose to reduce turnaround time at the Mod Center to a minimum.

The camera package would include a full trimetrogon configuration of three 6″ K-17 or K-22; Plus a choice of split vertical 24 or 40″ K-22 cameras or equivalent or the new Sonne Strip Camera; Plus one 12″ K-17 or K-22 forward oblique camera mounted in the most forward part of the nose assembly; This photo recon package would eliminate the requirement for a second airplane with long focal length cameras to fly in formation with airplanes equipped only with trimetrogon photo systems, a condition which existed in all previous photo recon mods.

The above proposal was presented in an open meeting at the Mod Center attended by Col. Elliot Roosevelt, Chief of Photo Intelligence operations and Don Marshall, general manager, and their staff personnel. At the conclusion of my presentation Col. Roosevelt raised his hands from the table and asked "What do you need from me?" I replied: "All we need is your authorization to proceed and the allocation of airplanes."

As I recall, within a few days we received a directive from the Air Material Command authorizing the full project and allocation of 350 P-38s for conversion to F-5Gs.

After finishing the design of the upgraded nose, Childs approached the Giberson Company with a contract to produce the required components. Giberson immediately went to work and in a very short time was turning out complete F-5G nose kits.

Army Air Force assigned 44-27231 to the Third Reconnaissance Command at Coffeyville, Kansas, shortly after it was modified. Here it served in the training role until November 1945 when it was declared surplus and turned over to the Reconstruction Finance Corporation at Altus Field, Oklahoma.

Altus was one of the five surplus depots to carry P-38s in their inventory. Initially, the Reconstruction Finance Corporation and the War Assets Administration decided to sell some of their unwanted surplus aircraft individually. By early 1946 most of the established reclamation or storage facilities were overflowing

James Harp shortly after completing the 2,000-mile race from Van Nuys to Cleveland. HARP COLLECTION

with airplanes. At that time the WAA deemed it more reasonable and cost effective to put entire depots up for bid. By July 1946 the depots at Kingman, Arizona; Walnut Ridge, Arkansas; Ontario, California; and others were purchased by salvage companies, which put an end to individual aircraft sales at those facilities. Altus, however, had a large inventory and was still actively selling aircraft when James Harp arrived to make his purchase. Harp recalled:

> During my spring semester in engineering at the University of Illinois, I started thinking about the Cleveland National Air Races, and the Bendix Trophy Race, in particular. I realized that a military fighter would undoubtedly win. If I selected the right plane and flew it properly, I would have as much chance as anyone else.
>
> I had flown my combat tour in P-47s (the only fighter I had flown) and I knew the advantages of having a turbo supercharger to compress air at high altitudes where high speeds could be maintained over long distances. I selected the P-38 because it had turbos and the photo version had a radio direction finder for navigation and a larger nose section for carrying added gasoline internally. Also, the price was a relatively inexpensive $1250.00.
>
> I purchased a P-38L-5-LO, serial number 44-27231, from the War Assets Administration, Altus Army Air Base, Oklahoma in July 1946. I picked out a P-38 with only 400 hours total time, looked new and had good tires. After reading the manuals on how to fly the P-38, and giving myself blindfold checks in the cockpit, I took off and flew to Joliet, Illinois, on 22 July 1946.
>
> My brother Ed, Bill Peel (an ex-Lockheed technician), and I stripped the armor from the plane, added three gas tanks in the nose, one under the canopy behind the pilot, and two 165-gallon drop tanks for a total fuel load at take-off of 910 gallons. We barely had time to paint my race number of "95" before I took off for Van Nuys, California and the start of the 1946 Bendix Trophy Race, held 30 August 1946.
>
> My race tactic called for firewalling the P-38 to a cruising altitude of 35,000 feet, then pull back the power to 35 inches of manifold pressure, 2400 rpm, and mixture in auto lean. According to the books, I should be able to get to 35,000 in about 15 minutes, then cruise at about 220 mph indicated which would give about 395 mph true airspeed.
>
> But, in talking to some of the other pilots the day before the race, when I told them I had 910 gallons on board, they wanted to know where I was planning to land enroute to refuel. When I told them I wasn't planning to land to refuel, they said they didn't think I could make it. So, the night before the race I got the books out and planned for maximum range. Climb at 35 inches of manifold pressure, 2,400 rpm, auto lean, and 160 mph indicated airspeed.
>
> The next day United States' greatest warbirds took off at 3 or 4 minute intervals headed for the Cleveland Municipal Airport, 2,045 miles away.
>
> My takeoff was uneventful, and immediately after takeoff, I pointed the nose toward Cleveland. I spent the next 45 minutes climbing to 35,000 feet altitude using a power setting of 35 inches manifold pressure and 2,400 rpm, auto lean, at an indicated air speed of 165 mph. At 35,000 feet I leveled off and my indicated air speed went up to 220 mph giving me a true air speed approximately 400 mph. Not too bad, I figured.
>
> I originally planned that both external tanks would run dry and be dropped before reaching Colorado Springs. But now I could see Colorado Springs up ahead and I was still running on the second tank. Should I drop it now where there would be no chance of hurting anyone on the ground, or should I keep it and run it dry? I decided to keep it. I ran dry some 50-75 miles after passing Colorado Springs, and I dropped it.
>
> Over Nebraska it appeared I was running long on fuel and considered pushing the throttles forward but then decided to play it safe and wait. Over Des Moines, I knew I was long on fuel and increased power to 40 inches manifold pressure, 2500 rpm, and auto rich, giving me an indicated air speed of about 230 mph for a true air speed of about 415 mph. Over Chicago I was considerably long on fuel and further increased power to 45 inches manifold pressure, 2600 rpm, auto rich which gave an indicated air speed of 240 mph and a true air speed of about 430 mph. At altitude that day we had a 60 mph tailwind, so my ground speed after passing Chicago was around 490 mph. As I approached Cleveland I started letting down while maintaining high speed, and zoomed across the finish line at Cleveland Hopkins Airport five hours and thirty-one minutes after starting my takeoff roll at Van Nuys.
>
> There were four P-51s in that race and I was fifth. The fourth place P-51 beat me by 2½ minutes. If I had stuck to my original race tactics, I would have beat one and maybe two P-51s.
>
> When considering the race results, it might be concluded that the P-51 was by far the better cross-country racer. In my opinion, however, I believe the P-38 and P-51 were comparable airplanes at each's best altitude. I believe the most important factor was the skill and experience of the pilot and the availability of funds to convert it to a racing machine. Paul Mantz and Jackie Cochran, who won first and second place had experience, skill, and money. Paul had sealed his wings to carry fuel, so he needed no external tanks. If Paul Mantz and Jackie Cochran had been flying P-38s, I

During the early 1950s N79123 could be seen near the Palwalki Airport in Illinois. The 301 on its lower nose indicates that it was the 301st P-38L to be converted to an F5G-6-LO. CLAY JANASSON VIA MILO PELTZER

think they would have again finished first and second or close to it.

When I look back on that experience at age 23, I sure must have been an optimist. To buy a P-38 1½ months before the race, prepare it for racing, and finish in the money now seems sort of incredible. I spent a total of $2,500 for the plane, gasoline and preparation. I won $1,500, sold the plane for $1,500, so made a profit of $500. Not a bad experience for a student during summer vacation at college.

Harp wasn't the only one to race a Lightning in the 1946 Bendix Trophy Race. Out of the 22 aircraft that competed in the 1946 Bendix Trophy Race, 14 were P-38s or F-5Gs. The reason for the P-38's overwhelming acceptance in 1946 as a long-distance racing plane probably stemmed from its war time reputation. It was also popular because it was one of the cheapest ($1,250) of the high power airplanes that could be purchased at that time.

A few months after the race, Harp sold N79123 to J. E. Howard of Champaign, Illinois. Two years later Howard sold the former Bendix racer to Ray Reinert of Arlington, Illinois. For a period of time, 79123 was kept at the Pal-Walkie airport near Wheeling, Illinois, but in 1950 the plane was sold to Carl C. Hughes of San Antonio, Texas, who four years later sold it for $2,800 to Joseph P. Jacobson. Unfortunately, little information exists on how this plane was utilized up to the time when Jack Hardwick purchased the plane in 1955.

Hardwick participated in the post-war air races and was also an avid aircraft collector who made his living supplying foreign air forces with surplus parts. In the early period of Hardwick's ownership a gloss black N79123 with white registration numbers could be seen parked along side of N29Q at Bracket Field at Laverne, California. Some time later the plane was moved to Hardwick's storage yard in El Monte, California. While there, the plane was more or less neglected. David Tallichet acquired N79123 from Hardwick in the early 1980s. The plane then spent time in several different re-build shops around the country before ending up at Cal Aero Field at Chino, California.

Presently, the aircraft is undergoing restoration at Tallichet's Military Aircraft Restoration Group facility in Chino, California. Volunteer help for the project is being supplied by Lockheed and the P-38 National Association. Some of the volunteers are former Lightning pilots and Lockheed-Burbank engineers who are hoping to get the plane back in the air soon.

One last footnote regarding N79123: In recent years the author has received numerous reports indicating that the airframe registered as N79123 was mistakenly identified as N505MH sometime before it was sold to Doug Arnold in 1988. Whether this purported identity swapping actually took place between N79123 and N505MH is presently still up for debate.

A weather-worn N79123 at Brackett Field, California. The landing gear doors on this plane were removed after being damaged in a wheels up landing.
DUSTIN CARTER (1954)

N79123 was later painted black after Jack Hardwick took ownership of the aircraft. DUSTIN CARTER (1958)

In the past few years N79123 has been undergoing restoration work at the Military Aircraft Restoration Corporation's facility at Chino, California. JOHN HARJO (1991)

N79123 was displayed for the public for the first time on June 19, 1992. It is decorated in the colors of one of Dick Bong's, America's leading ace, war-time P-38s. JOHN HARJO (1992)

Dick Bong's widow, "Marge" Bong-Drucker, and the aircraft's owner David Tallichet were on hand for the N79123's roll out ceremonies. JOHN HARJO (1992)

Survey Lightning

DURING THE LATE 1940S and throughout the 1950s, lucrative contracts were let by various governmental mapping agencies. Most of these contracts required the surveyor to supply clear, stable photographs scaled at one-inch per mile. To accommodate this provision, the competing survey companies were forced to seek an aircraft that could operate safely and reliably at altitudes in excess of 30,000 feet. In the near-post-war era the photo-recon variant of the P-38 proved to be a popular choice of airplane for high-altitude survey work. The Mark Hurd Mapping Company of Minneapolis, Minnesota, was one such company that strengthened its competitive edge by purchasing a number of Lockheed's twin-boom Lightnings.

In 1953 the Hurd company added a fifth F-5G to their fleet of Lightnings by purchasing N62441 from the Aero Exploration Company, Inc. of Tulsa, Oklahoma. Prior to Aero's ownership, N62441 was operated by Kargl Aerial Surveys, of Midland, Texas, who had purchased the plane in February 1946 from the War Asset's Depot 41 at Kingman, Arizona. The military history of N62441 dates back to May 1945 when P-38L-5-LO, Serial Number 44-53012 was accepted by the Air Force and sent to the Dallas Modification Center to be converted to an F-5G-6-LO. Not long after its conversion was completed, the plane was declared surplus and dropped from the Air Force's inventory.

Although Hurd's Lightnings performed well at altitude, they weren't necessarily the most comfortable airplanes from the crew's standpoint. One must remember that the P-38 was designed during a time when cockpit pressurization was still in the experimental stage. Therefore, the occupants of Hurd's P-38s were subjected to the frigid thin air of the lower stratosphere. Jack Ward, one time navigator and camera operator for the Mark Hurd Mapping Company, remembers one of his high-altitude experiences:

> I passed out one time at 36,000 feet. As we finished the line, I told my pilot that I wasn't feeling very well. He kiddingly said, "Well, I don't feel very well either." He then turned around and looked at me. I was having convulsions with my head down and it scared him. He dove the plane straight down and told me later that he pulled it out at 10,000 feet but he said the airplane had a tendency to do an outside loop and he couldn't pull it out. He finally did and it scared him to death. I had come to at the lower altitude and we attempted to go back up to do our job, but I started feeling bad again so we returned to the base and landed. We checked things out and discovered my oxygen regulator had a leak in it.

The air is so thin at 30,000 feet that a person will lose consciousness after only a few minutes of being

N501MH sharply decorated in the Hurd company colors of gray with blue highlight. The large bulge at the bottom of the plane's nose was configured so it could carry two large aerial cameras. MARKHURD CORPORATION (1958).

deprived of oxygen. To counter this hazard, most of the survey companies used what is called a pressure oxygen system. The pressurized system forces air into the pilot's lungs instead of the having him inhale in a normal fashion. In effect, it is like breathing in reverse. This type of system worked well; however, having to overcome the pressure in the mask just to exhale was very taxing on the pilot and the crew, so the Hurd company decided to try another approach to solve the problem.

In February 1954, N62441 was delivered to the Airesearch Aviation Service Company in Los Angeles for modification. Ward recalled:

> We had one P-38 that was pressurized, I guess it was the only pressurized P-38 in existence. The pressurization system was run off one of the turbo-superchargers. The pilot's seat was also moved six inches forward so the navigator could sit comfortably in tandem. However, this was very uncomfortable for the pilot as he had to sit with his legs straight out which made it hard for him to work the brakes and rudder. But the pressurization system worked so well that we didn't have to wear electric heated suits. I worked in it for a couple of years in shirt sleeves. The only thing was, you had to crawl through a little trap door, which was about one foot square. At some airports we couldn't get clearance to take off right away, and it would get mighty hot in that plane. But after we got into the air it was real comfortable. At 30,000 feet, we had to start using oxygen, but not very much. In our other Lightnings, we had to suck on 100 percent oxygen all the way upstairs to keep from getting the bends.

N62441's registration was changed to N501MH in March 1958, and the plane stayed in Hurd's service until 1965 when it was sold to Byers Airways, Inc., of Seattle, Washington. The following month Pacific Aerial Surveys, also of Seattle, acquired the 501MH for $12,000 and changed its registration to N517PA. In 1969 Pacific Aerial Surveys went bankrupt, and N517PA was sold at auction to Wally Peterson of Manson, Washington. Peterson operated the plane for a couple years before selling it to I.N. Burchinal of Paris, Texas.

Burchinal bought 517 to replace his P-38 (N5595V) that had been damaged in a landing accident. Over the next two years Burchinal attended airshows and used the plane in his Warbird Flight School. In 1973 he sold the aircraft to David Boyd of Tulsa, Oklahoma.

After getting N517PA to Oklahoma the plane was turned over to Doug Reeves and Rolin Standring of Starlite Aviation for restoration. Boyd wanted to bring the aircraft back to original fighter configuration, but

Pacific Aerial Survey's N517PA. MILO PELTZER COLLECTION (1967)

N517PA in Tulsa, Oklahoma, after being fitted with a P-80 nose and decorated in the 459th Fighter Squadron's twin dragon paint scheme.
MARK HOWARD VIA WARBIRD IMAGES (1981)

N517PA on display at the Yanks Air Museum in Chino, California. NICK VERONICO (1991)

there wasn't a fighter nose to be found. They, therefore, went about grafting a P-80 nose to the aircraft. The actual restoration took approximately a year to complete, at which time the plane was decorated in the "Twin Dragon" paint scheme of the 459th Fighter Squadron.

In 1981 Boyd sold 517 to Noel Wein who in turn sold the plane to Charles Nichols. N517PA was then moved to Chino, California where it was put on display with the other aircraft of the Yanks Air Museum.

Over the past few years the Yanks Air Museum has received numerous accolades for its impressive collection of vintage airplanes. The museum also has been recognized as having one of the finest restoration facilities in the country. According to the museum's curator, Stan Hoefler, they plan, as time permits, to restore the 517 back to its F-5G configuration. If so, it will be the only surviving Lightning to sport an original military recon nose, and will offer a welcome contrast to surviving fighter variants.

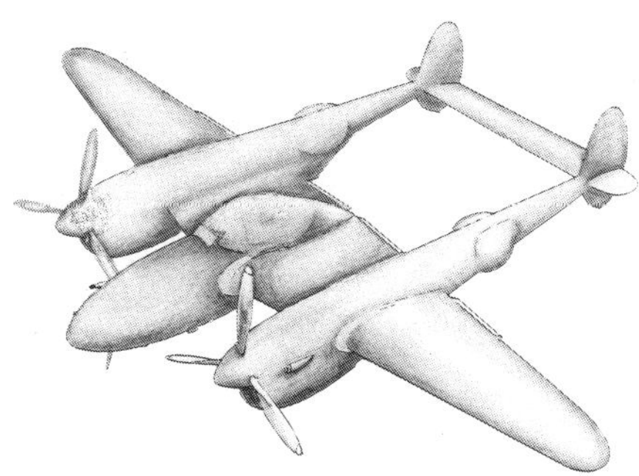

McGuire's Memorial

New Jersey's McGuire Air Force Base was dedicated in honor of America's second leading ace in September 1949. From its earliest beginnings, plans were made to construct a proper memorial in honor of the late Major Thomas B. McGuire. Twenty-two years later the idea was born to acquire and mount a Lockheed P-38 Lightning as a reminder of the late Major's war-time accomplishments. The lengthy search for a Lightning to commemorate the memory of Thomas B. McGuire finally came to an end when David Tallichet landed his P-38 (N9957F), which he had traded to Air Force Museum, at McGuire Air Force Base on September 18, 1981.

The plane that David Tallichet landed on that cloudy September day began its long, albeit discontinuous, journey to McGuire Air Force Base in June 1945. P-38L-5-LO serial number 4453015 was one of the many Lockheed Lightnings that were modified to F-5G-6-LOs during the summer months of 1945. Earlier in the war, military commanders from all theaters of conflict were pleading for more men and material. By mid-1945 the massive output of America's industrial might had overwhelmed the established logistical networks, and therefore, many of the aircraft that were produced during this period, including 44-53013, were placed directly into storage for future consideration.

In March 1946, Rex Mays, a popular young race car driver, arrived at the Kingman Field, Arizona, and purchased 53015 for $1,250. Prior to the war, Mays had made a name for himself in auto racing. He was the youngest (at age 21) driver to compete at the Indianapolis 500, and was also renowned for capturing four pole positions in the prestigious 500-mile race. When the United States entered the war, Mays joined the Army Air Force and served as a pilot. After his discharge in 1946 he aspired to purchase a Beechcraft Bonanza that he planned to fly from one auto racing event to another. He also had an interest in air racing and secured the MacMillen Oil Company as his sponsor in 1946 Bendix Trophy Race, in which he placed thirteenth. After the race Mays' F-5G was presumably used by the MacMillian company as a test vehicle for experimental lubricating oils, and as such was registered with the Civil Aeronautics Administration as NX57496.

Robert B. Utterbeck purchased 57496 from Mays in December 1948. Over the next few years the plane was operated in Costa Rica; however, it was never issued a Cost Rican civil aircraft license, and to what extent the plane was used during this time is unknown. On October 17, 1951, Edward C. Waterman acquired the plane from the Cost Rican government and re-registered it with the United States Civil Aeronautics Administration as N9957F. After returning to the United

Death of a Great Flyer

ILLUSTRATED BY T/SGT. DON BROCKELL

Officially, the major's death was due to "the operational failure of his aircraft." Actually, he died in an effort to save a friend. He was killed in a heroic violation of three rules of combat flying in a P-38; rules he himself believed in and taught to his men.

Maj. Thomas B. McGuire, Jr., was no novice. He had 38 planes to his credit, just two less than Maj. Richard I. Bong. He had 720 combat hours and 240 missions. His awards included nine Air Medals, five DFCs, the DSC, two Silver Stars, two Unit Citations, and the Purple Heart.

The 5th Fighter Command published his tips on combat tactics and used them as a bible for new pilots. Certainly, he knew what to do—and, more important, what not to do. He had written: *Don't get overeager. Don't try the impossible. Don't try to outmaneuver Jap fighters.* But when a friend called for help, McGuire forgot his own words, threw away his own book, and went to the rescue.

Who is to say why pilots—good sound pilots—suddenly disregard the rules? Unquestionably, his only idea was to save the life of another pilot. He acted on an involuntary impulse and was lost doing the things he had taught other men not to do.

Major McGuire was leading a flight of four Lightnings over a Jap-held airfield at 2,000 feet in the hope of catching some Nip planes while they were taking off. A lone Jap jumped them from out of the clouds and McGuire quickly led his flight into a tight Lufbery, snaring the Jap inside. The Jap made sharp turns in a frantic effort to break out of the trap, but the P-38s kept with him all the way down to 200 feet. There, the formation scattered, the Jap made a characteristically precise turn, and maneuvered into position right on the tail of one of the Lightnings. The attacked pilot called for help and McGuire tried to respond. His plane fell off and crashed into the ground.

McGuire had neglected his own lessons. *Never attempt combat at low altitudes.* He made his attempted attack at 200 feet. *Never let your speed fall below 300 mph while flying combat in a P-38.* He was going 180 mph when he tried a roll over. *Never keep your extra gas tanks in a fight.* His tanks were not released.

Of his death, Lt. Gen. George C. Kenney, commanding general Far East Air Forces, wrote, "Major McGuire was one of the most capable fighter pilots I have ever known. We will find it more difficult to carry on without him." ☆

Death of a flyer. COURTESY AIR FORCE MAGAZINE

The pit area at the Van Nuys Airport where the participants readied their aircraft for 1946 Bendix Trophy Race. BIRCH MATHEWES COLLECTION

States, N9957F was re-sold several times before it was purchased by the Hycon Manufacturing Company of Pasadena, California, in 1955.

Hycon had created a separate company to handle its rapidly growing aerial survey business, and N9957F was one of three of Hycon's original P-38-type aircraft that were given a longer nose configuration. This particular modification offered the company great flexibility in the types of equipment that could be carried. Hycon used its unique camera platforms to ride the tide in the vast sea of rich governmental contracts for the next four years. Late in 1959, however, contract offerings were on the decline, thus Hycon Manufacturing decided to get out of the aerial survey business and sold its fleet of aircraft.

Legendary movie stunt pilots Paul Mantz and Frank Tallman added N9957F to their private air force after purchasing the plane in 1962. When their airplanes weren't being leased by the movie studios they doubled as display pieces for the Talmantz Movieland of The Air Museum. Sadly, on July 8, 1966, Paul Mantz was killed while flying an airplane he had built for the movie "Flight of The Phoenix." As a result of his death, some of the aircraft in the Talmantz collection were sold at auction. Sometime later an ad in a paper caught the eye of Walter Erickson.

I think I saw an ad for N9957F in an Omaha newspaper. I was flying for Branniff at the time and on my next trip to Omaha I decided to drop by the Rosen Novak Auto Company who had purchased the plane at the Talmantz aviation auction. I then went out to

It took the famous young race car driver Rex Mays six hour, 15 minutes, and 16 seconds to complete his flight from Van Nuys, California, to Cleveland, Ohio. His average speed of 327.526 mph was good enough to earn him a 13th place finish out of 22 entries. His F-5G, nicknamed "MACMILLEN METEOR" (after his sponsor), was painted dark red. This photo was taken before Mays' race number 55 was added to the aircraft engine nacelles. H.G. MARTIN PHOTO FROM ROBERT J. PICKETT COLLECTION, VIA KANSAS AVIATION MUSEUM (1946)

Rex Mays (2nd from left) **and his race #55.** OSTROWSKI COLLECTION (1946)

California to make arrangements with Talmantz to make the plane ferriable. The plane had apparently sat around for about ten years without being run-up. The deal with Tallmantz never really worked, so I went back out there and got the plane running and made the worst test flight I ever had. The plane's glass was so crazed that I could hardly see out, and the left turbo blew-up and almost burned the boom off. But I got another turbo and ferried the plane to Falcon Field in Mesa, Arizona. There I got the drop tanks working and continued to Minneapolis St. Paul. After I got back to Minneapolis, I removed Hycon's ugly nose and replaced it with an F-5G nose. So many like the fighter nose, but I was partial to the F-5 nose configuration.

Despite the minor problems, for all the years that the P38 sat in Nevada and California, it performed great.

In 1972 David Tallichet bought N9957V from Erickson and replaced the plane's photo nose with fighter version. The gunfilled nose that he used is believed to have come from Wayne Rothgeb's old number 34 that was abandoned in New Guinea during World War II. Throughout the 1970s, N9957F was the featured attraction at several airshows around the United States. The highlight of this plane's airshow career is possibly its appearance at the Split S Society's

N5596V was one of three original Hycon F-5Gs to be given a new nose configuration. This setup gave the camera operator, who rode in the nose, more room while better accommodating a wide range of survey cameras and equipment. WARREN M. BODIE (1958)

A weather-worn N9957F during its 1960 to 1962 stay in Las Vegas, Nevada. MILO PELTZER COLLECTION

celebration of the P-38's 40th anniversary in 1977. The people that attended this event still talk about Tony LeVier's magnificent aerial demonstration, which further established him as one of the best P-38 pilots of all time.

Times changed in the 1980s and value of machines like the P-38 started to climb. Tallichet traded N9957F in 1981, along with a P-47 (N47DB), to the Air Force Museum in exchange for two Lockheed C-130A transport aircraft. The Air Force Museum had a standing promise to supply McGuire Air Force Base with the next available P-38, and Tallichet was given the honor of delivering the plane to the base.

The idea of taking an airworthy example of such a rare and valuable aircraft and allowing it to deteriorate in the harsh New Jersey weather appalled a great number of aviation enthusiasts. It also renewed the ongoing feud between the people who believe that airplanes should be flown, and the ones who ally with displaying such rare aircraft in museums. Despite these concerns, plans to display N9957V outdoors went forward. N9957F was decorated in the colors of Major McGuire's last P-38 and was given an overall covering with poly-sealant. It was believed that the protective coating would safeguard the aircraft from excessive corrosion. In 1988 the memorial aircraft was moved from

N9957F on display at Paul Mantz's and Frank Tallman's Movie Land Of the Air Museum in Santa Ana, California. MILO PELTZER COLLECTION (1966)

Aircraft collector David Tallichet had N9957F painted in the colors similar to that of Lt. Royal Frey's 20th Fighter Group wartime mount. Here the aircraft is shown at a P-38 Pilots reunion that was held in Minneapolis, Minnesota in 1975. DICK PHILLIPS' WARBIRD IMAGES

its pylon to a hangar for periodic maintenance and corrosion assessment. Unfortunately, the fears of those who opposed the idea of displaying the plane outdoors were realized, for many of the plane's outer components were severely corroded. The damaged components were immediately replaced with ones constructed out of stainless steel. In order to also protect the cockpit for harmful ultraviolet deterioration the original canopy glass was replaced with a UV filtering material. Lastly, an aggressive program of cleaning and polishing the plane every six months was adopted.

Although, concerns over the survivability of this rare plane continues to be an issue in the eyes of some, the personnel of McGuire Air Force Base should nevertheless be commended for their preservation efforts.

The Split S Society had no problem filling the seats at their P-38 symposium that was held to celebrate the Lightning's 40th birthday. N9957V was a featured attraction of the event. WARREN M. BODIE (1977)

Posing in front of N9957F during the P-38's 40th anniversary celebration are three great names in Lightning History. Left to right: **General Ben Kelsey, Kelly Johnson, and Tony LeVier.** LOCKHEED (1977)

N9957F's nose gear collapsed at the Memphis Airport while en route to McGuire AFB in early 1981. JEFF NICHOLS

On May 4, 1981, Tallichet completed the task of delivering the rare bird to McGuire AFB, New Jersey. USAF

DEDICATED TO THE MEMORY OF

MAJOR THOMAS B. McGUIRE, JR.

AND THOSE VALIANT AIRMEN WHO SACRIFICED THEIR LIVES IN DEFENSE OF OUR COUNTRY. CEREMONY PRESIDED OVER BY THE HONORABLE CASPAR W. WEINBERGER, SECRETARY OF DEFENSE.

DISTINGUISHED GUESTS PARTICIPATING

HONORABLE THOMAS H. KEAN, GOVERNOR, NEW JERSEY
GENERAL DUANE H. CASSIDY, COMMANDER IN CHIEF, MILITARY AIRLIFT COMMAND
MAJOR GENERAL FRANCIS R. GERARD, THE ADJUTANT GENERAL, NEW JERSEY
MAJOR GENERAL JACK W. SHEPPARD, COMMANDER, TWENTY-FIRST AIR FORCE
COLONEL JEROLD L. WEISS, COMMANDER, 438 TH MILITARY AIRLIFT WING
MR. WILLIAM J. DEMAS, PRESIDENT, MAJOR THOMAS B McGUIRE JR. MEMORIAL FOUNDATION
MRS. ROBERT E. BEATTY, JR. (FORMERLY MRS. THOMAS B. McGUIRE, JR.)

7 NOVEMBER 1986

The monument to commemorate Major Thomas McGuire's war time accomplishments was officially dedicated on November 7, 1986.
At left: **Dedication plaque.** AUTHOR'S COLLECTION (1988)

In 1988 the memorial aircraft was removed from its resting place and given a much needed face lift. Unfortunately, the sealant that was supposed to protect the aircraft didn't work as expected. Therefore, a new policy of cleaning and polishing the plane every six months was adopted. AUTHOR'S COLLECTION (1988)

PUGGY V is located in the middle of traffic circle just inside McGuire Air Force Base's main gate. AUTHOR'S COLLECTION

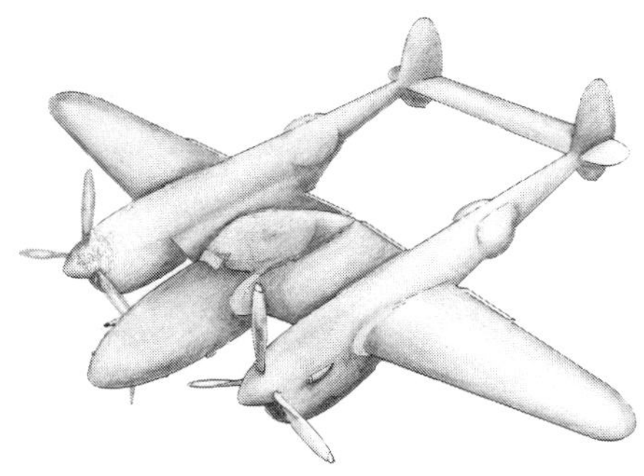

Experimental Aircraft Association's Lightning

The P-38 that is presently on display in the Experimental Aircraft Association's Museum has seen duty as a fighter, night fighter, and a civilian photo mapping platform. It began its career in June 1945 as a P-38L-5-LO, serial number 44-53087. It was then modified to fill the role of a night fighter. But the war ended too soon for it to see action and it was subsequently sent to Kingman, Arizona, for disposal.

Forrest M. Bird was a ferry service pilot and as such he kept his eye on the surplus aircraft that were accumulating at Kingman in the early months of 1946. When the word finally went out that the War Assets Administration was going to sell some of its aircraft, Bird was one of the first to take advantage of the low prices by purchasing 48 Lightnings (approximately 15 "M" models and 33 F-5Gs) for $1,250 each. However, not all of the items that the WAA had for sale were priced so cheap. For example the WAA's list price for a single Curtiss electric propeller was $3,800. This lopsided pricing policy offered Bird the opportunity to turn his investment around at a great profit by selling components (VHF radios and the like) from his aircraft, in some cases, for more than the original purchase price of the entire airplane. He then sold what was left of the airframes for anywhere from $350 to $900. He made a killing. In the end Bird retained only a few of his aircraft for his personal use. One of these was 44-53087.

Bird registered 44-53087 with the Civil Aeronautics Administration as N62887. He later sold the plane to David Bishop of Green Bay, Wisconsin. From that point, N62887's ownership passed through three other individuals before being exported to join the fleet of Spartan Air Services Ltd. of Canada in 1951.

The former N62887 officially entered the Canadian Aircraft Registry as CF-GDS in June 1952. Spartan mated their characteristic bubble nose to the plane and operated it as a mapping platform in many different areas of Canada. On April 19, 1953, CF-GDS was involved in a landing accident at Quebec's Island Airport. Pilot, James Lago, while attempting to land on an icy runway lost control of the plane when it veered off the runway into a snow bank. Lago emerged from the wreck unhurt, and damage to the aircraft was restricted to its undercarriage and nose section. CF-GDS was later repaired and continued to serve Spartan until 1956. At that time Spartan retired its Lightning-type aircraft by selling most of its fleet to Hycon Aerial Surveys, of Pasadena, California.

CF-GDS was recertified by the Civil Aeronautics Ad-

Like most of the Spartan Lightnings, CF-GDS carried the modified bubble nose. Here the aircraft is shown at Malton, Ontario, in April of 1955. JACK McNULTY

N1107V is being readied for a survey mission by Cartwright Aerial Surveys at the Oakland Airport in July of 1958. MILO PELTZER COLLECTION

ministration and registered as N1170V. Hycon operated the plane for only two years before selling it in 1958 to Cartwright & Co., which later became Cartwright Aerial Surveys. Cartwright used a Zeiss mapping camera, which projected vertically through the floor. The camera Cartwright was using was far more valuable than the entire airplane and, in fact, it was equipped with its own parachute. "It is interesting to note," said Vern Cartwright, "that the way to escape for the photographer—which was usually me, if something happened, was to pull a beautiful little cord and the camera and the photographer would drop out through the escape hatch together." Cartwright operated N1107V primarily in the western United States.

In 1961 Vern Cartwright sold N1107V to Lightning & Company, who are better known as Marvin "Lefty" Gardner and Lyold Nolen. As a result of this sale, N1107V became the Confederate Air Force's first Light-

Kucera extended N1107V nose an extra 26.5 inches. This was done so the aircraft could carry a second camera. JIM BUTLER (1965)

With such a long nose it was natural that N1107V would attract the nickname "Cyrano." This photo was taken in San Jose, California, shortly after Pete Kahn purchased the plane from the Wilson Flight Training Center of Kansas City. MILO PELTZER COLLECTION

ning. Gardner and his partners, Lloyd Nolen and Tom O'Connor, purchased another P-38, N25Y, in late 1963, so they decided to sell N1107V to Kucera & Associates, Inc. of Cleveland, Ohio. Kucera had obtained a contract to provide aerial mapping services to the Inter-American Geodetic Survey (an agency of the U.S. Army Corps). N1107V along with N6190C were sent to South America to fulfill these duties.

A.G. Wilson purchased N1107V from Kucera in March 1968. The following year the plane was dealt to Mark Hurd Aerial Surveys for a short time before returning to Wilson's Flight Training Center in February 1968. The following year Peter Kahn, of Danville, California, purchased the plane from Wilson. Kahn acquired a fighter nose from one of the P-38s that Metro Goldwyn Mayer had stored on its Culver City Lot 5, and used it to transform his photo Lightning back to a fighter. He also re-registered the plane with the FAA as N3800L. In 1973 N3800L's ownership went to Jack Flaherty who in turn traded the plane to Edwards & Edwards (Wilson C. Edwards aka "Connie" and Will P. Edwards, Jr.) of Big Springs, Texas, in September of the same year. Flaherty, in return for N3800L, received a Spanish version of the Bf 109 "Buchon" CASA 1112.

In 1981 the Edwards family donated N3800L to the Experimental Aircraft Association in memory of Bill Edwards, brother of Connie Edwards and husband of Patsy Edwards. Some years later the plane was dismantled for restoration. Major funding for the project

Kahn replaced the elongated photo nose with a fighter version that he acquired from one of the early model P-38s that were stored at one of Metro Goldwyn Meyer's Culver City movie lots. WARREN BODIE (1972)

A silver-colored N3800L shown at the EAA gathering 1973. BURTON KEMP COLLECTION.

was provided by Gary Levitz through a foundation endowment. The late John Sandberg also generously donated the time, expense and labor that was needed to overhaul the plane's Allison engines. The actual nuts and bolts of the lengthy restoration was carried out by EAA staff members and volunteers, all of whom where supervised by Daryl Lenz. When the restoration was completed, N3800L was accurately decorated in the colors of one of Dick Bong's P-38s and put on display in the EAA Air Adventure Museum's Eagle Hangar at Oshkosh. This hangar is dedicated to the brave individuals who put their lives on the line during the Second World War.

N3800L undergoing restoration at the EAA Facilities in 1988. The EAA was fortunate enough to have the following staff and volunteers to help with the project. DICK PHILLIPS (1988)

EAA STAFF:
Daryl Lens
John Hopkins
Ted Mosman
Duane Wilmer
John Lavin
Bauken Noack

VOLUNTEERS:
Tom Haug
John Davis
Clem Holzbauer
Frank Erm
Scott Fleagle
Chris Bortoluzzi
Kevin Jungwirth
Al Putzer
Scott McLain
Rich Sitzes
Bob McLaughlin
Ray Drexler
Lyle Milius

Experimental Aircraft Association's P-38 on display in their Eagle Hangar. DONNA BUSHMAN VIA EAA

Beautifully staged shot of the EAA's Lightning. EAA.

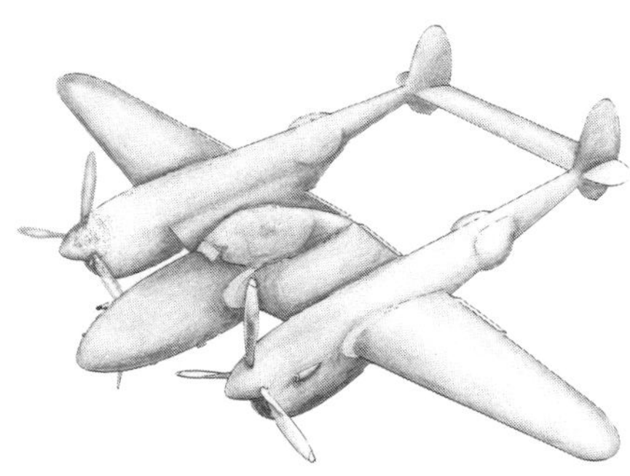

FORK TAILED DEVIL

THE P-38M-6-LO, SERIAL NUMBER 44-53095, which is currently owned by the Lone Star Flight Museum of Galveston, Texas, was but one of the many thousands of airplanes that were suddenly declared surplus at the end of World War II. The reality of handling tons of surplus property came as no surprise to the War Assets Administration, for as early as 1942 the then-Surplus Property Board began to formulate a contingency plan that dealt with the possibility of the war coming to an abrupt conclusion. This plan, later known as the Harvard Plan, called for the bulk of America's piston driven Air Force to be scrapped for usable parts and materials. Provisions, however, were also included that allowed some of these unwanted aircraft to escape the fate of being melted down for the price of aluminum by donating them to various approved educational institutions, as well as selling them outright to private individuals and friendly governments.

Honduras was one such country wishing to bolster its meager air defense capabilities by purchasing surplus World War II aircraft. Lt. Col. Malcolm Stewart, a former commander of the Fuerza Aerea Hondurena, organized the deal that eventually brought 44-53095 plus five additional P-38s, and three P-63 King Cobras to Honduras in the late 1940s. 44-53095 became FAH 506.

Most of the P-38s that went to Honduras were purchased from R.A Wardell and R.W. Martin of Jacksboro, Oregon. Regrettably, sales records pertaining to the Wardell/Martin Lightnings have long been lost, but it is believed that 44-53095 is one of the five Lightnings that Wardell and Martin delivered to Miami in 1947. It is also believed that 44-53095 was registered with the Civil Aeronautics Administration as N67745.

By 1955 it was apparent to the Honduran Air Force that the operational lives of its Allison engine aircraft were coming to an end. Therefore, ten Chance Vought F4U-4s were purchased to supplement its aging Air Force. Unfortunately, transition into the Navy fighters was delayed, and it wasn't until 1959 that the Honduran Air Force decided to officially retire the four Lightnings and two King Cobras that remained. In February 1960, Bob Bean, an aircraft dealer from Blythe, California, purchased FAH 506 along with the balance of the surviving Lockheed and Bell fighters for $15,000 each. Once each of the planes had been imported, and demilitarized, they were then properly registered with the Federal Aviation Administration. FAH 506 then became N9005R.

Apparently, Bean intended to resell his newly purchased relics, and the sight of several of Lockheed's famed fighters sitting in the desert certainly attracted the attention of aviation enthusiasts. But Bean would

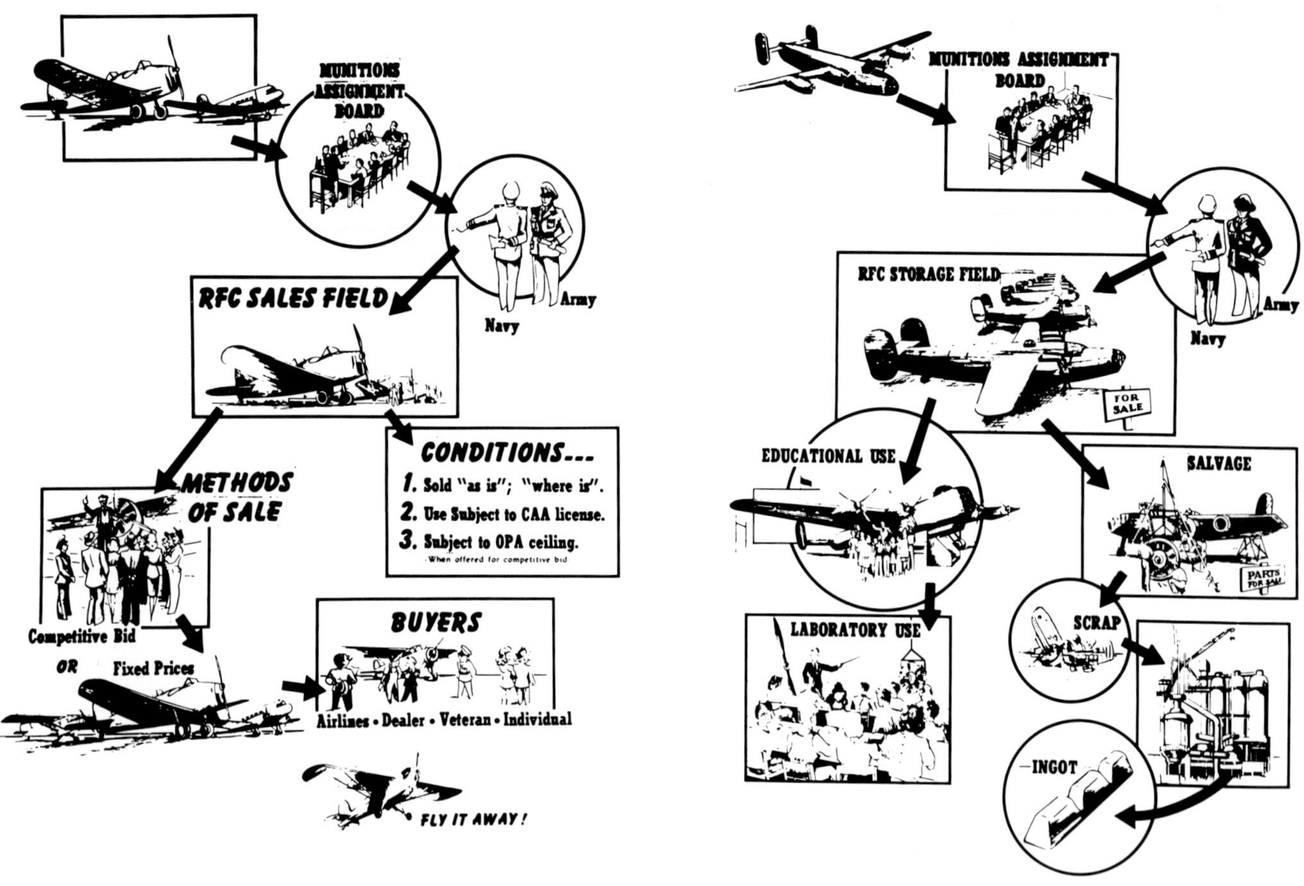

War Assets Administration promotional material. GSA (1945)

have to wait an additional eight years for the market value of the his P-38s to catch up with his asking price. Finally, in 1969, William Ross, a former Naval Aviator from Chicago, took an interest in Bean's aircraft and was lucky enough to persuade Bean to sell him N9005R. Although the plane was less than airworthy, it was in good condition, and its log indicated that it had only been flown 64 hours since departing Lockheed's assembly line in June 1945. Army Air Force records for 44-53095 also showed that it was one of the seventy-five "L" model P-38s that were converted to the night fighter variant of the Lightning at Lockheed's Dallas Modification Center.

A year passed before Bean delivered N9005R to Ross at the DuPage County Airport, and an additional year was needed for Ross to restore the plane. In 1972 Ross' highly polished natural metal Lightning made its public debut at TransPo' 72, which was held at Dulles Airport near Washington, D.C. Painted on the left side of the plane's nose was the name that made the P-38 forever famous: "Der Gabelshwanz Teufel" (Fork Tailed Devil). Ross' Lightning was a definite crowd pleaser and was widely regarded as one of the most aesthetically beautiful P-38s to have graced the airshow circuit during the 16 years that followed.

In 1986 Ross sold his "Fork Tailed Devil" to Air-Service, Inc. of Houston, Texas, and the plane was soon added to the Lone Star Flight Museum's collection at Houston's Hobby Airport. When the plane arrived in Texas it was obvious the plane's outer skin had some surface corrosion. It was, therefore, given a thorough going over and covered with a protective coating of silver paint. It was then decorated in the colors of Col. Charles MacDonald's "Putt Putt Maru." In 1990 the museum moved its collection of airplanes to its new facility in Galveston, Texas, where the now-registered N38RW took its place among the museum's growing collection of beautifully restored vintage aircraft.

DIGEST OF
"POGUE COMMITTEE" REPORT

GENERAL CONCLUSIONS:

AIR POWER IS TODAY THE KEY TO OUR NATIONAL SECURITY.

PRESERVATION, AS A NATIONAL ASSET, OF THE CAPACITY OF OUR PERMANENT AIRCRAFT MANUFACTURING INDUSTRY FOR RESEARCH, DEVELOPMENT AND PRODUCTION OF MODERN AIRCRAFT SHOULD BE A PRIMARY CONSIDERATION IN SURPLUS AIRCRAFT DISPOSAL.

DUMPING OF SURPLUS AIRCRAFT, REGARDLESS OF PRICE, IS NOT TO BE CONSIDERED. ON THE OTHER HAND, THE SCRAPPING OF ALL SURPLUS AIRCRAFT WOULD BE A DISSERVICE TO AVIATION AND A NEEDLESS DESTRUCTION OF NATIONAL WEALTH.

DISPOSAL IN AN ORDERLY MANNER, AT REASONABLE PRICES, UTILIZING NORMAL TRADE CHANNELS IS RECOMMENDED.

SURPLUS AIRCRAFT OF WHICH DISPOSAL HAS NOT BEEN MADE AT THE END OF THREE YEARS FOLLOWING THE CESSATION OF HOSTILITIES, SHOULD BE CLASSIFIED AS UNABSORBED SURPLUS TO BE UTILIZED ONLY FOR NON-FLIGHT PURPOSES, SALVAGE AND SCRAPPING.

CLASS A-TACTICAL AIRCRAFT

THE ONLY SIGNIFICANT MARKET WILL BE THE GOVERNMENTS OF FRIENDLY NATIONS. THERE MAY BE SMALL SPECIALIZED COMMERCIAL OR PRIVATE USE FOR A FEW TYPES, SUCH AS PHOTO-RECONNAISANCE AND OBSERVATION AIRCRAFT. IT MIGHT PROVE TO NATIONAL INTEREST TO HAVE A INTERNATIONAL AGREEMENT LIMITING OR PROHIBITING INTERNATIONAL SALE OF TACTICAL AIRCRAFT.

CLASS B-TRANSPORT AIRCRAFT

DURING THE PERIOD OF SHORT SUPPLY THE SURPLUS WAR PROPERTY ADMINISTRATOR MUST EFFECT AN EQUITABLE DISTRIBUTION AMONG DOMESTIC AND FOREIGN APPLICANTS. ULTIMATELY SUPPLY WILL EXCEED DEMAND. AIRCRAFT MANUFACTURERS SHOULD BE PERMITTED TO ACT AS THE GOVERNMENT'S SALES AGENTS, FOR REASONABLE FEE. AIRCRAFT SHOULD BE SOLD "AS IS," LEAVING PURCHASERS TO MAKE ARRANGEMENTS FOR OVERHAUL AND CONVERSION. METHODS OF DISPOSAL SHOULD INCLUDE LEASE, CASH SALE, INSTALLMENT SALE. PRICES SHOULD BE UNIFORM TO DOMESTIC AND FOREIGN PURCHASERS AND SHOULD REMAIN FIRM DURING THE DISPOSAL PERIOD.

CLASS C-PERSONAL AIRCRAFT (Useful for individual flying and training)

AIRCRAFT FOR WHICH THERE IS AN ACTIVE DEMAND SHOULD BE SOLD "AS IS" FOR CASH AS PROMPTLY AS POSSIBLE. AIRCRAFT FOR WHICH THERE IS LITTLE DEMAND SHOULD BE OFFERED AT A FIXED PRICE. REASONABLE NUMBER OF TRAINERS SHOULD BE STORED FOR FUTURE USE IN COLLEGE TYPE TRAINING PROGRAMS.

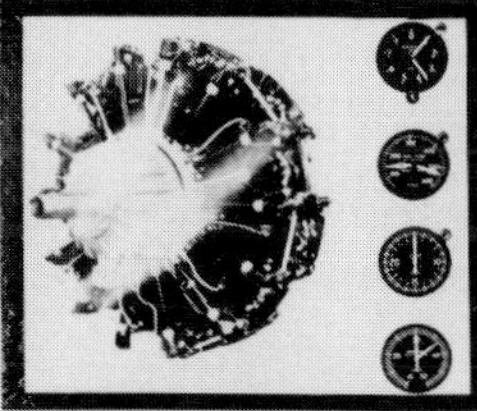

CLASS D-AIRCRAFT EQUIPMENT & COMPONENTS

SMALLER ITEMS, WITH A MAJOR MARKET IN THE NON-AVIATION FIELD, SHOULD BE SOLD UNDER POLICIES SIMILAR TO THOSE FOR PERSONAL AIRCRAFT. LARGER AND MORE COMPLEX ITEMS, SUCH AS ENGINES AND PROPELLERS, SHOULD BE CONSIGNED TO THE ORIGINAL MANUFACTURERS FOR INSPECTION AND DISPOSAL, THE MANUFACTURER ACTING AS SELLING AGENT FOR THE GOVERNMENT. PRICES SHOULD BE ON BASIS THAT WILL ENCOURAGE TECHNICAL DEVELOPMENT. LOW PRICES SHOULD BE SET FOR CERTAIN TYPES OF INSTRUMENTS, SUCH AS THE BLIND FLYING GROUP, TO ENCOURAGE THEIR USE FOR TRAINING PURPOSES.

CLASS E-UNABSORBED SURPLUS

MOST IMPORTANT USE WILL BE EDUCATIONAL, GROUND AND SHOP TRAINING. EXPERIMENTAL AND MEMORIAL USES ARE OTHER POSSIBLE METHODS OF UTILIZATION. NON-AVIATION USES OF AIRCRAFT PARTS AND COMPONENTS SHOULD BE GIVEN CAREFUL STUDY. ALL AIRCRAFT AND EQUIPMENT FOR WHICH NO ACCEPTABLE USES CAN BE FOUND SHOULD BE SCRAPPED UNDER THE SUPERVISION AND CONTROL OF THE DISPOSAL AGENCIES WITHIN SIX MONTHS AFTER THEIR TRANSFER TO THIS CLASS.

War Assets Administration promotional material. GSA (1945)

War Assets Administration promotional material. GSA (1945)

When FAH 506 was ferried to Bob Bean's facility in Blyth, California it was still decorated in official Honduran colors. BUDE DONATO (1960)

N9005R was considered by Bean to be the best of the four P-38s he purchased for the Honhurans. The P-47 in the background is presently housed with the Planes Of Fame Museum in Chino, California. BUDE DONATO (1960)

N9005R attracted a great deal of attention during the 1960s, but few buyers were willing to pay Bean's asking price. BRUCE PRUETT (1963)

A clean and shiny N9005R at DuPage Airport in April of 1970. JOHN LAW VIA PICKETT

Bill Ross (left) **giving Bob Hoover** (right) **a guided tour through the intricacies of a P-38 rebuild.** DICK PHILLIPS (1971)

Clearly one of the more ascetically beautiful aircraft to attend the EAA's 1976 convention in Oshkosh. BURTON KEMP COLLECTION

N9005R on display in the Lone Star's beautiful museum. AUTHOR'S COLLECTION (1992)

The staff of Lone Star Flight Museum spent a considerable amount of time restoring the N9005R. When they were finished it was decorated in the colors of Lt. Col. Charles MacDonald's "PUTT PUTT MARU." BRIAN SILCOX (1992)

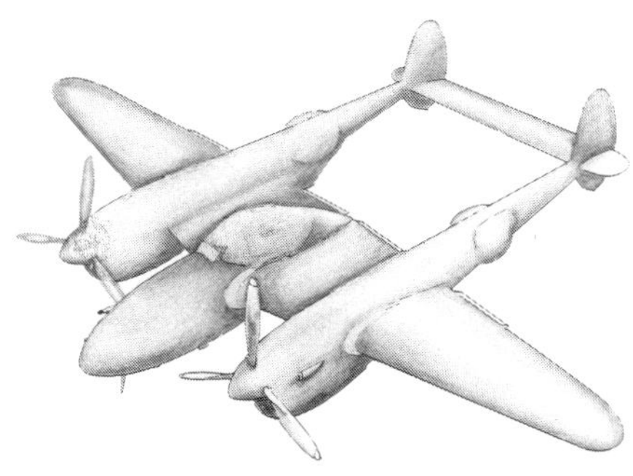

Night Lightning

The Champlin Fighter Museum of Mesa, Arizona, is home to one of the last surviving night fighter versions of the P-38. The Museum is also the home of the American Fighter Aces Association. Collectively, these two organizations have augmented a splendid assortment of vintage fighter aircraft with authentic memorabilia from the aces who made these planes famous.

The retrospective look into the history of the museum's Lightning begins in June 1945 when P-38L-5-LO, serial number 4453097, rolled off Lockheed's Burbank assembly line. Afterwards, this aircraft was immediately sent to the Dallas Modification Center. In late June its designation was changed to P-38M-6-LO when 44-53097, complete with ASH-type radar and brisling with blast suppressed armament, emerged from the center's massive hangar. Not long after Japan surrendered, however, officials of the Air Force decided that there was no longer a need for most of the P-38s that were in their inventory. So, in December, 44-53097 was declared surplus and sent to the Kingman, Arizona, disposal facility.

It was during this period that Dick Martin, long time aviator and aircraft restorer, started his lengthy, albeit intermittent, relationship with this chapter's subject aircraft. Dick Martin picks up the story:

> R.A Wardell, who was my partner at that time, and I purchased eleven P-38s from the Kingman depot in 1946. We sold five of these aircraft to a firm that was supplying Central American Air Forces with obsolete military aircraft. In the late 1940s myself and few other pilots flew five of the P-38s to a depot that was located in Miami. From there the planes were presumably delivered to Honduras.

As soon as these aircraft arrived in Honduras, they were quickly decorated in official state colors, and given appropriate identification numbers. 44-53097, which had been registered with the CAA as N67861, became Fuerza Aerea Hondurena 503. Unfortunately, little specific information exists on 503's operational history while serving with the Honduran Air Force. In general, however, it is known that a lack of qualified pilots and spare parts forced the Fuerza Aerea Honduras to keep their Allison powered Air Force grounded for much of its operational lifetime. Nevertheless, these Lightnings and King Cobras formed the backbone of the Honduran air defense for the immediate years that followed.

During the middle to late 1950s, the FAH replaced the four P-38s and two P-63s that remained in their Air Force with Chance Vought F4U Corsairs. On February 2, 1960, the FAH divested itself of its Allison-powered aircraft by selling the remaining four P38s to Bob Bean, of California. Each plane was then flown to Kelly Air Force Base where they were demilitarized before being officially turned over to Bean. From there Bean had the planes ferried to Blythe, California.

In 1968 Carl Kidd, of Atlanta, Georgia, purchased

FAH 503 at Blythe, California. PHOTO: BRUCE PRUITT

N3TF was painted in a sand and spinach scheme while under the ownership of Tom Friedkin. STEVEN HUDEK COLLECTION

FAH 503 (which had been registered with FAA as N9011R) from Bean, but never took possession of the plane. Al Hicks purchased the P-38 in 1972 and moved it to Palomar Airport, Carlsbad, California. A short time later, N9011R was sold to Thomas Freidkin, who contracted Dick Martin to rebuild the plane for him. Freidkin changed N9011R's registration to N7TF, and after operating the plane for only a year sold it to John Bolton of Matlin, Florida. Bolton re-registered his new P-38 with the FAA as N3JB but ended up selling the plane to John Stokes of San Marcos, Texas, in 1974.

During 1977 N3JB and one of its former Honduran sister ships (FAH 504 more commonly recognized as N38DH) made a guest appearance on NBC's "Black Sheep Squadron" television series. The list of pilots who participated in the filming of the episode, which was titled "Hotshot," read like a who's who of contemporary Lightning jocks. "We filmed that episode over a two week period," recalled Steven Hinton, master pilot and fighter rebuilder. "At that time we had several pilots flying. Tom Friedkin, Dick Martin, and myself flew N3JB and Dick Martin and Frank Tallman flew N38DH. The Ground shots were done at Magic Mountains's Indian Dunes, and the flight scenes were filmed out of Ventura Airport over the water near the Channel Islands off Oxnard. This was the first time I flew a P-38, so I have a lot of great memories of the flights for Black Sheep."

It is noteworthy to point out that both of the P-38s that appeared in the Black Sheep series had function-

John Stokes operated the rare M-model Lightning during the 1970s. The plane's registration number was not changed from N3JB in honor of the aircraft's late owner John Bolton, who was killed in a Mustang accident. DUSTIN CARTER (1977 CAF AIRSHOW)

Sun bursts above the classic silhouette of a P-38. DUSTIN CARTER (1977 CAF AIRSHOW)

ing turbo super chargers. This is important because the sound that emanates from these screaming power boosters is unique to the P-38, but unfortunately very few of the Lightnings that are actively flown today have such devices. Therefore, this show could quite possibly be one of the few sources that future Lightning admirers can access in order to experience the true sound of a "P-SCREAMER."

John Stokes decided to put N3JB up for sale shortly after the Black Sheep filming was completed. The ad he ran in "TradeA-Plane" truly touted this aircraft as being the "only one of its kind in the world," but the $250,000 asking price was a bit steep for the post-Vietnam era recession, and a couple of years would pass before the plane was finally sold to H. & E. Aviation, Inc. of Canby, Oregon. Cecil Harp and Bob Ennis operated N3JB until Ennis' unfortunate demise in a PBY accident. The plane was then sold to Doug Champlin in July 1983. Dick Martin was called on to deliver the plane to Champlin's museum.

At the time Champlin acquired the plane it was the only surviving example of its type to retain an original piggyback canopy configuration. But that changed in 1987 when the plane was modified to resemble the "L" model Lightnings that prowled the South West Pacific skies during the closing months of World War II. "Although I was delighted to add the plane to our collection, it didn't seem to fit the museum's theme," recalled Doug Champlin. "We, therefore, set out to locate parts that could be used to convert the plane back to a configuration that is more representative of the type the aces flew." Champlin was lucky enough to trade parts with John Stokes, who was resurrecting a derelict "J" model Lightning in San Marcos, Texas, and it wasn't long before N3JB was transformed to the way it must have looked prior to being re-worked as a night fighter.

Champlin's Lightning has not been flown in a number of years, but it is one of the many aircraft in the museum's inventory that is kept in airworthy condition. It is, therefore, comforting to know that this fine example will be around for many years to come.

N3JB taxiing by the crowd line during the Madera gathering of warbirds in 1980. One of the advantages of owning a P-38M is that the passenger behind the pilot doesn't have to bend forward to clear the canopy. SCOTT THOMPSON

Left: **Champlin's P-38 is seldom flown but it is kept in airworthy condition. Here one can clearly see the aircraft canopy conversion, which brought it back to "L" model specifications.** CHARLIE HYER (1989)

Below: **In 1993 N3JB was decorated like one of the P-38s that Fighter Ace John "Jack" Purdy flew during his combat tour with the 475th Fighter Group. Standing next to the plane is Champlin restoration crew:** (l to r) **Larry White, Charlie Hyer, Jack Purdy, Dave Gross, and Jack Reiser.** ALAN GRUENING (1993)

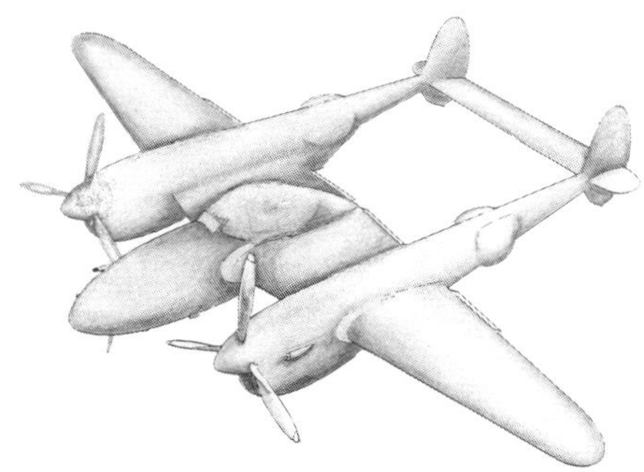

To the United Kingdom and Back

Mike Wright is one of the few pilots today that have the needed experience to ferry vintage warbirds across the frigid waters of the North Atlantic. In 1988 he was offered and accepted the opportunity to deliver David Tallichet's former P-38, N505MH, to England for noted warbird collector Doug Arnold. In the span of the following two years Wright would not only add his name to the list of airmen who have successfully ferried a Lightning across Atlantic, but would also add his name to the short list of pilots who have gone "To The United Kingdom And Back" in a P-38.

In the Summer of 1988 Wright flew to Chino to prepare the plane for its eventual flight. Wright recalls some of the problems he encountered:

> You never know what kind of condition an airplane is in. Most people make the basic assumption that a plane is well equipped once it has been rebuilt. In many cases, however, the surplus parts put into warbirds are simply made to work and not necessarily restored to zero time standards. This practice is fine for short domestic hops, but any time you prepare for long duration flights, especially if you are going to fly over water for any length of time, you have to begin the trip with everything working. This is important because invariably something always breaks on the road.
>
> I went out to California to check out the airplane, and shortly after I started ground runs I noticed that the left outboard coolant radiator was leaking. We got the radiator fixed and resumed ground runs when one of the other radiators sprung a leak. Well, this radiator episode almost got to be comical. In the end, all four radiators had to be completely rebuilt. This caused the scheduled delivery of the plane to England to be delayed by several months.
>
> The radiators were not the only thing that needed to be replaced in Arnold's P-38. The airplane's wet compass was really marginal. When you fly in the extreme northern regions of the western hemisphere, the difference between magnetic north and true north can be as much as fifty degrees. The typical difference in the U.S. is anywhere from zero to fifteen degrees, so a wet compass is not too bad of an instrument to use to navigate. But when you go as far north as Greenland, the airplane has to be absolutely stable for the magnetic compass to be of any use. To base the navigation strictly on a wet compass, while it's not impossible, it is extremely difficult. So, I installed an electric compass which tends to dampen out the errors associated with regular wet compasses. Over the winter I also hooked up some of the cockpit lighting.
>
> By the spring of 1989, things started to look up. Arnold had booked some airshows so we decided to set March as the "go date" to deliver the airplane to England. This was a little sooner than I wanted because the surface temperature in Canada at that time of year is about minus ten degrees celsius, and at altitude it is easily 40 degrees below zero. You have to remember that the center pod of the P-38 is very drafty. The amount of wind that leaks through is analogous to driving your car in the winter with its windows down. Anyway, during the time I was working on the

N62350 equipped with long-range external fuel tanks transverse the Atlantic in much the way its military counterparts did during World War II. ROGER BESECKER COLLECTION (PRESTWICK, SCOTLAND 1957)

Hurd incorporated a piggyback canopy configuration similar to the one that was used on the P-38M. They found that this configuration improved their mission productivity. MILO PELTZER COLLECTION (SANTA BARBARA 1959)

airplane I also tried to figure a way to heat the cockpit. When Lockheed designed the Lightning, they heated the cockpit by pushing air through an intensifier tube in the exhaust system. Only the left side of Arnold's P-38 was equipped with an intensifier tube, so I wired the heat open on that side because I knew I was going to need it.

The first leg of Wright's long trip began in March when he flew from Chino, California, to Albuquerque, New Mexico. Along the way he check the fuel system to make sure that all the tanks would feed properly, and he discovered that the right drop tank would only feed fuel for about twenty minutes. After he arrived in Albuquerque, New Mexico, Wright also noticed that the right engine's oil consumption was rather high. Although the oil consumption wasn't in the worry range it was nevertheless something to keep in mind. Later that afternoon he left for Nashville where he spent about a week sorting out some of the plane's minor problems before departing for the long colder legs of his journey.

In the early stages of the World War II the Army Air Force devised a plan, code name "Bolero," to

N505HM being readied for taxi test at Tallichet's Chino facility in 1988. ED DAVIES

rapidly deploy aircraft to the European war zone. This plan called for flights of two B-17s and six P-38s to be flown from the United States to England by way of Canada, Greenland, and Iceland. Although these missions proved to be successful, they also demonstrated the difficulties involved with operating aircraft through a frozen environment. Mike Wright, to some degree, experienced many of the same problems that plagued the men of the Bolero movement some forty years earlier. Wright picks up the story:

> When I landed in Montreal I could definitely feel the difference in the weather. I was traveling on a weekend so everything at the airport was closed, but the people there were kind enough to allow me to store the plane in a hangar for the night. After the 4.7-hour flight it became apparent that the right engine was leaking more oil than it was burning. But it wasn't really bad enough to delay the trip. The next day I made a 3-hour flight to Wabush where I filled the oil tanks and went on to Sheferville. There I took on fuel and headed out to Frobisher Bay.
>
> I was hoping to only spend the night but my stay at Frobisher Bay turned out to be an experience. When I got there, the ground temperature was 20 below with a 15 knot wind. While I was paying for the fuel, the operator of an FBO that had just opened approached me and asked if I would be interested in parking the plane near his hangar. He also told me that he had an engine pre-heating unit that I could use the following day. I gladly accepted his offer, but when it came time to park the plane, I couldn't find anyone to give me directions. So, I ended up parking it a safe distance from the FBO's hangar. The next day I discovered that the heater's power cord wasn't long enough to reach my airplane. The P-38 is a heavy plane and the ramp was covered with ice and snow, so it took us a couple hours to move the airplane. The heater they had could only handle one engine at a time, so we preheated the left engine first. Then during the hour or so it took to pre-heat right engine, I had to run the left engine periodically to keep it warm. Time was marching on but I figured I could still make it to Greenland before dark. However, the engine's circuit breaker would pop every time I tried to start the right engine. I then had to shut down the left engine, pull out the maintenance book, and start working on the airplane. It was so cold outside that I could only work for about 10 minutes at a time before having to return inside the hangar to warm up. To complicate matters even more, I had to wear gloves because when it's that cold your warm bare skin will stick to any metal it touches. It took a couple hours to trace the problem to the ignition vibrator. I then removed it from the plane and filed the vibrator's points (which is like the points on a car), roughly set the gap and finally got the engine running. By that time there wasn't enough daylight to make the trip to Greenland.

During his frozen ordeal with an ignition vibrator, Wright attracted the attention of the other FBO operator who allowed him to store the P-38 in their heated hangar for the night. The following day he departed for Greenland.

Mike Wright's drafty P-38 being refueled while on one of his stops in Greenland. MIKE WRIGHT COLLECTION

This particular leg, Frobisher Bay to Sondre Strom, is probably the worst leg I ever had in all my flying. Just about everything that could go wrong went wrong on this leg of the trip. Shortly after leaving Frobisher (the weather was IFR) the communication radio quit working. Mind you, it's −20 degrees in the cockpit and getting colder as I gained altitude. I believe if it had not been so breezy in the cockpit it wouldn't have been too bad. The best way to describe what it is like to fly a P-38 when it is in the minus temperatures is to go sit in a freezer with a fan blowing on you. I was bundled up to keep warm, but I was bundled up almost to the point that I couldn't function. I had on several layers of clothes underneath a snowmobile suit. I also had heated socks and two layers of gloves. Anytime I came across a navigation fix or some other item of importance, I would have to undress my hands to write it down. You have to keep good notes because the extreme cold can affect your memory. During the flight to Frobisher I could feel a little tingling in my fingers, but I couldn't see any visible effect of the cold. During the trip from Fobisher to Somdre Strom I could actually see a little black on my finger nails which means the frost bite is getting worse. Well, there wasn't much I could do about it because you have to write everything down. If you don't guard against hypothermia by keeping your mind active your memory will start to fade and you'll start making decisions based on, "It's too cold: I've got to get out of the airplane." In essence, you'll end up making some dumb-ass mistakes.

The cold also took its toll on the aircraft's flight instruments. (All I had were the old World War II type flight instruments.) The first thing to fail was the artificial horizon. After about an hour into the flight the directional gyro also acted up. I think the cold weather was causing the grease in the bearings of these instruments to freeze. Basically, after a few hours into the trip I had only the electric compass and the ball and slip indicator which was also electric. I was in and out of the clouds IFR then VFR while varying altitude every now and again to avoid icing. At some point I started thinking about what else could go wrong. Then the left turbo charger failed. The ADF was also giving me some problems so I decided to alter my flight plan and shoot straight for the west coast of Greenland. This is where the cold really started to affect my judgment.

I flew under weather so I could see the coast, and circled this little town in order to get my bearings. I

N505MH at Biggin Hill in 1989.
TRYGVE JOHANSEN

It is evident from this photo that Evergreen is serious about making its Lightning one of the finest examples of its type in the world.
WALTER DIETRICH (MARANA, AZ, 1992)

> had flown over this town enough times to know there wasn't an airport there, but the cold weather was affecting my brain. I ended up circling it a couple of times trying to find an airport that I knew didn't exist. I finally came to my senses and headed for Somdre Strom. The visibility was very low and all of a sudden a mountain seemed to jump out in front of me. All I could do was hang the plane on its props and head for altitude. I managed to clear the mountain, but I learned later the town's people thought I had crashed.

Wright managed to navigate through the low visibility and continued his trek to Sondre Strom where he informed Arnold of the turbo failure. He then returned to the United States on a commercial airline. It took about a month before the plane was repaired and at that time Wright returned to Greenland and completed the final two legs of the journey to England.

N505MH was one of the 2520 P-38L-5-LOs constructed at Lockheed Burbank in 1945. 44-53186, after its F-5G modification was completed, was put in storage at Kelly Field where it remained until February of the following year. At that time the plane was ferry-delivered to Kingman Field where it was deleted from the Air Force's inventory after it was turned over to the Reconstruction Finance Corporation. 53186 was then sold to the Kargl Aerial Surveys, Inc. of Midland, Texas, for $1,250, and was registered with the Civil Aeronautics Administration as N62350. The following year N62350 was sold to the Mark Hurd Mapping Company, who changed the plane's registration to N505MH in 1957. 505 served with the Hurd organization for twenty years before it was sold to Harrah's Club of Reno, Nevada, in 1967. Twelve years later the airplane was acquired by Dave Tallichet.

In the summer of 1990 Wright learned that Evergreen Airlines had purchased N505MH from Doug Arnold and he was again asked to pilot the plane back to the United States. Wright accepted Evergreen's request and completed a relatively uneventful Atlantic crossing.

Evergreen started a ground-up restoration, which is expected to take three years to complete. Afterwards Evergreen plans to attend airshows and display its Lightning in its museum, which is presently being constructed in Oregon.

Prior to its career with the Honduran Air Force, 44-53232 competed in the 1946 Bendix Trophy Race. However, race #11, piloted by J. Yandell, was forced out of the race in Kansas. N66678 was last registered to James L. Bledsoe of Miami, Florida, in 1947. WARREN M. BODIE (1946)

Yandell sold the future AFM Lightning to Ken Scribner, a fellow PAM AM pilot, shortly after the 1946 Bendix Race. Scribner painted the plane red and white and attempted to enter it in the 1947 Miami Air Races. However, the right engine of this F-5G caught fire prior to his qualifying run. Here the former racer is shown abandoned at Masters Field in Miami, Florida. WEINSCHENKER COLLECTION (1947)

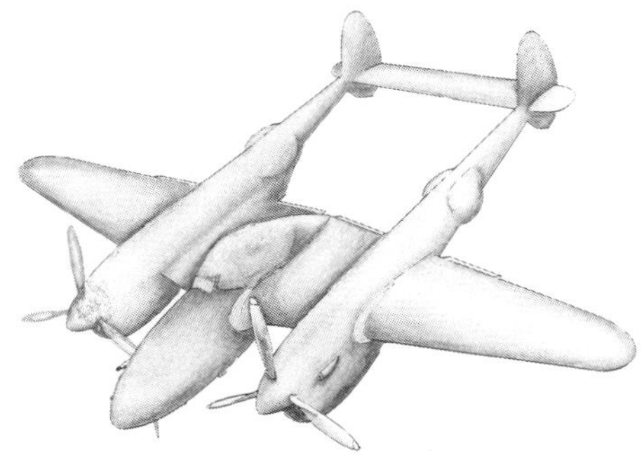

THE AIR FORCE MUSEUM'S LIGHTNING

The United States Air Force Museum has one of the largest collections of military aircraft in the world. The museum's main complex is located at Wright Patterson Air Force Base, near Dayton, Ohio, and is just a few miles from the location where the Wright Brothers actually developed the art of controlled-powered flight. Since its inception in 1923, the museum has strived to preserve the technology and the aircraft that were built for the Air Force. This was never more in evidence than at the conclusion of World War II.

In 1946 the museum's director, Mark Sloan, took on the task of collecting examples of the aircraft and aviation related artifacts that were developed during the war years. Over the next eight years, Sloan collected an impressive array of Air Force aircraft and historical memorabilia. However, most noticeably missing from the museum's fighter collection was an example of Lockheed's Fork-Tail Lightning.

Since the end of World War II, the performance of the Lightning, Mustang, and Thunderbolt, amongst other fighters, has been a continuous point of debate. The answer to which aircraft was the best fighter of this era, of course, depends to whom you direct the question. Typically a pilot develops and retains a fondness for the particular type he may have flown. This is certainly true for many of the pilots who flew combat in the P38.

Leslie E. Knapp, veteran fighter pilot who flew 26 missions in P-38s out of Foggia, Italy, with the 14th Fighter Group, 37th Fighter Squadron, recalls his first visit to the Museum.

> After being recalled to active duty during the Korean Conflict, and after a tour of flying L-20s with the 3rd Liaison Squadron, I returned to the States and obtained a Master's Degree from Stanford University. I was subsequently assigned to the Research and Development Command at Wright Patterson Air Force Base, Ohio.
>
> It was then I discovered that the best aircraft that ever flew was missing from the museum's exhibits. I called the museum Director, Major Robert Bryant Jr., to find out why this terrible oversight was allowed to continue. Major Bryant informed me that the museum was looking for a P-38 and asked me if I would be interested in flying the plane to the museum if they found one—needless to say, I said yes. I found out later that I was number six on the list of possible ferry pilots.

The top candidate to ferry any future P-38 acquisition to the museum was another veteran fighter pilot. Before joining the museum's staff in late 1959, Royal D. Frey had flown combat in the European skies in the P-38 with the 55th Fighter Squadron, 20th Fighter Group. During his tour he was officially credited with shooting down two Messerschmitt 110s. However, on

February 10, 1944, he was forced to bail out of his flak-damaged and burning aircraft over enemy territory, which resulted in his capture and subsequent internment as a prisoner of war.

Royal Frey, too, was surprised to learn of the museum's difficulties in obtaining a P-38. Fortunately, it wasn't long before the museum received a tip from Roger Besecker, an active member of the American Aviation Historical Society, as to the whereabouts of a Lightning which could possibly be acquired. Besecker's information turned out to be correct. The Philadelphia based Kaufman Foundation did, in fact, have a Lightning N90813 which they were willing to donate to the museum, but it was a photo version, F-5G, which had been operated for a number of years as a photo survey aircraft by Aero Service Corporation. The museum was interested in obtaining a fighter version of the Lightning because the conversion of an F-5 to a P-38 with five guns in its nose would require a considerable amount of money and man power. Regrettably, all of these commodities were in short supply, so the museum's director was forced to turn down the Kaufman Foundation's offer to donate their modified F-5G. It was at this time that Frey received a phone call from a fellow USAF Historian who had just returned from TDY at Kelly Air Force Base in San Antonio, Texas.

> At first I thought Martin Miller was pulling my leg, but he finally convinced me that he had seen an authentic P-38, complete with turbos and guns, on the ramp at Kelly. So I called Base Operations at Kelly, and they informed me that Bob Bean, an aircraft collector from Arizona, had traded a number of Chance Vought Corsairs to the Hondurans for two P-63s and four P-38s.

After a little research, it was learned that the plane Mr. Miller saw on the ramp at Kelly Air Force Base was P-38L-5LO, serial number 44-53232. This particular aircraft was manufactured in July of 1945 and was later modified to an F-5G6-LO at Lockheed's Dallas Modification Center. In September of the same year, 53232 was put into storage at Kelly Air Force Base and was officially declared surplus property in February 1946. The aircraft was then sent to the Kingman, Arizona, depot for disposal. Sometime later 44-53232, along with a number of other P-38s, was removed from the depot and sold to the Fuerza Aerea Honduras.

Bob Bean was contacted about the possibility of donating the Kelly P-38 to the museum, but due to

FAH 505 on display at Kelly Air Force Base's open house in 1960. USAF PHOTO (KELLY AFB, 1960)

Captain Knapp and 505 over Cincinnati, Ohio, while approaching Wright-Patterson AFB. AIR FORCE MUSEUM VIA WARREN M. BODIE (MAY 1961)

his financial situation, he was unable to donate the plane outright. He did, however, express an interest in trading his P-38 for the F-5G the Kaufman Foundation had offered the museum. Shortly thereafter, all parties agreed that the Kaufman Foundation F-5G would be traded to Bob Bean in exchange for 44-53232. In turn, the Kaufman Foundation and Bob Bean would jointly donate the ex-Honduran Lightning to the Air Force Museum.

One of the major provisions in the Kaufman-Bean transaction required the museum to undertake the responsibility of delivering the two planes to their final destinations. The job of ferrying the two planes was first offered to Frey.

> I was elated. Although the Air Force had grounded me in 1955 for poor eyesight, I still had a commercial multi-engine pilot's license at the time. So I got the Pilot's Handbook from the file and brought it home to bone-up. My wife asked me what I was doing, and when I told her, she put her foot down! She said flying worn-out F-84s on active duty was one thing, but flying a World War II P-38 as a lark was another matter. (We had lost several close friends in the Ohio ANG and USAF and she was not willing for me to risk my neck for my own personal fun.)

Three years had passed since Knapp had first added his name to the list of ferry candidates, so he was very surprised when Major Bryant offered him the opportunity to fulfill the museum's obligation to deliver the two Lightnings. Knapp first flew the former Aero Service Lightning to California for Bob Bean before flying to Kelly Air Force Base to pick up the museum's P-38.

When Knapp arrived at Kelly Air Force Base he found himself in the middle of a controversy. Apparently, Kelly's operations officer had not been informed that the museum was sending a pilot to fly the plane to Dayton. He, therefore, assumed that he was saddled with providing a qualified pilot. There was no shortage of hot-shot jet jockeys who wanted the job, but finding a truly qualified pilot was another matter. So the operations officer decided that the most reasonable thing to do was to select a pilot who had most recently flown a P-38. Knapp was understandably given the cold shoulder after he informed the opera-

Left to right: **Mark Sloan, Leslie Knapp, and K.T. York shortly after 505 was successfully delivered to Wright-Patterson AFB.**
USAF VIA LESLIE KNAPP (27 MAY 1961)

tions officer that he had been sent to ferry the Lightning. The officer then informed Knapp that he had already decided who was going to ferry the P38 and sarcastically asked Knapp when was the last time he had flown a P-38. Knapp calmly responded with, "two days ago!"

"The intentions were to fly the fighter version to Wright Patterson Air Force Base for an Armed Forces Day fly over," recalled Knapp. "however, due to a number of mechanical failures, the arrival was delayed. I was accompanied by a U-3A chase plane which was flown by Captain Smith and with him was an excellent mechanic from the museum. During the cross-country flights, the chase plane provided a radio link with the military flight facilities since the P-38 had no working radios."

In May 1961 Captain Knapp successfully delivered the museum's newest acquisition, and Major Frey was on hand to witness the big bird's arrival.

"When he got to Patterson Field, he buzzed the runway and pulled-up into a victory roll. That really got to me. So I got in my car and drove off. I couldn't stand to see him taxi in and shut down after doing what I had so greatly wanted to do."

Fortunately, the coming months would prove to be less of a disappointment to Major Frey.

At about the same time the Lightning arrived, I started to press for authenticity in the colors and markings of the displayed aircraft. When I came to the museum, the planes were painted in schemes which were not authentic but representative of all the units that had flown a specific type.

In August of 1961 I learned my Ohio ANG unit was to be recalled to active duty on October 1 and would probably be sent to Europe. One of the men in the restoration shop asked me how my own P-38 was painted, and I gave him a photo of the plane along with descriptions of the colors which were used to decorate the plane. In September, I went TDY to Orlando, Florida, for a week. When I returned, the shop people called me to the outdoor display lot. There was our new P-38, painted as my own plane had been painted. I can still recall the excitement I felt the first time I saw the plane. It was all a going-away present for me.

Ten years later the Air Force Museum officially opened its newly constructed permanent facility to the public. The new building offered the museum the opportunity to move most of its vast collection indoors. Today the much-sought-after twin-boom fighter, which played a special part in the lives of Captain Knapp and Major Frey, is preserved amongst its contemporaries in the World War II section of the main museum building.

Uncluttered view of the Air Force Museum's new Lockheed P-38 Lightning. EUGENE SOMMERICH (1960)

44-53232 decorated in the colors of Royal Frey's "Stardust" taking its place among the others on display at the Air Force Museum. BURTON KEMP (OCTOBER 1961)

Captain Knapp (left) **and Royal Frey standing on the wing of the museum's P-38.** USAFM.

The AFM's P-38 was given a fresh coat of paint before it was permanently moved inside the museum's new complex in 1970. It is noteworthy to point out the erroneous tail number that was added to this otherwise accurate paint scheme. WARREN M. BODIE

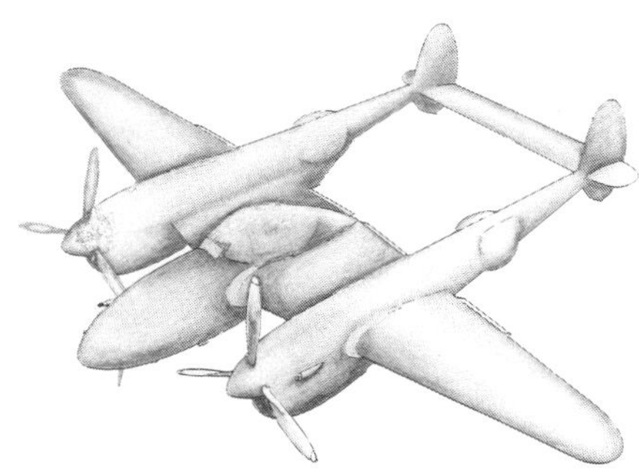

Lightning Memorial to America's Ace of Aces

OUT OF THE HUNDREDS of Fighter Pilots who flew the P-38 in combat, none were more successful than Major Richard Ira Bong. Through three combat tours, which culminated in one hundred forty six missions and nearly four hundred hours of combat time, Dick Bong scored an unprecedented forty aerial victories: earning him the Medal Of Honor and the distinction of being America's "Ace Of Aces."

Shortly after being credited with his last victory, Major Bong was withdrawn from combat duty and, subsequently, assigned to Lockheed as a test pilot. Tragically, on August 6, 1945, Dick Bong was killed while testing a Lockheed P-80 Shooting Star.

In the fall of 1947 the Richard I. Bong Post 435 of Superior, Wisconsin, approached state and local officials with a proposal to create a fitting memorial to commemorate Major Bong's war-time accomplishments. Bill Trinke, National Committeeman of the American Legion, and Wisconsin Governor Oscar Rennebohn, were among the men who presented this plan to Wisconsin Senators Alexander Wiley and Joseph McCarthy. In turn the request for a P-38-type aircraft was passed on to the newly established Department of the Air Force. The following year their request was approved and a plane was made available. Unfortunately, the donated aircraft was not airworthy, and the expense of moving a seven-ton fighter by land was far beyond Post 435's resources. However, after being advised of this problem, along with being pressured by Wisconsin's national representatives, the Department of the Air Force donated a P-38 that could be flown directly to Superior.

The history of the donated Lightning originates in July 1945 when the plane was delivered to the Army Air Force as P-38L-5LO, serial number 44-53236. This aircraft was first assigned to the 4146th Base Unit at Dover Field, Delaware. In September 44-53236 was transferred to the 4000th Base Unit, at Wright Field in Dayton, Ohio. The following January the plane was assigned to the 611th Base Unit at Eglin Field, Florida, where in July 1948 it was redesignated as a ZF-38. Finally, in August 44-53236 was returned to Wright Patterson Air Force Base.

On December 7, 1948, 44-53236, piloted by Lt. Donald Schultz, departed Wright Patterson Air Force Base for Superior, Wisconsin. En route, Lt. Schultz experienced mechanical difficulties with the aircraft's hydraulic system and landing gear. The runway length at Superior's airport was not long enough to accommodate an emergency landing of this type, so the aircraft's final destination was diverted to Duluth, Minnesota. Upon arriving in Duluth, Lt. Schultz executed an uneventful landing, and the plane was parked among the aircraft of the

After the plane was delivered to Duluth, parts were removed so it could not be easily flown again. Here the aircraft is shown being towed through Superior, Wisconsin. K.E. THRO VIA JOYCE ERICKSON (1949)

Joyce Bong Erickson's favorite picture of her famous older brother Richard Ira Bong. The photo was taken in Australia during his first combat tour. BONG-ERICKSON COLLECTION

newly commissioned 179th Fighter Interceptor Squadron of the Minnesota Air National Guard. Shortly thereafter, ownership of the plane was officially transferred to American Legion Post 435.

Representatives of Post 435 initially planned to move the Lockheed Fighter to the Tri-State Fair Grounds adjacent to the Superior Municipal Airport where Major Bong first learned to fly. However, Norman LaPole, president of the Richard I. Bong Memorial Foundation, Inc., recommended that the plane be brought to Bong's hometown of Poplar. In July 1949, the plane was dismantled and towed from the airport in Duluth through Superior to Poplar, Wisconsin. In the following years the plane was vandalized by souvenir hunters while financial difficulties thwarted any attempt to start the memorial's construction. But in the summer of 1954, construction finally commenced. Air Force mechanics from Duluth's Air Guard unit and the 515th Air Defense Group from Tinker Air Force Base, Oklahoma, worked together in restoring and placing the aircraft on the memorial site. On May 22, 1955, the Richard I. Bong Memorial was officially dedicated.

Major Bong's war-time commander, General George C. Kenney, remarked in his dedication address.

The dedication memorial's ceremony was opened with a formation of Minnesota National Guard F-89s and T-33s being led by a lone Lightning. The lead P-38 (actually an F-5G) was supplied by the Mark Hurd Mapping Company and is believed to have been flown by Mark Hurd himself.

BONG-ERICKSON COLLECTION (MAY 1955)

The Bong Memorial Foundation, which had been set-up with help from movie actor Clark Gable, had trouble attracting enough funds to erect a fitting memorial to Bong. In the interim the plane was stored in a lot where it was more or less obscured by weeds as the fund drive continued. In July 1949, a newspaper photo depicting the aircraft's deteriorated condition was published from coast to coast, which again brought attention to the project. The plane was then re-mated to its wings and moved, as shown here, next to Highway 2 so motorists could see it. BONG-ERICKSON COLLECTION (CIRCA 1952)

The memorial shortly after it was dedicated in 1955. Many of the parts that were used to restore this plane were donated by aircraft collector and parts dealer Earl Reinert. BONG-ERICKSON COLLECTION

To Major Richard Ira Bong ace of American aces of all of our wars, who is destined to hold that title for all time. With the weapons that are possessed today, no war of the future will last long enough for any pilot to run up a score of forty victories again. His country and the Air Force must never forget their number-one fighter pilot, who will inspire other fighter pilots and countless thousands of youngsters

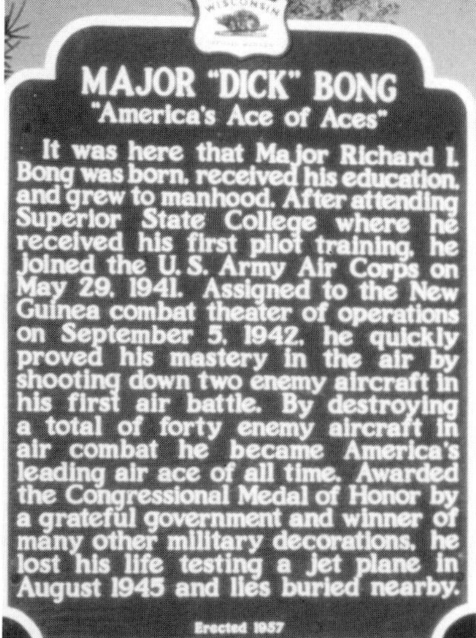

Memorial and dedication plaque during the late 1960s. DICK PHILLIPS

In 1988 the Minnesota Air National Guard was involved in redecorating the Bong Memorial in a more authentic paint scheme and for the first time adorned the plane with the image of Dick Bong's war-time sweetheart and later wife "MARGE." BONG-ERICKSON COLLECTION

The Richard Ira Bong Memorial today. BONG-ERICKSON COLLECTION

who will want to follow in his footsteps every time any nation or coalition of nations dares to challenge our right to think, speak, and live as a free people.

May this memorial building, donated by the veterans of Foreign Wars, and citizens of this community, serve as a shrine at which we may constantly resolve to see to it that we preserve our country, our ideals, and our freedom. May it also constantly remind us of our debt to our youth, which has always been willing to make any sacrifice to insure that the rest of us can keep and inherit this freedom. We owe a lot to our youth—youth typified by Dick Bong.

Today, tomorrow, and for all time, we salute you Dick gallant gentleman, hero, ace of aces.

The Bong Memorial was not dedicated and forgotten like many of the other outdoor memorials, which have been erected to commemorate the brave airmen of World War II. Since 1955 the actual aircraft has been cleaned and repainted a number of times. Most recently, it was refurbished by the 148th Fighter Interceptor Squadron of the Minnesota Air National Guard. The plane is currently decorated in the colors of P-38 (44-23964) in which Major Bong scored eight of his forty victories.

The Richard I. Bong Memorial Fund is striving to fulfill a forty-year-old dream of constructing a fitting museum building that will enclose the memorial aircraft. Contributions can be sent to The Bong Memorial Fund, P.O. Box 115, Superior, WI 54880.

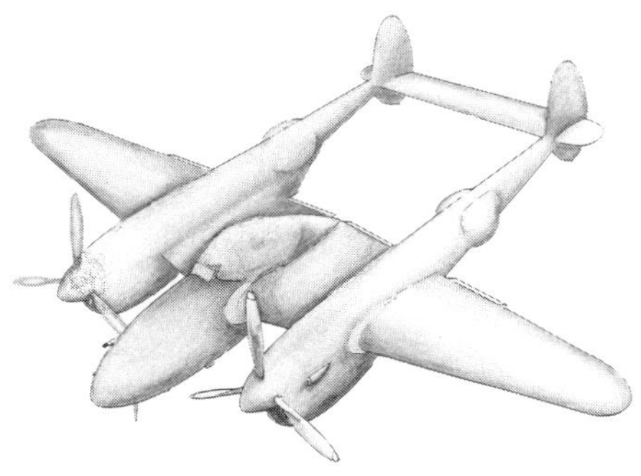

White Lightnin

Lefty Gardner's "White Lightnin" is one of the most recognized P-38s that survives today. Over the past thirty years Gardner, and his trusty racer number 13, have thrilled thousands of airshow and air racing fans with aerobatic performances that are reminiscent of the days when Lockheed's legendary test pilots first demonstrated the Lightning's capabilities. In the process, Gardner has clocked more time in the twin-boom fighter than any other pilot. The fact that his 49-year-old P-38 regularly endures the stress of stunt flying and pylon racing is a tribute to Kelly Johnson's design.

This aircraft is not only a contemporary air racing legend, but it also has a list of accomplishments, which date back to the post World War II Cleveland Air Races. Prior to beginning its post-war racing career F-5G-6-LO, serial number 44-53254 served with Army Air Force from July 24, 1945, until September when the plane was declared surplus and ferried to Kingman, Arizona. It was then purchased for $1,250 in April 1946 by the Lilee Products Co. of Chicago, Illinois, who registered the aircraft with the Civil Aeronautics Administration as N25Y. A few months later N25Y was sold for $1565.85 to Houston businessman and Beechcraft franchise owner J.D. Reed.

Reed was greatly interested in air racing and, after the war he purchased several ex-military aircraft. At the same time, he started the search for pilots he could trust to fly the racing machines that eventually emerged from his facility. One of the pilots Reed recruited to fly for him was a young man named Charlie Walling.

Charlie Walling was, and still is, the consummate pilot's pilot. His love of flying started at the tender age of 12 shortly before he soloed in an unregistered aircraft in 1933. From there he went on to acquire his Air Transport License, and after graduating from high school he began working for J.D. Reed's Air Activities company as an instructor. By the time the Second World War erupted, young Walling had also established himself as a top-rated air instructor with the Army Air Force, and after joining the Ferry Command he delivered B-17s and B-24s to various combat areas around the globe. He also had the opportunity to ferry a Martin A-30 to Accra, Africa, before being transferred to fly C47s and C-87s over the infamous Hump. Walling finished his Asian combat tour flying Northrop P-61s with the 427th Night Fighter Squadron before returning home in mid-1945.

Walling recalled:

> J.D. Reed helped me find a job with the Eastern States Petroleum Company shortly after I separated from the Air Force. I flew their twin Cessna (Bamboo Bomber), and Beach D-18 before hiring on with Superior Oil Company in April 1946. It was during the time that I was flying a Grumman G-21 for Superior that I heard about the surplus planes that were being sold for such cheap prices. I wanted to buy a Bell P-39

N25Y in-flight over the Houston area shortly after its second place finish in the 1947 Miami Air Races. COURTESY BAILEY STUDIOS

with the idea of racing it at Cleveland, so I talked to J.D. Reed about my plans and he mentioned that he was considering purchasing a P-38 to enter in the upcoming air races. (During the time I was in the Ferry Command, I had the opportunity to fly the P-39, P-40, P-43, P-47, and P-51, but never got into a Lightning.) As it turned out, I had a trip into Houston for maintenance not long after J.D. bought the plane, and I used this opportunity to fly a P-38 for the first time.

Shortly after Walling's first Lightning flight, J.D. Reed asked him if he would like to race the plane in the Miami Air Race that was coming up in January 1947. Walling eagerly accepted Reed's offer to race N25Y at the All American Air Maneuvers and set out to arrange for a short vacation from Superior Oil. Walling continues:

I got to Miami a few days before the time trials started in order to get a little experience in the airplane. I first structurally qualified N25Y, and then speed qualified it at around 310 mph. During the qualifying runs, the engines were turning at 3000 rpm, which was the takeoff rpm for the Allison, while pulling 64 inches of manifold pressure. In the straights my instruments indicated 400 mph even. In the turns the speed would only drop off to about 375 mph, so I knew something had to be wrong with the way I was timed. Not only was my qualifying speed low but all of the planes that were participating in the trials were being clocked much slower than indicated speeds. (Later I had the field surveyed and discovered that the course was actually 3 miles longer than the publicized 15-mile course.) Anyway, my qualifying speed of 310 mph was the highest speed until Paul Penrose's Mustang was clocked at about 10 mph faster.

J.D. Reed radically modified this aircraft during the summer of 1947. The cowls were modified to include a carburetor intake and water injector was added to the induction system. The exhaust was re-worked to expel the used gases in a conventional manner out the side of the engine cowls. The wings and propellers were also clipped to improve aerodynamic efficiency. COURTESY BAILEY STUDIOS

The Miami race was staged out of Masters Field, which was a very poor location to hold a race because of all the gun emplacements that littered the airport. So, before the race started, Steve Whitman and I stepped off the distance between the starting line and a runway that bisected our takeoff pattern. The distance we measured was only in the neighborhood of 2,000 feet, and to make matters worse, immediately on the other side of this runway was a deep ditch. We realized that it would be disastrous if we didn't get off by the time we were rolling on the pavement. Prior to this, J.D. had borrowed the Scotch tape trick that Tony LeVier successfully used on his P-38 in the '46 Cleveland race. We taped the flaps, and everything else that stuck up or had a gap in it. Therefore, we couldn't use flaps for take off or landing. So, when Mike Murphy, who was the starter for the race, began to raise the flag, I started to accelerate the engines to around 35 inches. It just so happened that the airplane was moving forward a bit when the starting flag was dropped. I then went to full throttle, and I waited until I was rolling on the bisecting runway's pavement before I pulled the yoke back and retracted the gear. I knew that if it didn't fly, I was going to do some sliding and possibly end up in the ditch. But it flew, so I went out to the scatter pylon and got on the race course. I lead for about three laps until Paul Penrose got squared away. (The guys in the single engine airplanes had a bad time getting off the ground due to the torque and having to really pour it to it on take off.) Penrose caught me after about three laps, and we finished the race one-two.

Charlie "Firewall" Walling had the hottest P-38 at Cleveland in 1947. Even Tony LeVier was impressed by the speed that was coaxed from the Lockheed design. However, problems with the exhaust system forced the Reed/Walling team to saw the P-63 style stacks off flush with the cowlings. This caused a great deal drag so the plane didn't perform as well as in the Sohio Trophy Race as it had during the qualifying run. Here Charlie Walling is shown ground checking the aircraft's engines performance. WARREN BODIE

N25Y on its way home after the 1947 Cleveland racing event. WARREN BODIE

J.D. Reed was very pleased with N25Y's second place finish and immediately started making plans to race the plane in the 1947 Cleveland National Air Races. Ivis Hill, who would also race the P- 38 "Green Hornet" for Reed in the '47 Cleveland races, was sent to Walnut Ridge, Arkansas, to pick up a fighter nose for N25Y. It was believed that replacing the photo nose with the fighter variant would increase the plane's top speed. Ironically, N25Y flew eight miles an hour slower with the gun type nose. Other ways of increasing the plane's top speed were considered. Charlie Walling continues:

J.D. asked me what I thought we could do to make the plane go faster. My first thought was to put a water injection system in the plane and change the supercharger ratio to where it would pull more manifold pressure. So, between January and September he removed the Y exhaust stacks from N25Y and put water tanks in slots where the Y stacks would normally go. The carburetor air scoops were moved to the top of the cowling, and the engine's exhaust was fitted with short exhaust stacks. Well, the distance from the exhaust ports to outside of the cowling on the P-38 is quite a stretch, so in order to use the short exhaust

In 1948, race number 14 returned to Cleveland with an attractive Inca Bronze paint scheme, but the aircraft suffered an engine failure which put it out of the races. WARREN BODIE

James P. Hagerstrom (World War II and Korean war ace) piloted N25Y to a fifth place finish in the 1949 Tinnerman Trophy Race. AARON KING

stacks, they had to extend the exhaust pipes approximately 15 inches before welding P-63-type stacks on the end of those. In order to keep them from bouncing around, they put two steel straps down on either side. J.D. also changed the 8.6 to 1 blower to the type that was installed on the P-40. This gave us a blower ratio of 10 to 1 and that, along with the water injection system, enabled us to pull 85 inches of manifold pressure. We also cut about a foot off each of the propellers in order to keep the blades under the sonic speed because we had increased the rpm to 3,200.

When we got to Cleveland, I went out to qualify, and the plane was extremely fast. As a matter of fact, Tony Levier said he never thought he would see a P-38 go that fast. I made a couple of trips around the race course, and the airplane was indicating 440 mph on the straits. But it turned out that during the qualifying run, I had blown six of these stacks off and burned the cowling a bit. We realized that there was no way to race this airplane under these conditions. So, we really didn't have any choice but to remove the short stacks. Unfortunately, we didn't have the time to remove the water tanks and put the "Y" stacks back on the airplane, and in any case, we didn't have old cowlings. So, we ended up putting a new set of manifolds on the engines. We extended the exhaust from the manifold to just outside either cowling by welding a short pipe to each of them, knowing full well that this would create a good deal of drag. When Tony LeVier and I took off at the start of the Sohio Race, Tony got slightly ahead of me, and I stayed the same distance behind him throughout the race. I was pull-

The former Cleveland racer spent much of its time during the 1950s and early 1960 at Harbor Field in Baltimore, Maryland.
ROGER BESECKER VIA DAVE OSTROWSKI

Vernon Thorpe stripped the plane of its old paint and brought the neglected aircraft back to flying standards during his period of ownership.
JOHN CAMPBELL COLLECTION

ing 85 inches of mercury and he was pulling 64. We wound up finishing the Sohio race one-two.

Fortunately, my qualifying speed was fast enough to get into the Thompson Trophy race. But, I experienced all kinds of problems with the water injection system so I had to leave the race in the second lap.

After the races were completed, J.D. Reed decided to purchase the P-51 that Paul Penrose had flown in the Thompson Trophy Race. Penrose flew the P-51, and Walling piloted the P-38 back to Houston. From there, Penrose rode piggyback with Walling in the P- 38 to Burbank, California. Walling agreed to rework some of the things that had been done to N25Y for the '47 races, and possibly increase the plane's performance for the 1948 National Air Races. It took about a year for Walling to complete the work, and in the meantime he enlisted Herman "Fish" Salmon to fly N25Y in the 48 races. Walling again picks up the story:

I finished replacing the old stacks on the 38, reinstalled the original cowling, and had the plane painted in an Inca Bronze color. Just before I left for Texas, Fish informed me that he had decided to race Charlie Tucker's P-63 instead of J.D.'s P-38 because he figured he would have a better chance of finishing the race in the money. Therefore, it was arranged for Johnny Hamp to fly N25Y, and I would fly J.D.'s P-51. Shortly after I delivered N25Y to Houston, Hamp and I set out for Cleveland, but along the way we got separated. When I arrived in Cleveland I inquired

Lefty Gardner's White Lightnin was first given the race number 25 before being later to changed to Lucky 13. MILO PELTZER COLLECTION

about Hamp and I was told that he had put down in Erie, Pennsylvania. The following day, he arrived in Cleveland, and I was sick when I saw the airplane. He had flown through several rain storms, which ruined the paint on the leading edges of the wings and stabilizers.

When we started our practice runs we didn't have the 200 octane triptane fuel we normally used for the race. So, I told Hamp not to go to high power on those Allison's with only 100 octane fuel because they would detonate and probably damage the engines. Well, that's exactly what happened! When Hamp came down the home stretch during his qualifying run, one of the engines detonated real bad and put him and N25Y out of the race. I was never sure of what manifold pressure he was pulling, but whatever it was, it was too much for the engines to handle.

Charlie Walling went on to qualify in Reed's Mustang but was forced to exit the Thompson Trophy Race in the 18th lap. The reason for his early departure was due to the plane's inadequate quantity of water for the injection system. Before the race, Walling had calculated that his aircraft would require approximately 90 gallons of water to run the 45 minute race at 400 miles an hour. Unfortunately, the water tanks that had been installed in his Mustang's gun bays only carried 30 gallons each. Therefore, it was evident to Walling that he would have little to no chance to win, but J.D. Reed wanted him to enter the race, nevertheless. Just as Walling had predicted, as soon as his water tanks went dry his plane's engine started to run rough and he was forced to exit the race.

The following year, which turned out to be the final year for the Cleveland National Air Races, N25Y returned to compete once again. Walling was unable to compete due to work obligations, so Reed enlisted the help of James P. Hargerstrom who was an ex-World War II ace. Hargerstrom collected $350 in prize money by piloting N25Y to a fifth place finish in the Tinnerman Trophy Race. However, the joy of placing in the money was soon overshadowed by the tragic loss of Bill Odom after he lost control of Jackie Cochran's "Beguine" and crashed into a nearby house, killing a woman and her child.

With the demise of the National Air Races, sport planes like N25Y were regarded by many to be nothing more than expensive conversation pieces. So, in 1953 J.D. Reed sold N25Y to Hugh Wells, of Baltimore, Maryland. Wells moved N25Y to Baltimore's Harbor Field where it remained for the next nine years. During this period ownership of this former racer changed several times, but the plane was seldom, if ever, flown. In 1962 Vernon Thorpe took an interest in the plane, and after a considerable amount of dickering with the plane's owner, purchased N25Y. Thorpe and his partner, Sylvan Laird operated N25Y for a little over a year before selling the plane to Marvin "Lefty" Gardner and his partners, Tom O'Connor and Lloyd Nolen. "Well, it kind of shows you how smart I am," said Thorpe. "I sold what is probably the most desirable P-38 in existence today for, would you believe, $4,000?"

Thorpe likes to poke fun at his level of intelligence for letting such an expensive aircraft get away, but don't be fooled. He is without question one of the most qualified warbird pilots in the country today. He is also one of the very few pilots who carries an instructor's rating for the P-38.

The list of Lefty Gardner's accomplishments would fill volumes. He started his aviation career at the outbreak of the Second World War by enlisting in the Air Force as a cadet. Gardner aspired to be a fighter pilot but after finishing cadet training he was sent to learn the ways of the heavy bomber, and eventually found himself in England where he flew with the Mighty Eighth Air Force. All totaled, he successfully completed 20 missions in B24s and 14 missions in B-17s. But when his tour was over, Gardner somehow felt that he wasn't quite finished with the war, so he volunteered to fly C-87s (cargo version of the B-24) on covert supply missions to aid the Norwegian underground. These missions were some of the most hazardous of the war. In order to avoid the Nazi-held Norway, each plane was required to fly unescorted from England, 1,700 miles over the North Sea along the Arctic Circle and land in dimly lit makeshift landing strips near Stockholm, Sweden. From there the supplies were smuggled into Norway. It goes without saying that this type of work was not for the faint at heart. Lefty completed 12 such missions.

After the war Gardner created a successful agricultural flying business, which is still thriving today. During the 1950s Gardner and his good friend the late Lloyd Nolen started collecting vintage warbirds. One day a prankster painted "Confederate Air Force" on their only Mustang. The name stuck and that day in 1957 is generally regarded as the unofficial beginning of what is now America's largest and most successful warbird organization. Lloyd Nolen once said, "Lefty, in many ways is responsible for making the CAF what it is today. He would go out take a look at a plane, do the work necessary to get it home, and fly the plane to Mercedes. Not many people have his natural ability as both a mechanic and a pilot."

After acquiring his P-38 from Vernon Thorpe in 1963, Gardner painted the aircraft in what was then the Confederate Air Force's official color scheme of white with red and blue trim. With the plane being white, it is natural that it would eventually be nick named "White Lightnin." In 1971 Gardner made his first trip to the Reno National Championship Air Races as a competitor and has competed and has performed precision aerobatics each year except 1991. The P-38 is not a particularly competitive racing airplane when compared to the Mustang, so Gardner also races his P-51, which is decorated like the United States Air Force's "Thunderbirds" demonstration team. Gardner captured the Reno championship in 1976 while piloting his Mustang. He has also experienced some success with his P-38 despite the Lightning's shortcomings as a pylon racer. He qualified N25Y in 1981 at 365.319 miles an hour, which is an unofficial course record for the P-38, and also placed second in the Bronze Race that same year.

Lefty Gardner's down-to-earth demeanor has earned him the reputation of being one of the more approachable warbird owners. He is has also known for giving a deserving soul the thrill of riding in his P-38 from time to time. The P-38 celebrated its 50th anniversary in 1989, and Gardner commemorated this event by highlighting his Lightning with the names of the individuals who made the Lightning forever famous. While attending an airshow in the Houston area Gardner's "White Lightnin" developed a leak in one of its coolant radiators. Gardner got in touch with Phil Turnbull, a Continental Airlines maintenance specialist, who helped him fix the problem. While Turnbull was working on the plane he noticed that the name of his friend Leo Childs, the designer of the F-5G nose, was painted on the side of N25Y. Turnbull then went on to tell Gardner a sad story which is better told by Leo Childs himself:

> In August 1945, I was "invited" by Ben Bramsom, chief test pilot at the Dallas Mod Center, to go for a piggyback ride with him on a full acceptance flight of a P-38/F-5G. Word got around that I was about to get his long-hoped for piggyback ride, and friends and fellow workers gathered in front of the flight shack to watch. Being 6′5″ tall and 148 pounds, I had to fold up like a grasshopper behind the pilot's seat.
>
> August in Texas can be pure hell, with temperatures often exceeding 107 degrees in the shade. We had been taxiing up, holding—taxiing and holding, repeatedly for about an hour by the time we turned onto the downwind leg of the taxi strip for takeoff. As we turned, I could see for the first time the long line of aircraft ahead of us, twenty- eight by my count. Once before I had suffered a mild heat stroke and didn't want another one. We kept creeping along the

Lefty Gardner and Gary Levitz often thrilled racing fans with their maneuvers around the race course pylons, 1980.
Inset: **Gardner at the controls of "White Lightnin".** NEAL NURMI

taxi strip for awhile longer and I began to feel dizzy and more than a little apprehensive. Also, I was beginning to feel the need to borrow Uncle Benny's relief tube. Then I began to think about what would happen if I got airsick. After all, this was to be a full production acceptance test flight. All these thoughts were racing through my mind. Engine overheating—I'm overheating—pilot relief tube—aerobatics and airsickness—Panic Time! I tapped Uncle Benny on the shoulder and made a motion to scrub the flight. My friends were waiting for me back at the flight shack and when we taxied up they all shouted out as one voice, "Childs chickened out." Uncle Benny said "Don't let them get to you. We will do it again next week." But within a few days the first atomic bomb was dropped on Japan, and hopes for a piggyback ride were consumed in the fall out.

In retrospect I have wished a thousand times since that day I had not chickened out, even if I had a heat stroke, pissed in my britches, and puked all over Uncle Benny. So what! I would have received my piggyback certificate and could have been enjoying telling friends and strangers alike about my ride in a P-38.

The following day Childs' son, Ryan, told him that Phil Turnbull had received several passes from Lefty Gardner for Sunday's airshow and that he should come to see N25Y's new paint scheme. Early the next morning Childs visited the plane and was amazed to his name painted in gold. When the official airshow festivities were over, Childs, Turnbull and Ryan returned to Gardner's P-38. Shortly after they arrived, Lefty Gardner asked Childs if he was ready for his much-belated piggyback ride. "I didn't ask any questions," said Childs.

There are pilots who go faster, but nobody flies a tighter pylon course than Lefty Gardner. NEAL NURMI

"I just folded up like a grasshopper and crawled into the space behind the pilot's seat. Deja Vu! As we taxied along, I began to reminisce about that day in August 1945 at Love Field."

After taking off they spent a good deal of time in the air before finally landing at Andrau Airport. Childs was puzzled by what was going on. He was also wondering how he was going get in touch with his son Ryan. But once he got on the ground he spotted his son and Phil Turnbull and the whole story came out of how they had cooked up the deal to get him out to see Lefty Gardner's P-38.

In 1990 Gardner and his white P-38 made their twentieth consecutive appearance at the Reno air races. He went on to win two out of the three Bronze race heats, and put on an aerobatic demonstration that few will forget. Sadly, the following year wasn't as kind to Gardner. On April 16, 1990, his long-time friend Lloyd Nolen passed away, and the on-going estate settlement that ensued forced him to attend the 1991 Reno Racing festivities without his trusty Race number 13. The sense of gratitude and endearing affection that race fans have for Gardner was apparent by the number of people who lined up in front of Kodak's film booth to get his autograph and wish him their best.

In 1992 Lefty Gardner and "White Lightnin" returned to Reno and to again race and perform for his fans.

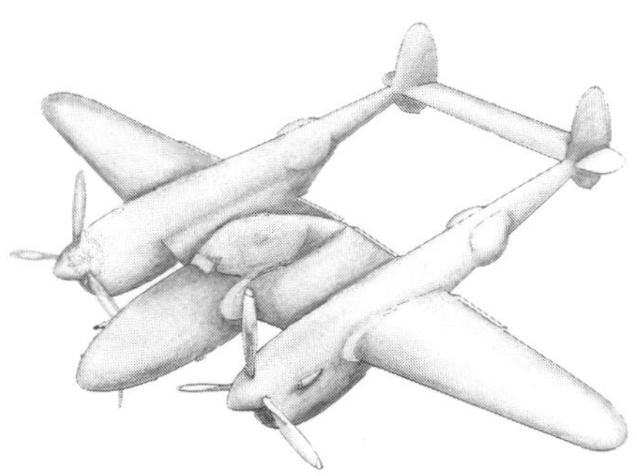

Other Survivors

Noted aircraft recovery specialist Gary Larkins has located several air-frames in New Guinea. Unfortunately, the PNG government has placed a moratorium against removing such items from their country. GARY LARKINS (1992)

Another of the P-38s discovered by Larkins. This one has the name Lt. E.G. Dickey and two Japanese flags painted on its side. GARY LARKINS (1992)

A P-38 re-build project surfaced at the Santa Monica Museum of Flying 1992 auction. This included the remains of an F-5G (N57496), which crashed near Bishop, California, during the late 1950s (see appendix B)**. Tom Reilly of Kissimmee, Florida, purchased the wreckage and will some day make a go at rebuilding this plane.**

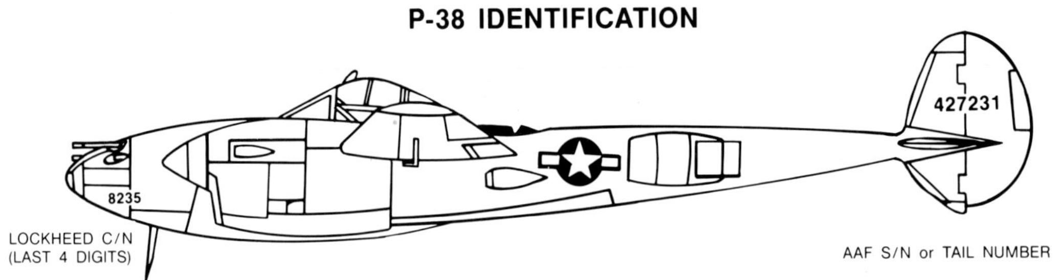

TYPICAL MARKINGS OF A L-MODEL LIGHTNING FRESH FROM THE FACTORY

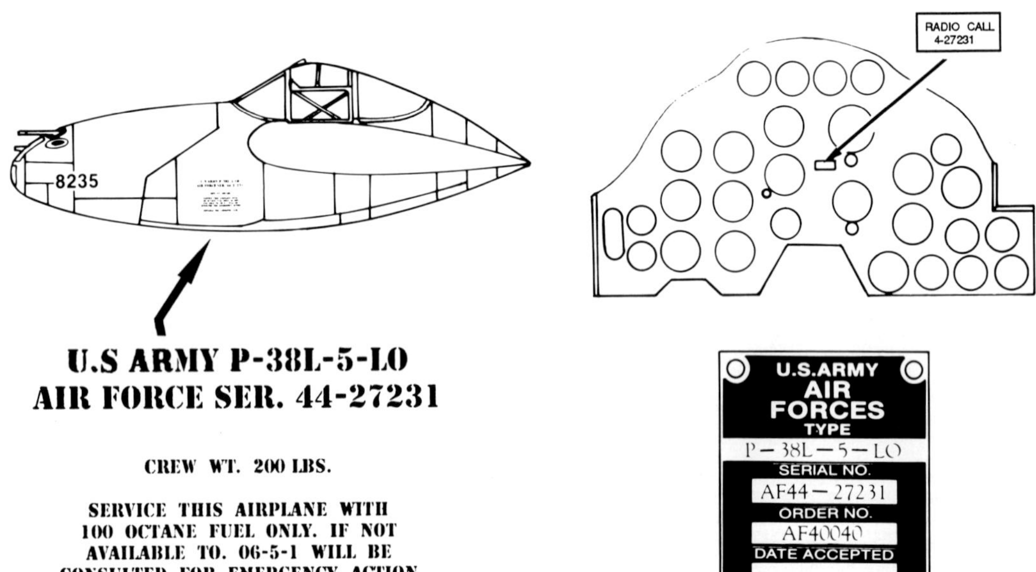

USAAF COCKPIT DATA PLATE

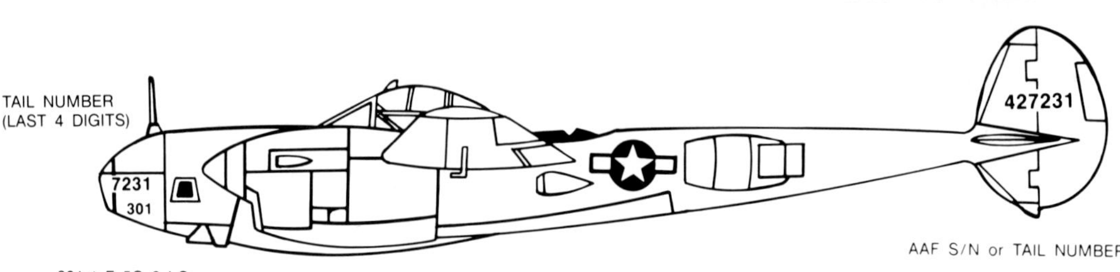

MARKINGS AFTER BEING CONVERTED TO A F-5G-6-LO

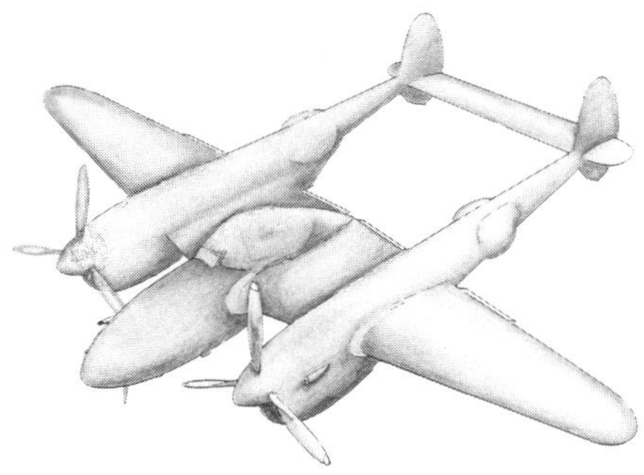

P-38 Identification

The Army Air Force serial numbers of some of the surviving Lockheed P-38 Lightnings are clouded by erroneous and inconsistent paper documentation. Some of these aircraft's identities are further compounded by the absence of their Army Air Force nomenclature or data plate. The lack of such fundamental sources of identification make necessary an explanation of the methods and theories that can use to identify a P-38 Lightning.

In General

During the war years, most P-38s were readily identified by their respective tail numbers (AAF serial number) or by the legend that Lockheed stenciled on the left side of each plane's center section. Lightnings fresh from the factory also sported the last four digits of their constructor's numbers (manufacturer's serial number). These numbers appeared on both sides of the plane's lower nose; but, the Air Force usually replaced them with the last four digits of the aircraft's AAF serial number, or deleted them altogether, shortly after the plane entered active military service. P-38s of this period also could be identified by the Army Air Force data plate that the manufacturer installed in the cockpit (just to the right of the starboard window crank) and by the radio call tag on the instrument panel of each aircraft.

Unfortunately, the Army Air Force serial numbers of airframes that exist today are not as easily identified. Very few of the surviving Lightnings are painted in such a uniform manner, and even fewer retain their data plate or radio call tag. Therefore, additional references such as Federal Aviation Administration files, Military Record Cards, and individual Army Air Force Aircraft Checker's Reports can be sought to aid in identifying the subject airplane.

Federal Aviation Administration's Records

The first document usually encountered in a particular aircraft's Federal Aviation Administration file is its initial bill of sale. For surplus military aircraft, this bill of sale document originates from the War Assets Administration. Amongst the other pertinent information included on this document are the aircraft's model number, manufacturer's serial number (constructor's number), and Army Air Force identification number (serial number). In theory, the Army Air Force serial number listed on the bill of sale should cross-reference (using Appendix A) to the plane's constructor's number and vice versa. However, this theory does not always hold true because some P-38 bill of sale documents contain numbers that do not directly

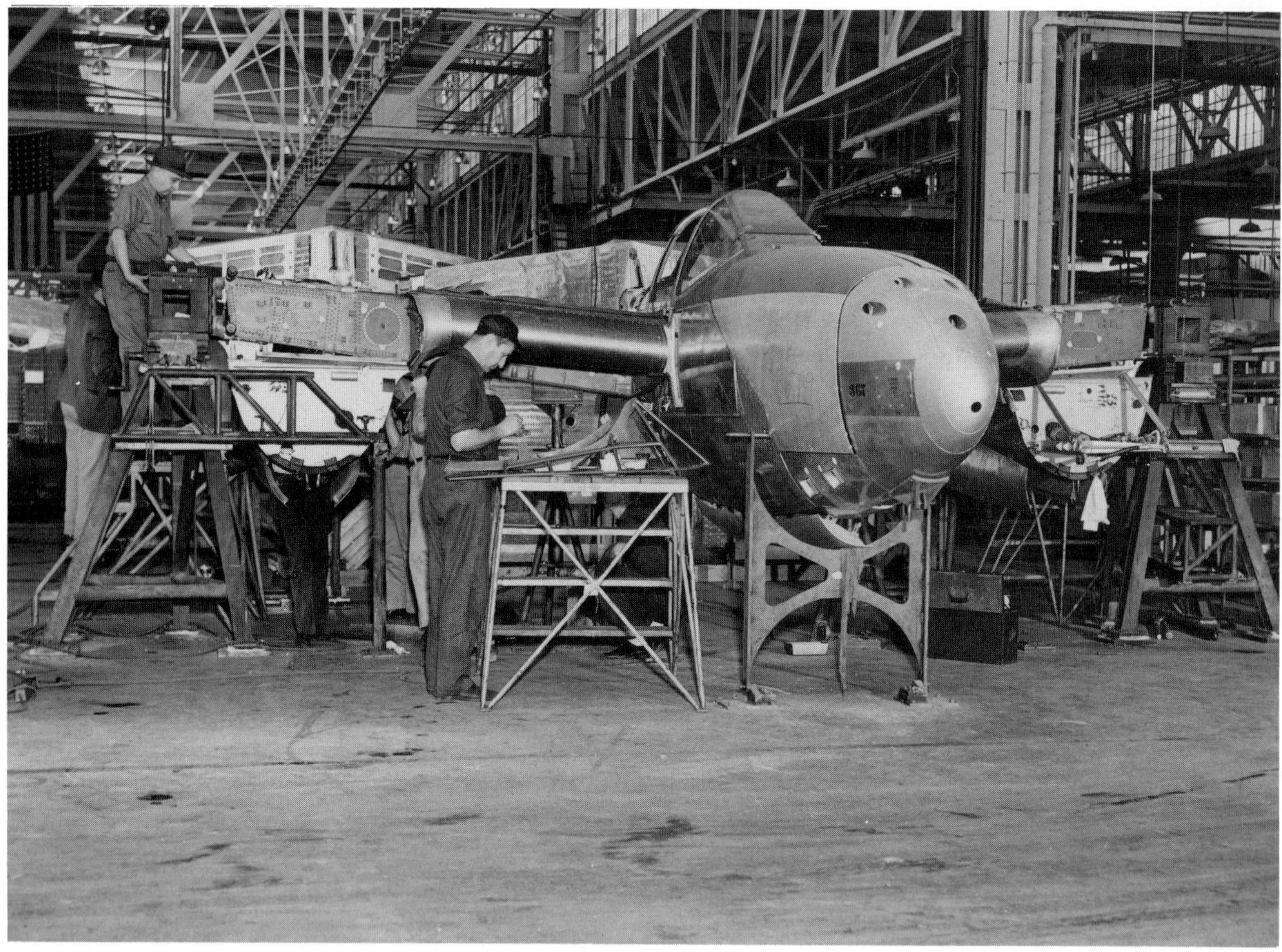

Lightning on the Lockheed assembly line. It is noteworthy to point out the constructor number 5679 that is grease penciled on the aircraft's gun access door. This is how Lockheed kept track of the planes along its assembly line. LOCKHEED

cross-reference. This is particularly true of the P-38s that were sold from the Kingman depot in Arizona.

The question of which number is correct may never be answered to suit everyone; but, the author's research in the area of aircraft identification has produced a reasonable new theory. This theory asserts that the Army Air Force serial number is probably the most reliable of the two numbers that appear on the bill of sale documents because it is the only number that could be obtained directly from the airplane.

The development of this theory began after interviewing Julian Myers, who managed the Kingman depot from 1945 to 1949. Myers recalled that he kept track of Kingman's aircraft by their tail numbers (AAF serial numbers) and that the tail number of each plane was checked to see that it agreed with the serial number on its data plate. Additional support for the previously stated theory came from a partial inventory listing of Kingman's P-38type aircraft. This document listed each aircraft's Army Air Force serial number and the serial numbers from each of its Allison engines but did not list any constructor's numbers. To prove further the Army Air Force number theory, most of the surviving aircraft in question have been physically examined. Only five of the existing eleven ex-Kingman P-38s retain their Army Air Force data plate, but in each case the number stamped on their data plate matches the Army Air Force serial number listed on their respective bills of sale. Therefore, it is reasonable to assume that the Army Air Force serial numbers listed on the War Assets Administration's bill of sale documents are accurate.

Where the Kingman sales representatives got the constructor's numbers that appear on their P-38 sale documents is unknown. It is likely, although it is yet to be proven, that these numbers originated from a Lockheed production list of P-38s. If this is the case, it is possible that something as simple as a minor mistake in calculating each plane's constructor's number could account for the errors. Another possibility is that Lockheed's production list is in error.

Lockheed Production List

The list of P-38 production block numbers (Appendix A) used with this publication came from Lockheed Aircraft Corporation of Burbank, California. Lockheed's P-38 production photographs are the only readily available source that can be used to verify Lockheed's bookkeeping. These photographs depict P-38s complete with their four-digit Lockheed constructor's number and their Army Air Force serial number (tail number). In every case tested, the numbers that appear in such photographs cross-reference without error when applied to Lockheed's production list.

Aircraft Checker's Report

Each aircraft that left Lockheed's assembly line was issued an Aircraft Checker's Report (Form 263A). The first part of this document contained the aircraft's vital statistics including its Army Air Force serial number and manufacturer's constructor number.

Military Aircraft Record Cards

Individual aircraft record cards are not generally helpful in sorting out conflicting identification numbers because the Army Air Force didn't use Lockheed's number system as a means of identification. Cards of this type merely contain the aircraft's Army Air Force serial number. Still, these record cards are helpful in determining the location of a plane at a particular place in time. This information can then be used to eliminate one of the two possible serial numbers by comparing dates and locations with those contained in the airplane's Federal Aviation Administration file.

Manufacturer's Data Plate

For unknown reasons, Lockheed chose not to install a manufacturer's data plate in their P-38 aircraft. Identification plates of this nature usually carry the manufacturer's name and constructor's number; the Army Air Force serial number; and the date of completion. It is important to note that the Lightning was the only large production fighter aircraft in World War II that did not have one.

When All Else Fails

None of the previously mentioned methods of identifying a P-38 are useful when the aircraft has no external markings, has no data plate or radio call tag, and has never been registered with the FAA. When all else fails, one must resort to looking for vintage photographs that might aid in its identification.

APPENDIX A

P-38 PRODUCTION BLOCK NUMBERS							
AAF MODEL #	LAC MODEL #	CONTRACT	A.A.F. S/N	L.A.C. C/N	DELIVERY SPAN	QTY	ENGINE MODEL
XP-38	022-64-01	AC -9974	37-457	022-2201	FEB. 1939	1	V-1710-C9
XP-38A	622-62-10	AC-13205	40-762	222-2233	DEC. 1942	1	V-1710-F2
YP-38	122-62-02	AC-12523	39-689 / -701	122-2202 / -2214	SEP. 40 - MAY 41	13	V-1710-F2
P-38	222-62-08	AC-13205	40-774 / -761	122-2215 / -2232	JUNE 41 - JULY 41	18	V-1710-F2
		"	40-763 / -773	122-2234 / -2244	JULY 41 - AUG. 41	11	"
P-38D	222-62-08D	AC-13205	40-774 / -809	122-2245 / -2280	JUNE 41 - SEP. 41	36	V-1710-F2
P-38E	222-62-09	AC-15646	41-1983 / -2097	222-5201 / -5315	SEP. 41 - APR. 42	115	V-1710-F4
	"	"	41 -2100 / -2120	222-5318 / -5338	MAR. 42 - APR. 42	21	"
	"	"	41-2172	222-5390	APRIL 1942	1	"
	"	"	41-2219	222-5437	FEBRUARY 1942	1	"
	"	"	41-2221 / -2292	222-5439 / -5510	FEB. 42 - APR. 42	72	"
							"
P-38F	222-60-09	AC-15646	41-2293 / -2321	222-5511 / -5539	MAR. 42 - APR. 42	29	V1710-F5
	"	"	41-2323 / -2358	222-5541 / -5576	MAR. 42 - APR. 42	36	"
	"	"	41-2383 / -2386	222-5601 / -5604	APRIL 1942	4	"
	"	"	41-2388 / -2392	222-5606 / -5610	APRIL 1942	5	"
	"	"	41-7486 / -7496	222-5613 / -5623	MAR. 42 - APR. 42	11	"
	"	"	41-7498 / -7513	222-5625 / -5640	APRIL 1942	16	"
	"	"	41-7516 / -7524	222-5643 / -5651	APRIL 1942	9	"
	"	"	41-7526 / -7530	222-5653 / -5657	APRIL 1942	5	"
	"	"	41-7532 / -7534	222-5659 / -5661	APRIL 1942	3	"
	"	"	41-7536 / -7538	222-5663 / -5665	APRIL 1942	3	"
	"	"	41-7542 / -7543	222-5669 / -5670	APRIL 1942	2	"
	"	"	41-7545	222-5672	APRIL 1942	1	"
	"	"	41-7547	222-5674	APRIL 1942	1	"
	"	"	41-7551	222-5678	APRIL 1942	1	"
P-38F-1-LO	222-60-15	AC-15646	41-2322	222-5540	JUNE 1942	1	V-1710-F5
	"	"	41-2359 / -2361	222-5577 / -5579	JUNE 1942	3	"
	222-60-12	"	41-2382	222-5600	JULY 1942	1	"
	"	"	41-2387	222-5605	APRIL 1942	1	"
	"	"	41-7484	222-5611	MAY 1942	1	"
	222-60-15	"	41-7485	222-5612	MAY 1942	1	"
	"	"	41-7497	222-5624	MAY 1942	1	"
	"	"	41-7514 / -7515	222-5641 / -5642	MAY 1942	2	"
	"	"	41-7525	222-5652	MAY 1942	1	"
	"	"	41-7531	222-5658	MAY 1942	1	"
	"	"	41-7535	222-5662	MAY 1942	1	"
	"	"	41-7539 / -7541	222-5666 / -5668	MAY 1942	3	"
	"	"	41-7544	222-5671	MAY 1942	1	"

	"	"	41-7546	222-5673	MAY 1942	1	"
	"	"	41-7548 / -7550	222-5675 / -5677	MAY 1942	3	"
	"	"	41-7552 / -7680	222-5679 / -5807	MAY 1942	129	"
P-38F-5-LO	222-60-12	AC-21217	42-12567 / -12666	222-7001 / -7100	JUNE 42 - MAR. 43	100	V-1710-F5
P-38F-13-LO	322-60-19	BR-A-242/AC-31707	43-2035 / -2063	322-3144 / -3172	AUG. 24 - OCT. 42	29	V-1710-F5
P-38F-15-LO	322-60-19	BR-A-242/AC-31707	43-2064 / -2184	322-3173 / -3293	SEP. 42 - OCT. 42	121	V-1710-F5
P-38G-1-LO	222-68-12	AC-21217	42-12687 / -12766	222-7121 / -7200	AUG. 42 - OCT. 42	80	V-1710-F10
P-38G-3-LO	222-68-12	AC-21217	42-12787 / -12798	222-7221 / -7232	SEP. 24 - OCT. 42	12	V-1710-F10
P-38G-5-LO	222-68-12	AC-21217	42-12799 / -12866	222-7233 / -7300	AUG. 42 - OCT. 42	68	V-1710-F10
P-38G-10-LO	222-68-12	AC-21217	42-12870 / -12966	222-7304 /-7400	OCT. 42 - MAR. 43	97	V-1710-F10
	"	"	42-12987 / -13066	222-7421 / -7500	NOV. 42 - DEC. 42	80	"
	"	"	42-13127 / -13266	222-7561 / -7700	JAN. 43 - MAR. 43	140	"
	"	"	42-13327 / -13557	222-7761 / -7991	MAR. 43 - MAY 43	231	"
P-38G-13-LO	322-68-19	BR-A-242/AC-31707	43-2185 / -2358	322-3294 / -3467	NOV. 42 - JAN. 43	174	V-1710-F10
P-38G-15-LO	322-68-19	BR-A-242/AC-31707	43-2359 / -2391	322-3468 / -3500	JANUARY 1943	33	V-1710-F10
P-38G-15-LO	322-68-19	BR-A-242/AC-31707	43-2392 / -2558	322-3502 / -3668	JAN. 43 - MAR. 43	167	V-1710-F10
P-38H-1-LO	422-81-20	AC-21217	42-13559	422-1005	MARCH 1943	1	V-1710-F17
	"	AC-24636	42-66502 / -66726	422-1013 / -1237	MAY 43 - AUG. 43	225	"
P-38H-5-LO	422-81-20	AC-24636	42-66727 / -67101	422-1238 / -1612	JUNE 43 - DEC. 43	375	V-1710-F17
P-38J-1-LO	422-81-14	AC-21217	42-12867 / -12869	422-1001 / -1003	MARCH 1943	3	V-1710-F17
		"	42-13560 / -13566	422-1006 / -1012	JULY 43 - OCT. 43	7	V-1710-F17
P-38J-5-LO	422-81-14	AC-24636	42-67102 / -67311	422-1613 / -1822	AUG. 43 - APR. 44	210	V-1710-F17
P-38J-10-LO	422-81-14	AC-24636	42-67402 / -68191	422-1913 / -2702	OCT. 43 - DEC. 43	790	V-1710-F17
P-38J-15-LO	422-81-22	AC-35374	42-103979 / -104428	422-2813 / -3262	DEC. 43 - FEB. 44	450	V-1710-F17
	"	"	43-28248 / -29047	422-3263 / -4062	JAN. 44 - MAY 44	800	V-1710-F17
	"	"	44-23059 / -23208	422-4063 / -4212	APR. 44 - MAY 44	150	V-1710-F17
P-38J-20-LO	422-81-22	AC-35374	44-23209 / -23558	422-4213 / -4562	MAY 44 - JUNE 44	350	V-1710-F17
P-38J-25-LO	422-81-22	AC-40040	44-23559 / -23768	422-4563 / -4772	JUNE 44 - NOV. 44	210	V-1710-F17
P-38K-1-LO	422-85-22	AC-21217	42-13558	422-1004	SEPTEMBER 1943	1	V-1710-F15
P-38L-1-LO	422-87-23	AC-40040	44-23769 / -25058	422-4773 / -6062	JUNE 44 - NOV. 44	1290	V-1710-F30

P-38L-5-LO	422-87-23	AC-40040	44-25059 / -27258	422-6063 / -8262	OCT. 44 - JUNE 45	2200	V-1710-F30
	"	AC-40040	44-53008 / -53327	422-8263 / -8582	MAY 45 - AUG. 45	320	"
	"						
	"	CANCELLED	44-53328 / -54707	N/A			
	"						
P-38L-5-VN		AC-760	43-50226 / -50338	N/A		113	V-1710-F30
		CANCELLED	43-50339 / -52225	N/A			
PHOTO RECONNAISSANCE LIGHTNINGS BUILT BY LOCKHEED AIRCRAFT CORPORATION							
F-4-1-LO	222-62-13	AC-15646	41-2098 / -2099	222-5316 / -5317	MARCH 1942	2	V-1710-F4
	"	"	41-2121 / -2156	222-5339 / -5374	MAR. 42 - MAY 42	36	"
	"	"	41-2158 / -2171	222-5376 / -5389	APR. 42 - JUN. 42	14	"
	"	"	41-2173 / -2218	222-5391 / -5436	MAY 42 - AUG. 42	46	"
	"	"	41-2220	222-5438	AUGUST 1942	1	"
F-4A-1-LO	222-60-13	AC-15646	41-2362 / -2381	222-5580 / -5599	AUGUST 1942	20	V-1710-F4
F-5A-1-LO	222-68-16	AC-21217	42-12667 / -12686	222-7101 / -7120	AUG. 42 - DEC. 42	20	V-1710-F10
F-5A-2-LO	222-62-16	AC-15646	41-2157	222-5375	JULY 1942	1	V-1710-F4
F-5A-3-LO	222-68-16	AC-21217	42-12767 / -12786	222-7201 / -7220	OCTOBER 1942	20	V-1710-F10
F-5A-10-LO	222-68-16	AC-21217	42-12967 / -12986	222-7401 / -7420	NOV. 42 - JAN. 43	20	V-1710-F10
	"	"	42-13067 / -13126	222-7501 / -7560	DEC. 42 - JAN. 43	60	"
	"	"	42-13267 / -13326	222-7701 / -7760	MARCH 1943	60	"
F-5B-1-LO	422-82-21	AC-24636	42-67312 / -67401	422-1823 / -1912	SEP. 43 - OCT. 43	90	V-1710 F17
	"	"	42-68192 / -68301	422-2703 / -2812	DEC. 43 - JAN. 44	110	"
STATE SIDE MODIFICATION CENTER CONVERSIONS							
F-5C-1-LO	422-81-20	AC-24636	NOT IN SEQUENCE			123	
XF-5D	222-68-16	AC-21217	42-12975	222-7409	SEPTEMBER 1943	1	V-1710-F10
F-5E-2-LO	422-81-22	AC-35374	NOT IN SEQUENCE			166	V-1710-F-17
F-5E-3-LO	422-87-23	AC-40040	NOT IN SEQUENCE			705	V-1710-F30
F-5E-4-LO	422-87-23	AC-40040	NOT IN SEQUENCE			369	V-1710-F30
F-5F	422-81-22	AC-35374	NOT IN SEQUENCE				V-1710-17
F-5F-3-LO	422-87-23	AC-40040	NOT IN SEQUENCE			111	V-1710-F30
F-5G-6-LO	422-87-23	AC-40040	NOT IN SEQUENCE			357	V-1710-F30
P-38M-6-LO	422-87-23	AC-40040	NOT IN SEQUENCE			75	V-1710-F30

LIGHTNINGS PRODUCED FOR EXPORT							
322-F	322-61-03	A-242					V-1710-C15
322-B	322-61-04	BR-A-242/AC-31707	AE-978 - AE-980	322-3001 / -3003	MARCH 1942	3	V-1710-C15
P-322-I	322-61-04	BR-A-242/AC-31707	AE-981 / -999	322-3004 / -3022	DEC. 41 - JULY 42	19	V-1710-C15
P-322-II	322-62-18	BR-A-242/AC-31707	AF-100 / -220	322-3023 / -3143	JAN. 42 - JULY 42	121	V-1710-C15
LOCKHEED PRODUCTION TOTAL: 9924							
LOCKHEED & VULTEE PRODUCTION TOTAL: 10037							
QUANTITY TOTALS IN BOLD PRINT ARE APPROXIMATE.							

Army Air Forces Serial Numbers

Author's note: The passage of time coupled with flawed reference material has made the task of compiling an accurate list of the P-38s that were modified to fill the photoreconnaissance and night fighter role almost impossible. The list of serial numbers which follows, although admittedly incomplete, was derived from a variety of reference sources including AAF Aircraft Record Cards, FAA documents, and photographs.

F-5C-1-LO

ALL SERIAL NUMBERS PREFIXED WITH "42-"

67263, 67105-67134, 67236-67239, 67241-67254, 67261, 67273, 67279, 67529-67550, 67552-67569, 67572/-57577.

F-5E

42-104081: First F-5E.

ALL SERIAL NUMBERS PREFIXED WITH "43-"

28285-28334, 28422-28625, 28909, 28938, 28948-28961, 28963-28965, 28968, 28970, 28972-28974, 28977, 28979/-28980, 28980, 28990, 28992-28993, 28995-29009, 29015-29016, 29018-29037, 29044.

F-5E-2-LO

ALL SERIAL NUMBERS PREFIXED WITH "44-"

23211-23216, 23218-23247, 23249-23290, 23312-23313, 23336.

F-5E-3-LO

ALL SERIAL NUMBERS PREFIXED WITH "44-"

23602-23611, 23687, 23690-23768, 23983, 23985, 24087-24088, 24093, 24095-24109, 24225-24260, 24262-24274, 24276-24301, 24465, 24467-24471, 24474-24479, 24481-24488, 24491, 24493, 24495, 24508, 24530, 24553-24581, 24583-24588, 24648, 24652, 24655, 24667, 24672-24674, 24678, 24683-24731, 24748, 24891-24937, 24961-24972, 24974-24999, 25702.

F-5F-3-LO

ALL SERIAL NUMBERS PREFIXED WITH "44-"

24732-24743, 24789, 24938-24960, 24973, 24992, 25096-25099, 25102-25110, 25117-25119, 25127-25129, 25133-25137, 25140, 25152, 25154, 25157, 25161, 25163, 25165-25166, 25168, 25174-25175, 25179, 25181-25182, 25190-25193, 25231, 25333, 25366-25547, 26041-26046, 26052-26062, 26070, 26750.

F-5G-6-LO

ALL SERIAL NUMBERS PREFIXED WITH "44-"

25067, 25173, 25768, 25776, 25779, 25781, 25788, 25790, 25811-25814, 25816, 25822-25823, 25825-25826, 25828, 25884, 25900, 25904, 25908-25909, 25911, 25913, 25915, 25920, 25927-25929, 25932-25933, 25939, 25948, 25953, 25955, 25958, 25970, 25972, 25991, 25994, 26063, 26120-26131, 26137-26145, 26227-26237, 26244, 26247-26276, 26393, 26400, 26402, 26406, 26416-26430, 26432-26446, 26448-26449, 26451, 26453-26456, 26458, 26460-26461, 26565, 26588, 26592, 26609, 26612, 26614-26616, 26622-26636, 26642-26644, 26646, 26648-26649, 26656, 26666, 26670, 26679, 25583-26685, 26688, 26690, 26693, 26699, 2672526729, 26731-26738, 26740-26744, 26751, 26756, 26759, 26760-26761, 26775-26776, 26778, 26780-26783, 26827, 26855, 26871, 26873-26874, 26877, 26884, 26918, 26920-26923, 25950, 26952-26964, 26969, 26972, 26990, 26992-26996, 26998, 27001-27002, 27004-27006, 27009, 27011-27013, 27015, 27021-27088, 27092, 27210-27213, 27215, 27218, 27230-27232, 27235, 53008-53009, 53012-53013, 53015, 53024, 53026-53028, 53036-53038, 53044-53045, 53105, 53170-53171, 53173, 53176, 53178-53179, 53181-53183, 53185-53205, 53212, 53220, 53229, 53232, 53239, 53241, 53244-53249, 53251-53258, 53260, 53262, 53282-53283, 53291.

P-38M-6-LO

ALL SERIAL NUMBERS PREFIXED WITH "44-"

26831, 26863, 26865, 26892, 26951, 26997, 26999, 27000, 27108, 27233-27234, 27236-27238, 27245, 27249-27252, 27254, 27256-27258, 53011, 53017, 53019, 53020, 53022-53023, 53025, 53029-53032, 53034-53035, 53042, 53050, 53052, 53056, 53062, 53063, 53066-53069, 53073-53074, 53076-53077, 53079-53080, 53082-53090, 53092-53098, 53100, 53101, 53106-53107, 53109, 53110, 53112.

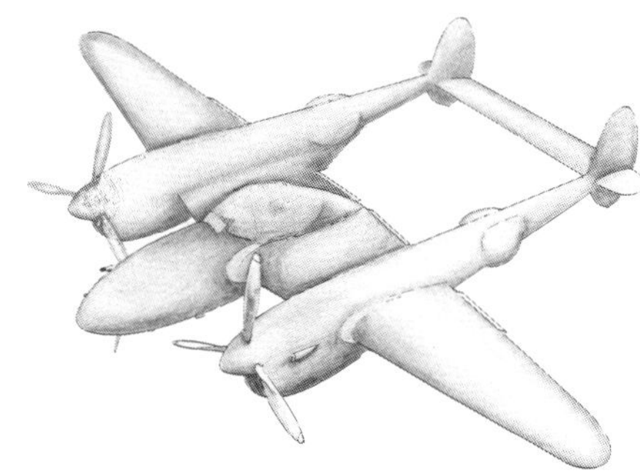

Appendix B: Civilian Lightnings

The late Malcolm L. Gougon recognized the importance of keeping records on the surplus military aircraft that entered the civilian registry long before it became fashionable to do so. In 1973 Gougon produced a list of "CIVILIAN LIGHTNINGS," which became more or less a standard guide for researchers and aspiring P-38 historians. Gougon was assisted in this task by many well-known names in the field of historical aviation research. Most notable are Jack Barbery, Harry Gann, Dan Hagedorn, William T. Larkins, Norman Malayney, Larry Smalley and probably many others of which the author is unaware. Although the original list is very informative, it is not without fault. The question of identity (true Army Air Force serial numbers vs. Lockheed constructor numbers) was not resolved. The project was also hampered by the lack of Federal Aviation Administration information on the subject aircraft. In 1987 the author and Gougon joined forces with the hope that a combined effort might provide answers to some of the questions that have become embedded in civilian P-38 lore. The results of this collaboration follows. Unfortunately, many of the obstacles that obstructed the original body of research are still present today. However, every effort has been made to expand its scope by incorporating new information as well as correcting errors that were included in the original text. It is also noteworthy to point out that the constructor's numbers (C/N) contained in this appendix are based on the Army Air Force serial numbers (AAF S/N) that appear on the aircrafts' identification plates or original bill of sale documents.

Sadly, Malcom Lloyd Gougon passed away on June 12, 1990. His loss will always be felt by the many that endeared him. This appendix is included in this volume not only to give the reader a better understanding of civilian P-38s but as a tribute to the man who first blazed the trail that many have followed.

1. N1107V—See Listing #26.

2. N1201N—P-38L-5-LO. C/N 422-8013. AAF S/N 44-27009. Converted to a F-5G-6-LO. Purchased from the Kingman, Arizona depot in April 1946 by R.A. Wardell of Portland, Oregon, who modified the plane to carry a passenger behind the pilot's seat. Aircraft was destroyed in a crash on November 11, 1950, while under the ownership of the Babb Co., Inc., of Glendale, California.

3. N1208N—P-38L-5-LO. C/N 422-7674. AAF S/N 44-26670. Converted to a F-5G-6-LO. Purchased for $1,250 from the War Assets Administration's Depot 41 (Kingman Field, Arizona) in April 1946 by R.A. Wardell. Last FAA Inspection Report was 1954, registered to Giorgi S. Moody, Vero Beach, Florida. Last U.S.C.A.R. listing was 1965. Disposition unknown.

6. PICKETT—KAMM

7. PICKETT—KAM

4. N1219N—P-38L-5-LO. C/N 422-8026. AAF S/N 44-27022. Converted to a F-5G-6-LO. Purchased from the Kingman, Arizona, depot in April 1946 by R.A. Wardell. N1219N was demolished on May 25, 1948.
5. N138X—See Listing #24.
6. N1502V—P-38L-5-LO. C/N 422-8439. AAF S/N 44-53184. Converted to a F-5G-6-LO. Ex-N33697 (1946), ex-1502V (1951) and CF-GKH (1953). Purchased from the Kingman, Arizona, depot by pilot/owner John Carroll in 1946. Race #22, registered as N33697, placed 11th in 1946 Bendix Trophy Race (Time: 6:03:46.6, Speed: 337.880 mph). Exported to Canada in 1953 as CF-GKH. On July 31, 1953, CF-GKH was lost in a crash near Dawson, Yukon, while under the ownership of Spartan Air Service, Ltd. of Canada. Pilot James Lago and camera operator E. M. Benoit were killed in the accident.
7. N21764—See Listing #34.
8. N21765—P-38L-5-LO. C/N 422-8300. AAF S/N 44-53045. Converted to a F-5G-6-LO. Obtained from the Kingman, Arizona, depot by pilot owner Harold S. Johnson in January 1946. Race #63 finished 10th in the 1946 Bendix Trophy Race (Time: 5:57:57.0, Speed: 343.380 mph). In 1947 #63, piloted by Jane Page Hlavcek, placed 9th (Time: 8:15:59.6, Speed: 247.812 mph) in the Bendix Race. Sonny Hlavcek also piloted #63 to a fifth place finish in the 1947 Sohio Trophy Race with an average speed of 270.197 mph. Exported to Canada in 1954 as CF-HSC. On June 25, 1956, CF-HSC was lost near Prince George, B.C. Crash investigators listed that the probable cause of the accident was negligent flying due to pilot intoxication. Pilot Frank S. Pynn and a 15-year-old passenger, who was being given a ride, were killed in the crash.
9. N25Y—P-38L-5-LO. C/N 422-8509. AAF S/N 44-53254. Converted to a F-5G-6-LO. Obtained surplus from the War Assets Administration by the Lilee Products Company of Illinois in 1946. Highly modified post-World War II air racer. Race #14 finished 2nd in the 1947 Miami and Sohio Races. Also placed 5th in the 1949 Tinnerman Trophy Race. Presently owned and operated by Marvin "Lefty" Gardner.
10. N26927—P-38L-5-LO. C/N 422-7931. AAF S/N 44-26927. Owner H.L. Pemberton entered race #48 in the 1946 Bendix Trophy Race after purchasing the plane from the surplus depot at Walnut Ridge, Arkansas. Pilot H. Calloway and #48 failed to complete the long-distance race due to mechanical problems near Toledo, Ohio. It was later sold to the Bolivian Air Force. N26927 was destroyed in Nov. 1949 near Washington National Airport, Washington, D.C., after colliding with an Eastern Airlines DC-4. Bolivian pilot Eric Rios

8. WARREN BODIE PHOTO

9. BOB BAILEY STUDIOS

10. WARREN BODIE PHOTO

Bridoux was flying this P-38 at the time. All aboard (4 crew and 51 passengers) the Eastern Airlines DC-4 were killed. Bridoux survived the crash with a broken back. In 1949 this crash was considered the worst in history.

11. N2897S—P-38L-5-LO. C/N 422-7765. AAF S/N 44-26761. Converted to F-5G-6-LO. Ex-N5054N (1948), ex-CF-GKE (1951), ex-N6190C (1956), and N2897S (1981). Purchased surplus in October 1947 from the Altus, Oklahoma, surplus depot by Everett L. Moore of Tulsa, Oklahoma. N5054N was exported to Mexico in 1949 by Luis Struck. It was later exported to Canada and re-registered as CFGKE. During its tenure in Canada, CF-GKE served with both Kenting Aviation, Ltd. and Spartan Air Service, Ltd. From 1956 to 1958 the now registered N6190C was used by Hycon Aerial Surveys (1956-1958), Cartwright Aerial Surveys (1958-1962) and Kucera Surveys as a photo mapping platform. On January 5, 1965, N6190C was damaged and subsequently abandoned after its gear collapsed while on a mapping project in Paraguay. Aircraft was finally recovered from Paraguay in 1974 by Bob Diemert of Canada. In 1981 N2897S was purchased by Kermit Weeks and put on display six years later at the Weeks' Air Museum near Miami, Florida.

12. N29Q—See Listing #22.

13. N3JB—P-38L-5-LO. C/N 422-8352. AAF S/N 44-53097. Converted to a P-38M-6-LO. Ex-N67861 (1946), ex-N9011R (1960), ex-N7TF (1972), and N3JB (1973). The former N67861 is believed to be one of several Lightnings that were purchased from the Kingman Arizona surplus depot by R.A. Wardell. From 1949 to 1960 this aircraft served with the Honduran Air Force as FAH 503. In 1960 aircraft collector Bob Bean purchased 503 and three additional P38s from the Hondurans and exported them to the U.S. In 1989 the aircraft's original "M" canopy setup was re-configured to "L" model specifications. N3JB is presently on display at the Champlin Fighter Aces Museum in Mesa, Arizona.

14. N3145X—P-38J-10-LO C/N 422-2054. AAF S/N 42-67543. Converted to a F-5C-1-LO in October 1943. During World War II 4267543 served in the training role with the 37th and 36th Photo reconnaissance Squadrons. History of this aircraft between 1945 and the mid-1960s is unknown. Recovered by the Confederate Air Force sometime during the 1960s from Ragsdale Flying Service in Austin, Texas. In 1988 the future N3145X was sold to aircraft collector Stephen Grey who moved the plane to Fighter Rebuilders of Chino, California. In 1992, N3145X, the last remaining F-5C, flew for the first time in more than possibly 40 years. It was later shipped to England and decorated in the colors of Jack Ilfrey's "Happy Jack's Go Buggy."

15. N3005—P-38L-5-LO C/N 422-8448. AAF S/N 44-53193. Converted to a F-5G-6-LO. Ex-N34993 (1946), ex-CF-NWM (1961), and N3005 (1969). Originally obtained surplus from the Kingman, Arizona, depot by former Woman Airforce Service Pilot (WASP) Nadine Ramsey. Ramsey entered this F-5G in the 1946 Bendix Trophy Race but didn't compete. N33993 served with Aero Service Corporation from 1951 to 1961. It was then exported to Canada as CF-NWM. While in Canada CF-NWM was operated as a photo mapping ship by Bradley Air Service and Kenting Aviation, Ltd. In July 1965 the plane's registration was deleted after it was sold to the Age Of Flight Museum near Niagara Falls, Canada. Four years later the newly registered N3005 was brought back to the United States and put on display at the Aidair Museum in Wilmington, Delaware. Later it was moved again to the Colonial Flying Corps Museum Near Toughkenamon, Pennsylvania. In July 1977 Pete Sherman, of Maitland, Florida, purchased N3005 and mated a P-80 nose to the aircraft which he nicknamed "Glamorus Glyness." While on Route to Oshkosh, Wisconsin, in 1978 Pete Sherman and his wife were killed when their P-38 crashed near White House, Ohio. The exact cause of the crash was not determined; however, no fuel was found

14. PETER HADINGUE PHOTO, COURTESY JOHN HARTO

15. PICKETT—KAM

in or near the wreckage. Witnesses stated that the aircraft was rolling with a nose down attitude just before it struck the ground. The NTSB suspected the plane's engines shut off due to fuel starvation which caused the plane's aileron boost servo's to malfunction. A few days prior to the accident N3005 registration was changed to N38PS; however this registration never appeared on Sherman's Lightning.

16. N33638—See Listing #24.

17. N33697—See Listing #6.

18. N33698—P-38L-5-LO. C/N 422-8366. AAF S/N 44-53111. Converted to a F-5G-6-LO. Obtained surplus from the Kingman, Arizona depot by pilot/owner Andrew Grant. Race #82 finished 17th in the 1946 Bendix Trophy Race (Time: 7:49:44.0, Speed: 261.665 mph). N33698 was deleted from the civil registry in February 1951 after it was disassembled for parts.

19. N345—See Listing #50.

20. N34992—P-38L-5-LO. C/N 422-8209. AAF S/N 44-27205. Ex-N57210 (1946). Operated by Fairchild Aerial Surveys for nine years starting in 1947. It was painted bright orange and a small radiator was installed in the plane's nose. This radiator provided heat to the nose compartment via a parallel connection to one of engine's glycol return lines. In 1956 N34992 was exported to Canada where it saw service as CF-JJA with both Kenting Aviation and Survey Aircraft, Ltd. On Nov. 30, 1961 the plane was exported to Argentina as LV-HIV. Eventual disposition unknown.

21. N34993—See Listing #15.

16. BUDG DONOTO PHOTO (1961)

18. WARREN BODIE PHOTO

22. N38BP—P-38J-20-LO. C/N 422-4318. AAF S/N 44-23314. Ex-N29Q (1954), and N38BP (1989). During the Second World War, Army Air Force S/N 44-23314 was used as a training ship. In 1945 it was donated to the University of Southern California. It was later turned over to The Hancock College of Aeronautics, Santa Maria, California, which USC leased to become their aviation campus. Nine years later Allan Hancock sold the aircraft to Jack Hardwick who in 1959 donated the plane to Ed Maloney's Planes of Fame Museum. In 1989 newly registered N38BP returned to airworthy status after a lengthy period of restoration. Presently it shares time between Planes of Fame Museum East & West.

23. N38DH—See Listing #85.

24. N38LL—P-38L-5-VN. C/N N/A. AAF S/N 43-50281. Ex-N33638 (1946), ex-N138X (1961), and N38LL. One of 113 Lightnings that were produced at Consolidated Vultee's plant at Nashville, Tennessee. Served with Fairchild Aerial Surveys from 1946 to 1963. Purchased by Darryl Greenamyer in September 1963 and decorated it to resemble Lockheed's 5000th P-38 "Yippee." Placed fourth in the 1965 Lancaster Air Races. After being sold to Revis Sirmon in 1968 the aircraft was restored and nicknamed the "SCATTERBRAIN KID." N38LL was destroyed in a landing accident at the Lafayette Airport during October 1974. Pilot George Harper was killed in the crash. Derelict airframe (possibly 44-104088) that was donated to the CAF by Gary Levitz (see listing #42) was obtained by Paul Fournet. Parts from the first "SCATTERBRAIN KID," as well as parts from a P-38E 41-2260, which crashed 20 miles east of Portland, Oregon, on March 26, 1943, were used to rebuild "SCATTERBRAIN KID II." First flight of the new "KID" took place in San Marcos, Texas, on February 28, 1992.

25. N38PS—See Listing #15.

26. N3800L—P-38L-5-LO. C/N 422-8342. AAF S/N 44-53087. Converted to P-38M-6-LO. Ex-N62887 (1946), ex-CF-GDS (1951), ex-N1107V (1956), and N3800L (1973). One of 48 Lightnings purchased from the Kingman, Arizona, depot by Forrest M. Bird of Long Beach, California. N62887 was exported to Canada as CF-GDS in 1952 by Spartan Air Service, Ltd. Purchased in 1956 by Hycon Aerial Surveys who re-registered it as N1107V. During the early 1970s Pete Kahn replaced N1107V's photo nose with a fighter version, which was acquired from an early model P-38 that sat on Metro Goldwyn Meyer's Culver City back lot #5. In 1981 N3800L was donated to the Experimental Aircraft Association Museum in Wisconsin by owner Connie Edwards of Big Springs, Texas. N3800L is presently on display in the association's Eagle Hangar.

20. MOLSON PHOTO

21. PICKETT—KAM

27. N4530N—P-38L-5-LO. C/N 422-8151. AAF S/N 44-27147. Originally purchased from the Walnut Ridge, Arkansas, depot by J.D. Reed, of Houston, Texas. Race #66, piloted by Ivis Hill, placed third in the 1947 Sohio Race with an average speed of 347.391 mph. N4530N was painted emerald green and was known as the "Green Hornet." On September 23, 1951, it was destroyed in a landing accident at Starkville, Mississippi. The pilot Major Kenneth J. Snedden was ferrying the aircraft from Meridian to Starkville for owner Dr. Harold Flinsch, who was the dean of the School of Engineering at Mississippi State University. While on approach (gear and flaps down), the aircraft's left engine failed and the plane spun-in, killing Major Snedden.

28. N4532N—P-38L-5-LO. C/N 422-8278. AAF S/N 44-53023. Converted to a P-38M-6-LO and purchased surplus from the Kingman depot by Martin Wunderlich in October 1946. Wunderlich's salvage company also purchased Kingman's entire inventory (5,000 plus aircraft) in July 1946. It is, therefore, possible that this P-38 could be the last aircraft to be sold from Kingman. Robert J. Harlow purchased N4532N from Wunderlich and entered it in the 1947 Sohio Race; however, race #36 failed to start the race. N4532N was permanently retired and presumably scrapped in 1956.

29. N49721—P-38J-10-LO. C/N 422-2085. AAF S/N 42-67574. Converted to a F-5C-1-LO. Arthur D. Knapp, president of Mechanical Products Inc., of Jackson, Michigan, became the first civilian owner of a P-38 when he purchased 42-67574 from the WAA's depot at Bush Field, Georgia, for $18,000. In 1946 race #51 (aka "Connie") and new pilot/owner James De Santo placed sixth in the Sohio Trophy Race with an average speed of 303.682 mph. Pilot John Saum purchased the plane in 1947 and entered it (race #63, a.k.a. "Jill") in the 1947 Sohio Race, but was forced to leave the race in the first lap with mechanical problems. In 1948 Saum won the Sohio event in what is regarded as one of the most exciting races of the post-war Cleveland era; however, he was later disqualified for low flying. After the 1948 races N49721 was dealt to the Aircraft Salvage Corp. of Baltimore, Maryland, for $486.00 and was presumably scrapped.

30. N501MH—See Listing #39.

31. N5016N—P-38L-5-VN. C/N N/A. AAF S/N 43-50312. Ex-NL5016N (1946). One of three Vultee Lightnings to be given civilian registrations. Originally purchased surplus in June 1947 for $500.00 by Pat Brandenburg of Metal Products Company, Amarillo, Texas. In August of the same year ownership of N5016 passed from Brandenburg to Edward

27. PICKETT—KAM

28. WARREN BODIE PHOTO (1947)

29. WARREN BODIE PHOTO

34. MARKHURD CORP. PHOTO

Browder and finally to Arthur Roscoe of Burbank, California. NL5016N was later exported to Cuba and operated by its Air Force before being scrapped. The aircraft's U.S. registration was cancelled by the CAA on March 20, 1948, because "Purchaser failed to comply with Civil Air Regulations."

32. N502MH—P-38L-5-LO. C/N 422-8087. AAF S/N 44-27083. Converted to F-5G-6-LO. Ex-N75551 (1946), and N502MH (1957). Served with Mark Hurd Aerial Surveys until middle 1960s. Was then purchased by Bruce Pruett of Livermore, California. N502MH is presently being restored.

33. N503MH—P-38L-5LO.—C/N 422-8006. AAF S/N 44-27002. Converted to F-5G-6-LO. Ex-N53753 (1946), and N503MH (1957). Served with Mark Hurd Aerial Surveys until the middle 1960s. Same current disposition as listing #32.

34. N504MH—P-38L-5-LO. C/N 422-8333. AAF S/N 44-53078. Ex-N21764 (1946), and N504MH (1957). This aircraft became the first P-38 to be sold from the Kingman depot when Lockheed test pilot Tony LeVier purchased it on January 23, 1946. LeVier and his bright red race #3 finished second in the 1946 Thompson Trophy Race with an average speed of 370.193 mph. In 1947 Race #3's average speed of 360.866 was good enough to earn first place in the 1947 Sohio Race. It also placed fifth in the 1947 Thompson Trophy Race. N21764 served with the Mark Hurd Aerial Surveys for 12 years (1953-1965). In 1965 N504MH was sold to J. Byron Roche who was later killed (August 4, 1965) while test flying N504MH near Los Olivos, California. Some of the remains of 504 were used to re-build N3145X in the early 1990s.

35. N505MH—P-38-L-5-LO. C/N 422-8441. AAF S/N 44-53186. Converted to a F-5G-6-LO. Ex-N62350 (1946), and ex-N505MH (1957). Originally obtained from the Kingman, Arizona, depot by Kargl Aerial Surveys, Inc. of Midland, Texas. From 1947 to 1952 N62350 was operated by Aero Exploration of Tulsa, Oklahoma, until it was sold to Mark Hurd Mapping Co. in 1952. N505MH was sold in 1967 to the Harrah's Club and put on display in Reno, Nevada, before being sold to David Tallichet. In 1989 aircraft was ferried across the Atlantic to England by Mike Wright for new owner Doug Arnold. The following year 505 was returned to the United States again by Mike Wright after it was purchased by Evergreen Airlines. When Evergreen completes N505MH's restoration its registration will probably be changed to N38EV.

36. N5054N—See Listing #11.

38. LOCKHEED PHOTO

37. N5056N—P-38L-5-LO. C/N 422-7616. AAF S/N 44-26612. Converted to a F-5G-6-LO. Obtained surplus by Kargl Aerial Surveys of Midland, Texas, from the Altus Depot on October 2, 1946. Also was used between the years of 1947 and 1949 by Tulsa, Oklahoma's Aero Exploration Corp. In 1952 the plane was purchased by the Minneapolis-Honeywell Regulator Company and was used to test advanced auto-pilot systems, approach couplers, and fire control couplers. As a result of this research, many of Honeywell's control systems were later incorporated in more advanced airplanes such as F-89s, F-100s and other century series fighters. N5056N was later lost in a crash at the San Antonio Airport not long after it was purchased by Jack Ammann Photogrammetric Engineers, Inc. Pilot Norman Bergman survived the accident.

38. N5101N—P-38F-15-LO. C/N 322-3290. AAF S/N 43-2181. The only known "F" model Lightning to enter the civil aircraft registry after being acquired in June 1947 from the Walnut Ridge, Arkansas surplus aircraft depot by Ivis Hill for Houston Beechcraft dealer J.D. Reed. Before leaving Walnut Ridge N5101N's early model Allison engines were replaced with new V1710-111 and 113 models. Later this aircraft was sold to hotel and oil magnate Glenn H. McCarthy, who moved the plane to Van Nuys, California where it was modified to compete in the 1947 Bendix Trophy Race. During its Bendix departure pilot James Rubel lost the P-80-type fuel tank that was attached to the right wing tip. Later a turbo supercharger fire forced Rubel to bail out of #88 over Arizona. Race #88's color scheme was P-80 gray with kelly green lettering and white flash lines.

39. N517PA—P-38L-5-LO. C/N 422-8187. AAF S/N 44-27183. Converted to a F-5G-6-LO. Ex-N62441 (1946), ex-N501MH (1957), and N517PA. Purchased surplus from the Kingman, Arizona depot by Kargle Aerial Surveys, who later sold the aircraft to Aero Exploration Co. of Tulsa, Oklahoma. In 1953, N62441 was sold to Mark Hurd Aerial Surveys who lengthened the cockpit to accommodate tandem seating and modified it for pressurization. Registration was changed from N501MH to N517PA when it was sold to Pacific Aerial Surveys, of Seattle in 1967. N517PA was restored in 1973 by new owner David Boyd. In the process its photo nose is replaced with a P-80 type gun nose. Presently, N517PA is on display at the Yanks Air Museum at Chino, California.

40. N5260N—P-38J-?-LO. C/N ?—AAF S/N ?
One of two P-38s that Page Aircraft Industries of Yukon, Oklahoma, acquired from surplus aircraft dealer Dale M. Myers. Page's request to register this P-38 with the CAA as N5260 was turned down because of an incomplete chain of title. Unable to secure the proper documents for registration, Page cancelled the request. It is believed that this mystery P-38 was previously owned by Interstate Aircraft Corp. In 1969 the remains of the airframe was sold to Gary Levitz who removed parts to complete his restoration of N345. Later the airframe was donated to the Confederated Air Force and was subsequently used to rebuild N38LL. The serial number that is listed in the FAA documents is 43-21917, which is a serial number for a Douglas A-20G.

45. BOB STUCKEY VIA WARREN BODIE

46. WARREN BODIE PHOTO

41. N5261N—P-38L-?-LO—C/N ?—AAF S/N ?
The second of two P-38s that Page Aviation Service purchased from Dale Myers. Again Page's request for registration was denied due to an incomplete chain of title. On June 8, 1953, Page withdrew his request and scrapped the plane for parts. The AAF serial number listed in N5261N's documents is 44-24189; however, there is a considerable amount of doubt about the accuracy of this serial number.
42. N53752—See Listing #44.
43. N53753—See Listing #33.
44. N5596V—P-38L-5-LO. C/N 422-8000. AAF S/N 44-26996. Converted to a F-5G-6-LO. Ex-N53752 (1946), ex-CF-GCH (1952), and N5596V (1956). Served as a training ship until it was put in storage at Kingman Field, Arizona, in late 1945. Purchased for $1,250 in March 1946 by Aero Exploration Corp. of Tulsa, Oklahoma. In 1951 N53752 was exported to Canada by Spartan Air Service, Ltd. Spartan utilized the newly registered CF-GCH as a photo mapping platform for five years before selling it to the California-based Hycon Aerial Surveys. In 1970 pilot/owner I.N. Burchinal crashed N5596V while landing in a rain storm. It was later sold to John Silberman of Tampa, Florida, in 1979. After seven years of painstaking restoration, N5596V made its first public appearance in the spring of 1986. N5596V was later sold to the Santa Monica Museum Of Flying and subsequently auctioned off to General William Lyons for $1.55 million in 1990.
45. N5597V—P-38L-5-LO. C/N 422-8029. AAF S/N 44-27025. Converted to a F-5G-6-LO. Ex-N64506 was exported to Canada as CF-GSQ on November 27, 1950. In 1956 it was sold to Hycon Aerial Surveys, Pasadena, California. In 1957 the aircraft was sold to a Spanish Marquis and ferried to Madrid by famous ferry pilot Max Conrad. Later its ferry registration, EC-WNU, was changed to EC-ANU. EC-ANU's

48. PICKETT—KAM

52. PICKETT—KAM

Spanish registration was cancelled on 17 October 1969 after the aircraft was damaged in an accident. Final disposition is unknown.

46. N56687—P-38L-5-LO. C/N 422-8438. AAF S/N 44-53183. Converted to a F-5G-6-LO. Post-World War II air racer. Entered the 1946 Bendix race, but pilot Herman "Fish" Salmon was forced to return Race #74 to Van Nuys due to mechanical problems. The following year this plane (nicknamed "Martha J. II") and pilot/owner Bill Lear, Jr. placed ninth in 1947 Bendix Trophy Race (Time: 6:59:57.4, Speed: 292.680 mph). Exported to Canada as CF-GCG on Nov 29, 1951. Aircraft was lost on March 17, 1955, after it crashed, nose first, into MacGregor Lake in Quebec. Aircraft was not recovered.

47. N57492—See Listing #101.

48. N57496—P-38L-5-LO. C/N 422-8497. AAF S/N 44-53242. Converted to a F-5G-6-LO. Owner Tom P. Mathews entered the aircraft in the 1947 National Air Races at Cleveland, Ohio, but Race #47 didn't compete due to mechanical problems. In 1948 N57496 was sold to Ball-Ralston of Hillsboro, Oregon, where its pilot seat was moved forward five inches to make room for a rear passenger. From March 1948 to September 1955 the plane was owned by California Electric Power Company. In 1955 it was sold to Weather Modifications, Inc., Redlands, California, and was used to conduct cloud seeding and other weather experiments. N57495 was lost when it crashed near the Bishop Airport in California. Pilot Chester A. Janes was killed in the accident. The remains of N57496 were later salvaged by Joel Bishop, who in turn sold the wreckage to the San Monica Museum of Flying. In 1991 N57496 was auctioned off to Tom Reilly of Kissimmee, Florida.

49. N57497—P-38L-5-LO. C/N 422-8282. AAF S/N 44-53027. Converted to a F-5G-6-LO. Registered in 1946 to M.E Jenkins of Van Nuys, California. No other information available.

50. N577JB—P-38L-5-LO. C/N 422-8091 AAF S/N 44-27087. Converted to a F-5G-6-LO. Ex-65485 (1946), ex-N345 (1958), ex-N345DH (1983), and N577JB (1984). Purchased from the Kingman, Arizona, depot by Russell Reeves of Tulsa, Oklahoma. During the early 1950s N65485 was operated as a photo-mapping ship by the Tennessee Valley Authority and Aero Service Corporation. In 1957 it was purchased by Jim Cook of Dallas, Texas. Cook used the plane to conduct weather research from 1958 to 1969. It was then sold to Gary Levitz, who raced #38 until 1983. In 1984 the plane was sold to aircraft collector John MacGuire. Presently, N577JB is on display at the War Eagles Air Museum in Santa Teresa, New Mexico.

54. E.C. HANEY PHOTO VIA ROGER BESECKER (1961)

55. MILO PELTZER COLLECTION

51. N58540—P-38L-5-LO. C/N 422-?. AAF S/N ?. Converted to a P-38M-6-LO. FAA documents list C/N as 5792. However, 422-5792 doesn't cross-reference to any P-38L that was converted to a night fighter. Registered in 1946 to R.A. Wardell of Hillsboro, Oregon. Disposition unknown.

52. N61121—P-38L-5-LO. C/N 422-8425. AAF S/N 44-53170. Converted to a F-5G-6-LO. Originally purchased surplus by James B. Redwine of Kansas City, Missouri. Aircraft was entered in the 1946 Bendix Trophy Race but failed to compete in the event. The following year pilot/owner John Thompson clipped race #27's wings and replaced its photo nose with one that was fabricated from a 300-gallon drop tank. This highly modified air racer placed 4th in 1947 Sohio Trophy Race. The aircraft was painted Army Navy yellow (chrome yellow) and was known as the "Teterboro Special." Thompson donated the plane to the Teterboro School of Aeronautics of Teterboro, New Jersey, shortly after the 1947 races. It was later damaged by a storm and subsequently scrapped.

53. N61470—P-38L-5-LO. C/N 422-8475. AAF S/N 44-53220. Converted to a F-5G-6-LO. Registered in 1946 to Emile Lewis Cernich of Albia, Iowa. Disposition unknown.

54. N6190C—See Listing #11.

55. N62345—P-38L-5-LO. C/N 422-8437. AAF S/N 44-53182. Converted to a F-5G-6-LO. Ex-World Wide Surveys, Inc. aircraft. Registered to Reed Pigman of Fort Worth, Texas. Disposition unknown.

56. N62350—See Listing #35.

57. N62354—P-38L-5-LO. C/N 422-8451. AAF S/N 44-53196. Converted to a F-5G-6-LO. Registered to Reed Pigman of Abilene, Texas. Disposition unknown.

58. N62441—See Listing #39.

59. N62805—P-38L-5-LO. C/N 422-8337. AAF S/N 44-53082. Converted to a P-38M-6-LO. One of 48 P-38s purchased from the Kingman, Arizona, Depot by Forrest M. Bird. NX62805 was later exported to Cuba and operated by the Fuerza Aerea Cubana for several years before being scrapped. Last known photograph of N62805 was taken by Warren M. Bodie in Detroit, Michigan during the late 1940s.

60. N62807—P-38L-5-LO. C/N 422-7966. AAF S/N 44-26962. Converted to a F-5G-6-LO. Registered in 1946 to Wynn Motors (Mark Wynn) of Los Angeles, California. Disposition unknown.

59. WARREN BODIE

61. OSTROWSKI COLLECTION

65. WILLIAM T. LARKINS

61. N62828—P-38L-5-LO. C/N 422-8293. AAF S/N 44-53038. Converted to a F-5G-6-LO. Post-World War II air racer. Jack Hardwick piloted race #34 to a third place finish in the 1946 Sohio Trophy Race (Speed: 322.625 mph). Aircraft was highly decorated with a fish on its nose, green checkerboard tail, and dragon teeth on its engine nacelles. Believed to have crashed after catching fire in flight over Ohio during the early 1950s.

62. N62835—P-38L-5-LO. C/N 422-8274. AAF S/N 44-53019. Converted to a P-38M-6-LO. One of 15 "M" model Lightnings acquired from the Kingman, Arizona, depot by Forrest M. Bird. Disposition unknown.

63. N62875—P-38L-5-LO. C/N 422-8449. AAF S/N 44-53194. Converted to a F-5G-6-LO. Purchased in 1948 by Eugene Akers of Oxnard, California. It was later sold to Jack Hardwick who apparently planned to ship the aircraft to Cuba.

72. WARREN BODIE PHOTO (1946)

73. PICKETT—KAM

N62875 is believed to have been confiscated by the FBI before it was exported. Disposition unknown.

64. N62887—See Listing #26.

65. N62898—P-38L-5-LO. C/N 422-8261. AAF S/N 44-27257. Converted to a P-38M-6-LO. Purchased from the Kingman, Arizona, surplus depot by Forrest M. Bird. Last registered to Archie A. Baldocchi who mostly operated out of El Salvador and Honduras. Only known photograph of this plane was taken in August 1946, at Oakland, California Airport, by William T. Larkins. Aircraft was painted black with American and Mexican flag on its nose. On its nose was also the name CUSCATLAN painted in red. Believed to have been exported to Mexico.

66. N63300—P-38L-5-LO. C/N 422-8263. AAF S/N 44-53008. Converted to a F-5G-6-LO. Last owned by Engineering Service Corporation, 235 Montgomery Avenue, San Francisco, California, in 1965. Disposition unknown.

67. N64083—P-38L-5-LO. C/N 422-8311. AAF S/N 44-53056. Converted to a P-38M-6-LO. Exported to the Honduran Air Force (FAH 501) and was subsequently destroyed.

68. N64426—P-38L-5-LO. C/N 422-?. AAF S/N ?. Converted to a P-38M-6-LO. FAA documents list C/N as 5790. However, 422-5790 doesn't cross-reference to any P-38L that was converted to a night fighter. Registered to Jack Hardwick and Checkerboard Airways of Durango, Colorado, in 1947. No other information available.

75. PICKETT—KAM

69. N64506—See Listing #45.
70. N65419—P-38L-5-LO. C/N 422-8211. AAF S/N 44-27207. Modified to a F-5G-6-LO. Post-World War II air racer (race #2). Pilot Earl Ortman placed fifth in the 1946 Sohio Trophy Race with an average speed of 265.995mph. Disposition unknown.
71. N65485—See Listing #50.
72. N66108—P-38L-5-LO. C/N 422-8389. AAF S/N 44-53134. Converted to a F-5G-6-LO. Post-World War II air racer (Race #99). Pilot H.L. Marshall placed 12th in the 1946 Bendix Trophy Race (Time: 6:05:52.8m Speed: 335.938 mph). Disposition unknown.
73. N66613—P-38L-5-LO. C/N 422-8281. AAF S/N 44-53026. Converted to a F-5G-6-LO. Post-World War II air racer (race #71). Pilot/owner William Lear Jr. finished fourteenth in the 1946 Bendix Trophy Race (Time: 6:15:45.6, Speed: 327.105 mph). Aircraft was damaged at Twin Falls, Idaho, on September 16, 1946. Lear was performing an aerobatic air show act when his left engine over-heated. While on final approach he also lost power in the right engine, again due to overheating, and landed about 100 feet short of the runway. Both propellers and gear boxes departed the plane before it came to a stop. It was learned after the crash that the seals in both coolant pumps had failed during Lear's lengthy inverted aerobatic routine. The aircraft was later given to an aviation technical school in Pocatello, Idaho.
74. N66678—P-38L-5-LO. C/N 422-8487. AAF S/N 44-53232. Converted to a F-5G-6-LO. Post-World War II air racer (race #11) known as "Country Boy II." Entered the 1946 Bendix Trophy Race by pilot/owner J. Yandell, but was forced out of the race at Kansas City, Missouri. Served with the Honduran Air Force (from 1948-1960) as FAH 505. Five-zero-five returned to the United States in 1960 after being purchased by Bob Bean. Aircraft was then donated to the Air Force Museum where it is currently on display.
75. N66692—P-38L-5-LO. C/N 422-7549. AAF S/N 44-26545. Post-World War II air racer (race #36) known as "Pumpkin." Pilot John Shields entered #36 in the 1946 Bendix event, but failed to complete the race. N66692 was scrapped for parts by Earl Reinert during the early 1950s.
76. N66808—P-38L-5-LO. C/N 422-8204. AAF S/N 44-27200. Originally obtained from the Kingman, Arizona, Depot in May 1946 by S.A. Smith. Later sold to Lawrence F. Niel of San Diego, who had the aircraft canopy converted to that of a P-38M. In 1947 the aircraft was sold to George C. Stamets and exported to the Dominican Republic. Disposition unknown.
77. N67247—P-38L-5-LO. C/N 422-8258. AAF S/N 44-27254. Converted to P-38M-6-LO. Registered to L.B. Ramseyer of Long Beach, California. Disposition unknown.
78. N67745—See listing #97.
79. N67849—P-38L-5-LO. C/N 422-? AAF S/N ?
Converted to a P-38M-6-LO. FAA documents list C/N as 3142. However, 3142 doesn't cross reference to any P-38L that was converted to a night fighter. Registered to the BABB Company of Glendale, California. NC67849 was later exported to Cuba and operated by its Air Force before being scrapped.
80. N67861—See Listing #13.
81. N67863—P-38L-5-LO. C/N 422-8355. AAF S/N 44-53100. Converted to P-38M-6-LO. Registered to the BABB Company of Glendale, California. No other information available. NX67863 was later exported to Cuba and operated by the Fuerza Aerea Cubana (Cuban Air Force) for several years before being scrapped.
82. N67864—P-38L-5-LO. C/N 422-7999. AAF S/N 44-26995. Converted to F-5G-6-LO. Post-World War II air racer (race

82. WARREN BODIE (1947)

#34) known as "Batty Betty II." Number 34, piloted by owner Jack Hardwick, placed sixth in the 1947 Sohio Trophy Race (Time Handicap: 86.0 sec., Speed: 312.655 mph) and fourth in the 1949 Tinnerman Trophy Race (Speed: 328.470 mph). Aircraft is believed to have crashed near Vasques Rocks, California, during the early 1950s.

83. N68123—P-38L-5-LO. C/N 422-8009. AAF S/N 44-27005. Converted to a F-5G-6-LO. N68123 was purchased by Spartan Air Services, Ltd. from Richard G. Koplitz and exported to Canada, as CF-GSP, on March 31, 1950. On November 25, 1950, CF-GSP made an emergency landing at Minneapolis-St. Paul Airport, receiving substantial damage. Aircraft was salvaged following this accident.

84. N68394—P-38L-1-LO. C/N 422-4806. AAF S/N 44-23802. Post-World War II air racer (Race #25) owned and piloted by Howard S. Gidovlenko. Finished second in the 1948 Sohio Race (Time Handicap: 1.5 sec., Speed: 317.952 mph). Race #25 also competed in the 1949 Tinnerman Trophy Race, but Gidovlenko was forced to leave the race with mechanical problems in the third lap. Aircraft was last seen in April 1950 at the Chicago Municipal Airport while under the care of Col. Wilson V. Newhall. Disposition unknown.

85. N6961—P-38L-5-LO. C/N 422-7965. AAF S/N 44-26961. Converted to a F-5G-6-LO. Ex-Honduran Air Force FAH 504 (1948), ex-N74883 (1960), ex-N38DH (1976), and N6961 (1977). Returned from Honduras in 1960 after being purchased by Bob Bean. During the mid-1960s N74883 was added to Ed Maloney's Air Museum collection. Later N74883 was owned by World War II ace Larry Blumer who decorated it like his famed war-time mount "SCRAPIRON IV." In 1971 "SCRAPIRON IV" (a.k.a. race #59), piloted by Ward Clemmo, appeared at the Reno National Air Races and won first prize money ($600) in the Medallion Race with an average speed 276.49 mph. On April 9, 1981, N6961 experienced an engine failure on take-off from the Salt Lake City airport. Pilot/owner John Deahl of Denver, Colorado, was killed in the subsequent crash.

86. N69800—P-38L-5-LO. C/N 422-8314. AAF S/N 44-53059. Purchased surplus from Kingman, Arizona, depot by Anderson Air Activities of Milwaukee, Wisconsin, in June 1946. Post-World War II air racer (Race #58). Finished sixteenth (Time: 6:17:53.8, Speed: 325.295 mph) in the 1946 Bendix Trophy Race (pilot M.W. Fairbrother). In early 1947 the aircraft's new owner, Hugh I. Wells took N69800 to Peru for the purposes of collecting data on the operation of Allison engines and Curtiss electric propellers at high altitudes. Wells intended to use this data to seek CAA approval for use of this engine and prop combination in commercial aircraft. N69800 was later abandoned in Peru and subsequently sold to Elizabeth Walker of Coconut Grove, Florida, in 1949. There is no record of the plane ever returning to the U.S. It is believed, however, to have later been sold to the Bolivian Government. Disposition unknown.

87. N69902—P-38L-5-LO. C/N 422-8435. AAF S/N 44-53180. Converted to a F-5G-6-LO. Registered in 1946 to Harry Renkert of Canton, Ohio. One of Hycon Aerial Surveys' three original Lightning-type aircraft that were converted to carry the elongated Hycon photo nose. Aircraft was destroyed in a crash at the Greater Pittsburgh Airport on August 23, 1957. Pilot Gilbert Mendoza and photographer John L. McPherson were killed in the accident.

88. N7TF—See Listing #13.

89. N70005—P-38L-5-LO. C/N 422-8030. AAF S/N 44-27026. Converted to a F-5G-6-LO. Purchased surplus from the Kingman, Arizona Depot by R.A. Wardell of Oregon on April 22, 1946. Post-World War II air racer (race #50) spon-

83. WALTER ERICKSON

84. PICKETT—KAM

sored by De Ponti Aviation as "Minnesota Gopher II" (pilot Walter Bullock). Finished ninth in the 1946 Bendix Trophy Race (Time: 5:45:21.0, Speed: 355.908). Crashed during the time trials at the 1949 Cleveland National Air Races.

90. N70087—P-38L-5-LO. C/N 422-8428. AAF S/N 44-53173. Converted to a F-5G-6-LO. Post-World War II air racer (race #70). Pilot/owner Harvey Hughes, finished eighth in the 1946 Bendix Trophy Race (Time: 5:44:50.8, Speed: 356.428 mph). It was sponsored by The Paul Bunyan Clan and the nose of the aircraft was decorated with an image of the mythical lumberjack and his blue ox Babe. It was later sold to Spartan Air Service Ltd. of Canada who cannibalized the aircraft for parts.

91. N73467—P-38L-5-LO. C/N 422-8356. AAF S/N 44-53101. Converted to P-38M-6-LO. Last registered to Jack Hardwick of Englewood, California. Disposition unknown.

92. N74883—See Listing #85.

93. N75551—See Listing #32.

94. N75632—P-38L-5-LO. C/N 422-8461. AAF S/N 44-53206. Obtained surplus from the Walnut Ridge, Arkansas, depot by Neal Bradshaw in September 1946. Later sold to George Darnielle and then to Clarence Page. Purchased from Page Aviation Service, Yukon, Oklahoma, by Spartan Air Services, Ltd. and exported to Canada on June 6, 1953, as CF-HDI. Spartan painted the aircraft black and used it as a training ship. Spartan personnel referred to the plane as "The Black Widow." Destroyed May 2, 1955, near Ottawa. Pilot C.P. McEvoy was killed in the crash.

95. N75666—P-38L-5-VN. C/N N/A. AAF S/N 43-50310. Purchased surplus from the Altus, Oklahoma, depot in May 1947, by N.B McCreary of Little Rock, Arkansas. In August of the same year, N75666 was sold to Tulsa's Southwestern Aero Company. NL75666 was later exported to Cuba and operated by the Fuerza Aerea Cubana (Cuban Air Force) before being scrapped.

96. N79123—P-38L-5-LO. C/N 422-8235. AAF S/N 44-27231. Converted to a F-5G-6-LO. Post-World War II air racer (race #95). Pilot/owner James Harp placed fifth in the 1946 Bendix Trophy Race (Time: 5:31:47.8, Speed: 370.447 mph). N79123 was purchased in the 1950s by Jack Hardwick. In 1982 the aircraft was acquired by David Tallichet. The plane is presently undergoing restoration at Tallichet's facility in Chino, California.

97. N9005R—P-38L-5-LO. C/N 422-8350. AAF S/N 44-53095. Converted to a P-38M-6-LO. Ex-67745. One of six P-38s that were exported to Honduras during the late 1940s. Served

85. MILO PELTZER COLLECTION

86. WARREN BODIE PHOTO

with the Honduran Air Force as FAH 506. Reinstated on the U.S. Civil Aircraft Registry in 1960 as N9005R after being purchased by Bob Bean. Later the plane was sold to Bill Ross, who operated it for a number of years before selling it to the Lone Star Museum of Flight in 1986. N9005R is presently on display in the Lone Star's museum near Galveston, Texas. It is decorated in the colors of Col. Charles MacDonald's "Putt Putt Maru."

98. N9011R—See Listing #13.

99. N90813—P-38L-5-LO. C/N 422-8502. AAF S/N 44-53247. Converted to a F-5G-6-LO. Purchased surplus from the Kingman, Arizona, Depot in February 1946 by Wesley M. Grey, Long Beach, California. Subsequently sold to famous WASP Nancy Harkness-Love. N90813 was sold to former Grumman test pilot Cecil W. Kenyon in October 1946. Kenyon used this aircraft to test flight gyros, auto pilot systems, and stabilizing equipment for radar and camera platforms. In 1951 N90813 became one of Aero Service Corporation's first Lightnings. Nine years later N90813 was traded to Bob Bean in exchange for the "L" model Lightning that is currently on display in the Air Force Museum. In 1972 Bean donated N90813 along with a number of other artifacts to Air Force Museum for six surplus HU-16 aircraft. This aircraft was subsequently put on loan to the Pima County Air Museum where it was authentically restored and configured as a F-5G-6-LO. In 1988 N90813 was traded to France's Air & Space Museum for a Lepere Lusac II. On May 17, 1990, the former N90813 was destroyed in a fire at the museum's storage facility near Bourget, France.

100. N91300—RP-38E. C/N 222-5266. AAF S/N 41-2048. Modified by Lockheed to investigate the compressibility phenomenon. Later in the war it was used as a general flying

89. PICKETT—KAM

90. PICKETT—KMA

test bed. Known by Lockheed employees as "Old Nosey" or "Swordfish." Purchased surplus by Lockheed in March 1946, who continued to used the plane for a number of years as a flight component testing platform. Sold to Hycon Aerial Surveys where it was radically modified to accommodate much of the later "L" model parts. It was also one of three original Hycon Lightnings to receive the Hycon Photo Nose. In 1960 Hycon concluded its use of the P-38. N91300 was sold to Don May, Phoenix, Arizona in 1962. Believed to have been lost in a fatal crash sometime between 1962 and 1963. Disposition unknown.

101. N9957F—P-38L-5-LO. C/N 422-8270. AAF S/N 44-53015. Converted to a F-5G-6-LO. Ex-N57492. Purchased surplus from the Kingman, Arizona, Depot in March 1946 by famous race car driver Rex Mays. Race #55 nicknamed "MacMillian Meteor" was entered in the 1946 Bendix Trophy Race. Mays and his red colored Lightning placed 13th in the event (Time: 6:15:16.6, Speed: 327.525 mph). N57492 was deleted from the civil aircraft registry in 1948 after it was exported to Costa Rica by Robert Utterback. In 1954 the now registered N9957F returned to the U.S. and was later purchased by Hycon Aerial Surveys of Pasadena, California. During the 1960s ownership of N9957F passed through the Tallmantz' "Movie Land of The Air" museum in Santa Ana, California, and Walter Erickson before ending up with David Tallichet in 1970. N9957F was then traded to the Air Force Museum in 1981 for two surplus Lockheed C-130A aircraft. Presently this plane is on display at McGuire AFB, Wrightstown, New Jersey as a memorial to the late Major Thomas McGuire. The memorial aircraft is decorated in the markings of Major McGuire's "Puggy V."

94. COURTESY PADDY GARDINER

99. WARREN BODIE

100. WARREN BODIE

Bibliography

Books

Alexander, Jesse. *P-38 Lightning.* Osceola, WI: Motorbooks International, 1990.

Andrade, John M. *U.S. Military Aircraft Designations and Serials.* Leicester, England: Midland Counties Publications, 1979.

Bodie, Warren M. *The Lockheed P-38 Lightning.* Hiawassee, Georgia: Widewing Publications, 1991.

Brown, Joseph E. *Yesterday's Wings.* Garden City, NY: Doubleday & Company, Inc., 1982.

Buehl, Fred W. and Harry S. Gann. *The National Air-Race Sketchbook.* Los Angeles, CA: Floyd Clymer, 1949.

Chapman, John and Geoff Goodall. *Warbirds Worldwide Directory.* Leicester, England: Midland Counties Publications, 1979.

Christy, Joe and Jeff Ethell. *P-38 Lightning At War.* New York, NY: Charles Scribner's Sons.

Craven, Wesley F. and James L. Cate. *The Army Air Forces In World War II, Volumes One through Seven.* Chicago, IL: The University of Chicago Press, 1948.

Ethell, Jeff and G.L. Walbrun. *EAA Warbirds Of America.* Paducah, KY: Turner Publishing Co., 1989.

Francillion, Rene J. *Lockheed Aircraft Since 1913.* Annapolis, MD: Naval Institute Press, 1987.

Farmer, James H. *Celluloid Wings.* Blue Ridge Summit, PA: Tab Books Inc., 1984.

Frey, Royal D. *Flying Combat Aircraft of the USAAF-USAF* (chapter 13). Ames, Iowa: The Iowa State University Press, 1975.

Kinert, Reed. *Racing Planes and Air Races, Volume IV through XIII.* Fallbrook, CA: Aero Publishers, Inc., 1968.

Maloney, Edward T. *Lockheed P-38 Lightning.* Fallbrook, CA: Aero Publishers, Inc., 1968.

Orriss, Bruce Wm. *Museum and Display Aircraft of the United States.* American Aviation Historical Society, 1976.

Stafford, Gene B. *P-38 Lightning In Action.* Carrollton, TX: Squadron/Signals Publications, Inc., 1976.

The Greenland Expedition Society. *Lost Squadron Recovery Program.* Atlanta, Georgia: The Greenland Expedition Society, 1991.

Tigler, John. *Gentlemen You Have A Race.* Severna Park, MD: Wings Publishing Company, 1984.

Articles

Brown, D.F. "Question of Survival," *Air Classics,* December 1981, pp. 39–42.

Childs, Leo, "PiggyBacking with Uncle Benny and Lefty Gardner," April 1, 1991.

Childs, Leo. "The Lockheed Modification Center Love Field—Dallas, Texas," August 6, 1991.

Conly, Robert. "Men Who Measure the Earth," The National Geographic Magazine, March 1956, pp. 335–64.

Cummings, Urban. "The Driver Of The Fork Tailed Devil, Lefty Gardner and White Lightnin," *National Air-Racing Group,* April 1987, pp. 4–7.

Davisson, Budd. "Twin Tales Of A P-38," *Aviation Review,* Fall 1978, pp. 75–80.

Davisson, Budd. "School For Warbirds," *Air Progress,* July 1971, September 1971, and October 1971.

Gimlett, James L., Kenneth E. Hunter and John C. Whitaker. "How The Nuclear Precession Magnetometer Aids Exploration," *Engineering and Mining Journal,* May 1957, pp. 89–90.

Hegge, Robert. "Der Gabelshwanz Teufel Flies Again," *Air Classics,* May 1975, pp. 37–43 and 76–77.

Hess, Karl. "P-38 Purchased As Personal Plane," *Aviation News,* September 17, 1945.

Hoy, Bruce. "Tropical Lightning, Survivor," *Flightpath,* Volume 4, Number 2, pp. 20–25.

Huvard, Todd H. "Lost And Found," *The Southern Aviator,* August 1992, pp. 28–34.

Johnson, J.T. "The Lost Squadron," *Popular Mechanics,* May 1984, pp. 78–81 & 196–97.

Lichtblau, Eric, "Lightning Still Full of Fight," *Los Angeles Times,* November 11, 1991.

O'Leary, Michael. "Lightning Airborne," *Air Progress Warbirds International,* November/December 1988, pp. 42–49.

Pratt, Don. "Zero-Seven-Victor Where Are You?," *Air Classics,* May 1972, pp. 46–53.

Madison, Pete. "An Exciting Day!!," *Tam News,* Summer 1988.

Melayney, Norman, "Warbird Reports," *Air Classics,* May 1975, p. 15.

Shelly, J.M., "Dream of Owning P-38 Comes True For Pilot," *The Shreveport Times,* February 14, 1971.

Smith, Eugene and Dorothy. "Snuffy Smith Reunited With *Japanese Sandman,*" *Warbirds Of America,* January/February 1987.

Surface, Melvin. "Flying Enthusiast Leads Big Industry Here," *Abbeville Meridional,* March 19, 1970.

Veronico, Nick. "P-38 Lightning Celebrates Golden Anniversary," *In Flight Aviation News,* January 1989.

Veronico, Nick. "Big Money Spent At Auction," *In Flight Aviation News,* June 1990, pp. 16–17.

______. "England People Help Restore Vintage P-38," *Tiger Talk,* May 1978, p. 8.

______. "Col. Gary Levitz Initiates Maintenance Program, Donates P-38 and F8F," *CAF Dispatch,* February 10, 1972.

______. "Charge Of The Lightning Brigade," *CAF Dispatch,* March/April 1977, p. 9.

______. "Vintage Planes Crashes Along Highway Here," *Paris News,* May 24, 1971, p. 1.

______. "Warbird Report," *Air Classics,* August 1975, p. 15.

______. "Hycon Plans New Method of Geophysical Exploration," *Star-News,* March 4, 1955.

______. "Death of a Great Flyer," *Air Force,* April 1945, p. 58.

———. "Lightning Strikes Kelly Flight Line," *Flying Times*, February 12, 1960, p. 10.

———. "Weeds Almost Obscure Bong Memorial P-38," *Chicago Daily Tribune*, August 29, 1949, p. 24.

———. "Bong Airplane Stands Alone," *The Milwaukee Journal*, May 30, 1952.

———. "P-38 Equipped to Photograph Weather, Radar Presentation," *Aviation Week & Space Technology*, March 1, 1965, p. 51.

———. "P-38s Adaptable for Photo Survey Job," *Aviation Week & Space Technology*, January 14, 1957, pp. 115–16.

———. "Funeral Services Held Wednesday For Major Snedden," *The Starkville News*, September 28, 1951, pp. 1–6.

———. "University of Southern California Spends Millions for Surplus Aircraft," *RFC Surplus Property News*, November 1945, p. 6.

Special Documents

Federal Aviation Administration. "Civil Registration and Airworthyness Documents for Individual Aircraft," 1946–1992.

Hassell, B.R.J., Captain AAF. "Recovery Operations BW-1," July 25, 1942.

Hycon. "Hycon Mfg. Co. Annual Report," 1954 & 1955.

Hycon. "Hycon News," 1956–1959.

McGuire Air Force Base. "P-38 Memorial," 1981.

Markhurd Corporation. "Markhurd History," January 1989.

National Air & Space Museum's curatorial file on P-38J, serial number 42-67762.

NTSB. "Pilot/Operator Aircraft Accident Report, N38LL," October 19, 1974.

Stone, John N., Colonel, AAF. "Bolero Movement," August 7, 1942.

USAAF. "Roster of Bolero Movement Personnel," June 16, 1942.

USAAF. "Monthly Return Of Enemy Aircraft Casualties Claimed In Combat," 1942–1943.

USAAF. "History Of The 39th Fighter Squadron," June 23, 1945.

USAAF. "Signal Operations Instructions," June 23, 1942.

USAAF. "Operational Report On Tomcat Yellow," July 1942.

USAAF. "Report On BW-8," July 7, 1942.

USAAF. "Bolero Ferry Plan," June 18, 1942.

USAAF. "Individual Military Aircraft Record Cards," 1942–1945.

USAAF. "Report of Aircraft Accident, P-38G, serial number 42-13400," January 1, 1945.

USAAF. "Report of Aircraft Accident, RP-38E, serial number 41-2260," March 26, 1943.

United States Air Force Museum curitorial file on P-38L, serial number 44-43232.